The Lady of Booger Hill

The Lady of Booger Hill

Sallie Krickel

ISBN: 1523630507
ISBN 13: 9781523630509

Dedicated to my grandchildren:

Nathaniel Edward Krickel, b. 2004

Robert Bradford Wilson, b. 2005

Andrew Lamar Wilson, b. 2010

Sarah Evans Wilson, b. 2014

Part I

Three Score and Ten

Prologue

WELL, HERE I am.

Seventy years is the life span of mankind. Psalm 90 tells us that "the days of our years are threescore and ten...and then we fly away...." Dante's *The Inferno* echoes the Psalm, telling us that Dante, at age thirty-five, was "midway upon the journey of life...."

I traveled with Dante, and now I, too, have neared the end of my journey, as I have lived my allotted "three score and ten." In the last seventy years, I have neared the edge of Dante's abyss, myself, and I, too, have caught a glimpse of bliss. At the end of my Biblical lifespan, I have arrived at a state of great reflection, mindful that the Psalm also exhorts us to "number our days." In doing so, I recall the somber and the happy, the joy and the sadness, the pain and the blessings of my rather ordinary life.

I began my memoir as an homage to my husband, Edward. My grandchildren have never known their grandfather, and I wanted desperately for them to become acquainted with this genius of a man—to identify him as more than a part of their lineage, but as part of themselves.

During the course of writing about Edward and me and our family life on the little farm on the Booger Hill Road, I could speak of practically nothing without mentioning my own childhood--the relatives who had peopled my world and the events which formed my life and values. So, there was nothing to do but to write about my early years, also.

Thinking about my childhood and youth, I realize that I have hung on to some memories, while other memories have hung on to me. I have no control of either the remembering or the forgetting. I also know that memory is an unfaithful muse. However much I want the narrative of my life to be objective, I know that it is not. What I have written is "my truth." Others may have theirs.

The most significant part of my life began in December 1966, when I married. I left Savannah, returning only to visit and later to take care of my mother. But we never, none of us, ever really leave our childhood. What's more, I've discovered that, even if we lived in the same house, my brothers and I didn't share the same childhood. No two siblings have the same parents.

Rather than a chronological account, I have written a series of vignettes. I don't want to "confuse time with its mathematical progression…." As Faulkner observed, "The past is not a diminishing road, but instead a huge meadow." From this meadow of my childhood, I have chosen and picked the flowers, the weeds, and some of the thorns. The result is a full, if lopsided, bouquet.

The House that Groaned

When I was a child, our household was large and diverse. There were ten of us altogether: my mother and father, my four brothers, me, my widowed maternal grandmother (Sissy), her unmarried sister (Aunt Sarah), who was blind, and her unmarried brother (Uncle Jack) after he retired. My childhood memories date from the late 1940s to the mid-1950s. I was a teenager in the soporific era of the 1950s and the turbulent, radical years of the early 1960s. We lived in various houses in Savannah, Georgia, some rather nice and the others, after my father lost his health and business, rather shabby.

I unabashedly and unapologetically love the entire clutch of my four brothers. I've been closer at certain times to one and then to another, as life has taken its various twists, but I adore them in a way that neither Edward nor my children could understand, with a profundity that surprises even me. When I was growing up, after poverty, uninvited, squatted in our house, nearly making "squatters" of us all, I occasionally found a spot alone, uninhabited by either people or frustrations. Sometimes I gave myself over to a grim, secret little game, a game which even now makes me ashamed. By this time Sissy, Aunt Sarah, and my father had all died. That left us five children, our Great Uncle Jack, and my mother. I speculated that, if there were fewer of us, life would be easier and there would be more money to spread around. I mentally began to figure out who was expendable. I discounted our mother immediately, for understandable reasons. I discounted my Uncle Jack, though I'm not sure why, probably because he contributed to the household income. I'd painstakingly go through the list of brothers. I pondered life without them, one at a time. I dispassionately reminded myself of who they really were and how much they individually meant, weighing their "worth" on imaginary scales. I always came to the same conclusion. The truth is that I couldn't imagine living without each and every one of them. I was inextricably bound to them. I loved and needed them all.

Of course that doesn't deny that I would have liked a little more money, too.

My brothers' lives speak for themselves. Even after all these years, they have continued to mean an awful lot to me, all four: Ranny, Windell, Neil, and John.

RANNY: THE FIRST BORN

I grew up as "one of the boys." Though we always lived in Savannah, we spent many summers in Asheville, North Carolina, and I had only brothers and boy cousins to play with. I wore borrowed jeans (which we called "dungarees") and tee-shirts to climb mountains, while my frilly dresses hung in the closet. At the beach I wore hand-me-down boy trunks, long before topless suits were in vogue. I climbed trees with the boys, ran with them, though badly, played tug of war and football. I envied their ability to relieve themselves so quickly and efficiently, and regretted that I could not, which Sigmund Freud would have appreciated.

My father, like his own, had not been a good money manager. In addition, his many years of illness had strained the budget until it snapped. I note wryly that we became *nouveau pauvre* at a time when the rest of the world was becoming *nouveau riche*. In the 1950s prosperity was not only being played out daily on television, but seemed ripe for the taking in real life, too. While the rest of the world sang and danced, life must have been unbearable for my mother, losing her own mother with whom she had always shared a house, then her mother-in-law and her husband, all three within the span of a single year. Her light dance became a determined stride. She might have stumbled a time or two, but she didn't fall.

Our financial and social status had already plummeted. Though we continued to live in a nice neighborhood, circumstances on the inside of our house became increasingly desperate. Mother's fancy shoes grew moldy in the back of the closet, and she ended up with only "work clothes," and few of them. After she started teaching school, she alternated her three acceptable outfits, so that, at least, she never wore the same dress two days in a row. She usually worked two jobs, moonlighting with part-time jobs, as well as putting in a full day in the classroom. She used to laugh at herself when she thought back on her days as a young matron, those days when she felt herself terribly overburdened by life, rushing from bridge games, to sorority functions, to church circle meetings, to tailoring classes, all the while with a mother, an aunt, and several servants at home to take care of the hearth and the children. Though her life became unbearable, she bore her public self admirably, in an awe-inspiring way.

Ranny was the oldest. He was christened Brazil Ransom Bradford IV, and he resented both the ponderous sound of his name and the fact that he was our father's namesake. They never really hit it off. But as the first born, he was doted on by everyone else. He had a whole bevy of admirers and he always remained a favorite. He got to know all the extended family in a way that the others of us did not. After all, it was easier to cart around one adorable little baby than a whole passel of children. He still has a strong sense of history and family and has known everyone for several generations, especially the most important ones.

Later on, after our father died, Ranny became the "man" of the family, and he felt a heavy mantle of responsibility. Though just a teenager himself, he played the role of a surrogate parent and was free with advice and criticism, which most often were not appreciated. I can remember Neil telling him, in a most emphatic fashion, that Ranny was not, indeed, his father, and that Neil didn't have to do what Ranny wanted. Ranny even at one point tried to be a physical disciplinarian, metaphorically dusting off our father's unused belt, but that didn't work at all. Neil, especially, was as strong (and bull-headed) as he. Ranny insisted on doling out rules to his little sister, too, rules of his own making. I rejected his insistence that I skip my senior year of high school and enroll in college. I would have no conversation about making my debut. Even if some of my cousins did, the notion was not only absurd to me but repugnant. Mother could hardly afford one fancy gown, much less a whole season's wardrobe. Besides, such things have never mattered to me.

He was, though, the reason that I became a foreign language major. When I was in high school, he urged me to take Latin for the third year. He pointed out, in the great wisdom of a brother only five years older than I, that most students stopped their language courses after the second year, and they, therefore, endured only the drudgery of grammar, not the thrill of literature. I followed his advice in this case and ended up taking four years of Latin, instead of three, the only fourth-year student in the school. My major and career were determined due to his wise counsel.

The most touching example of his kinder nature and his feeling of paternal responsibility was one particularly gloomy Christmas. Mother said that she had no money for gifts that year, and Ranny, barely in his twenties, played the role of Santa Claus. He took his own time and his own money on Christmas Eve and bought John, Neil, and me presents and placed them under the tree. When I learned later that it was he who played Santa, that explained the rather strange gifts that I received: the shell part only of a bright orange sweater set, and a train case to complete my non-existent set of luggage. I smile even now. But, the truth of it is that, other than the year I was given a shiny blue bicycle, that was the only Christmas morning that I remember.

I feel forever tender about my eldest brother's love and generosity, his concern and compassion. My younger brothers were still in the just-beyond-belief stage, and they would have been devastated on Christmas morning to find nothing under the tree. And I, in my sensitive teen years, was able to save face with my friends by telling them that Santa had brought me "clothes and luggage." Most of all, Ranny, in his compassion and with as much generosity as he could muster, saved John and Neil's belief in goodness and magic.

As a young child, Ranny was artsy and sensitive. He was encouraged by our mother and grandmother to paint, to read, and to put on little neighborhood plays. He now says that he felt keenly the disappointment of my father that he wasn't a good athlete, not interested at all in sports, but I knew none of that then. As he grew older, his tastes remained intellectual, and I thought he was the smartest, most sophisticated person who ever lived. He knew important people and he did important things. He talked about history, literature, and politics. Tchaikovski's *1812 Overture* boomed from his stereo, and Puccini's *Tosca* broke the spell of a hot, gloomy afternoon. He knew the brand names of clothes. He was outspoken and witty.

He started working at an early age. He delivered packages for the Little House, a small, private bookstore. He was paid something like twenty cents a package, which he loaded onto his bike and pedaled to the post office. He loathed the job, finding the work demeaning and the owners condescending. Once he was a salesman at Sears in, I think, something unlikely like the outdoor equipment section. He liked that job not much better, though the salary was an improvement.

One of his jobs was at a small grocery store in an impoverished part of town, a black slum area. He worked for Marino Orsini, whose father before him had owned the store and whose daughter was a poster child for polio victims. Ranny, in my memory, worked many, if not all, Sundays. I remember Sissy preparing him a plate of our Sunday dinner, always delicious, and our driving down to Orsini's. I remember feeling sad as we left him to eat alone, sitting on a stool behind the shabby counter, while the rest of us sat around the dining room table. When he closed up Orsini's at night, he had to bring the proceeds home. Oftentimes, if not always, he had no ride and had to call a taxi. He carried a pistol carefully placed on the bundle of money, then camouflaged the lot by draping a towel over his arm. He was only sixteen years old, even then a pacifist who lacked the courage and conviction of shooting a gun.

Sallie Krickel

He claimed once to have told the Savannah High English teacher, Miss Virginia Hudson, who, as he pointed out, bore an uncanny resemblance to the picture of George Washington hanging on her wall, that "he wanted to pull her long, blond hair out by its short black roots." I realize now that he never actually said that to her face (he was brought up better than that), but back then I hung onto his every word and was excited by his cleverness and boldness. In fact, I believed all his stories well into adulthood, and some of them were too fantastic for even the most naïve to be taken in by. As an adult, I have realized that he was such a good storyteller that he didn't let a little thing like truth get in the way of a good narrative. That, in addition to his intelligence and diligence, was what made him such an exciting and memorable professor.

He scandalized the whole high school by wearing Bermuda shorts and argyle knee socks with his tux jacket and cummerbund to the prom. The faculty held an impromptu meeting, again going only by his reports, with all the chaperones huddled in a group, to decide on whether or not to let him in. They did. (I can't help but think of my son who scandalized the school when he wore a tie-dyed tee-shirt and some Vans without socks to his graduation. If he were proving a point to Edward and me, he was sorely disappointed. We didn't notice. The teachers did, and there was much a-do. It was because of him that a strict written dress code for graduation was drawn up.) For his junior picture Ranny wore a jaunty hat cocked at an impertinent angle, and there was some talk about not letting his picture be placed in the yearbook, or the "annual" as we called it back then. But it was. Naughty and imaginative, he was also engaging and had superb manners. I was in awe.

He ran around with the semi-elite of Savannah and was a popular escort at debutante balls. Though he didn't actually date a whole lot, when he was in high school he took the principal's daughter to dances, and when he was in college, he escorted the president's niece. He was smart and had a compendium of knowledge. He was avant-garde in his opinions of politics and of race relations, which were just coming into national consciousness. He campaigned for progressives. He was a Civil Rights activist. He hated Joe McCarthy. He devoted himself to developing fine tastes in everything. I would have referred to him back then as "urbane," if I had known the word.

After he graduated from the local "junior college," Armstrong, Ranny enrolled at Emory University in Atlanta. Again, he made it a point to know and be known by the right people. By that time, our family circumstances had been "humbled," to put it mildly, for several years, so he, instead of joining an expensive fraternity, became an outspoken GDI (g-damned independent), who railed about the vacuousness of Greek life. He came back to Savannah briefly, ostensibly to help mother out with us younger children who were giving her "teenager problems," and he taught history at Armstrong, the youngest teacher ever hired. He got me dates, and we frequented bars on the black side of town, just to be rebellious. My dates also took me to concerts, and I was impressed with myself. I tried to stay awake and look appropriately appreciative and, at the same time, nonchalant, but I doubt that I succeeded. It was not until several years later that I actually began to like classical music. I enjoyed my first and last espresso, learning that I could hold my liquor far better than I could handle my caffeine. My heart and mind both raced for days.

Ranny graduated from Emory with a degree in history and headed to the University of London for graduate school. He bummed around throughout Europe. His letters back to Savannah were thrilling, and I envied him his adventuresome nature and his wealth of experience. While in Switzerland, he met his future wife, Ann Shook, a steel heiress from Birmingham, Alabama. After a courtship of less than a year, they married.

Sallie Krickel

Our family had been quasi-prominent in Alabama in the old days and Ann's father had known a few of them, so my brother had a modicum of social creds, but, as a young, idealistic, penniless, and volatile liberal, he was far from Ann's father's choice as a suitable mate for his daughter. Everyone carried on in a genteel fashion. For the fantastic, extraordinary week of prenuptial parties, Mr. Shook had reserved the entire country club for our family. I commented to Mother that I couldn't imagine living in the extraordinary luxury of their world. She replied, not to worry, that it would have been just as hard for them to imagine living in ours.

I was proud and happy for my brother and I loved Ann very much, but I was uncommonly sad at their wedding. There was no reason that I could figure out, and I decided that it was the few drinks every night for a week that I was not accustomed to. But the cloud of uncertainty didn't leave. The newlyweds took the *Queen Elizabeth II* to London, where they lived on Sloan Square for several years before they moved to the south of France, and finally to Munster, Germany, where they settled. To me, it was a fairy-tale life. To him, it must have been the fulfillment of a life-long dream. As the oldest child, Ranny had been in his sensitive teen years when our family lost its ersatz fortune, whatever it was. He smarted desperately from the turns of fate, the public embarrassment, and the destitution of our lives. As the result, so I thought, position and wealth were particularly important to him. Finally he could live the role of the *bonhomme*, a respected professor with a wealthy wife. He could have been a character, a century earlier, in a Henry James novel.

He fathered a wonderful son. The three of them, Ranny, Ann, and Alfred, settled in a picturesque house on the river in Raestrup, a little village near Munster from which he commuted every day to the University. They planted a garden. He and Ann, a gourmet cook, entertained extensively.

If there are people in this world who still think that sexual orientation is a choice, they don't know my brother. He tried hard to deny his essential nature and to play the role that society expected of him. He pursued the dating game, in some small way, in high school and college. He tried to live a conventional, acceptable domestic life. He really worked hard at being "normal." Nobody could have wanted any more than he a life of respectability, and few people had as much to lose for not being able to have it.

It must have been ghastly as he was growing up to realize that his own inclinations were, in the eyes of society, unacceptable at best, and damnable at worst. Ardently religious, even to obsession, he felt that his church rejected his very essence. He probably even felt that his God did, too. I cannot imagine what self-loathing he must have suffered. Ranny's closet door had stayed tightly closed and firmly locked. He had grown up under the burden of this shameful secret, playing his role so successfully that none of his family had any inkling of his so-called "orientation," not even Windell, despite the fact that they had always shared a bedroom and had gone to high school and college together.

Living in Europe, he spent hours in therapy, even undergoing "gay conversion therapy" a process whereby homosexuals were broken from their "perverse" nature. He told me that electrodes were attached and shocks were sent through his body whenever he responded to pictures of men. (In much the same way, we have buried electric fences to send tremors through our pets if they, God forbid, follow their natural inclinations and step outside their boundaries.) But even such brutal tactics had no effect. Ranny was, simply put, gay.

His marriage dissolved, and the pain of this rupture has not lessened these long decades later. He and I talk a lot. He struggled desperately to overcome social and financial mediocrity. He loved Ann immensely. He couldn't be who she wanted and needed him to be. He has remained a charming conversationalist and an erudite professor. But behind the veneer of his sophistication and charm, he remains a broken man. All of those long, dark shadows from childhood, then on into adolescence, and into adulthood won't disappear. He couldn't outrun them, couldn't hide them, and even now can't shake them off.

Of all the disappointments I have encountered, this one, the cruelty of Ranny's life, the impossibility of realizing his dreams through no choice of his own, pricks at my heart and continues to grieve me to the point of tears. (He died in August 2013.)

WINDELL: THE SHY IDEALIST

Windell, the second born, was a gentle child. He was named Windell Robertson Bradford, the namesake of my maternal grandfather and my uncle, Windell Arthur Robertson Sr. and Jr., respectively. I never knew my grandfather, but my compassionate brother Windell bore no resemblance at all to my brutal uncle. While Uncle Windell was whipping his powerful stallion into submission, brother Windell was fading back to the end of the pack, catching my hand and helping me to keep up with the rest. For, although I was merely "one of the boys," I was pathetically unathletic. Try as hard as I could, I couldn't run fast enough, couldn't pull hard enough, couldn't climb with nearly as sure a foot. As the whole lot of brothers and boy cousins dashed ahead, leaving me a frustrated straggler, Windell stopped, turned around and came to pull me along. He always had a soft spot for the underdog, drawn like a magnet to the helpless and the needy. He was my hero.

Ranny was not only older but he had a more dominant and assertive personality. It's amazing how well the older two boys got along, considering their vast differences in personality. I don't ever remember seeing them fight physically or even argue, certainly not the way that my mother's two brothers did, not even the way that my own two younger brothers did. Windell agrees, saying that, early on, they merely went their separate ways and did their own things.

Windell admits that Ranny, through his example, inspired his interest in history and politics and introduced him to classical music. But, whereas Ranny showed no interest in athletics or outdoorsmanship, Windell was avid about sports of whatever kind. With him, there was always a ball to be tossed. He played on a softball team and was such an ardent supporter of the local Savannah Indians that he didn't miss a single home game for several years. He loved to be outside, and his fondest memories of childhood are the summers we spent in Asheville and at Lake Lure. He loved climbing mountains, camping out on the weekends, swinging bare chested on the monkey vines next door. (Poor Ranny was teased for forty years or more for rolling down the mountain like a barrel and landing, plop, at the bottom.)

Especially painful for Windell were the family Sunday afternoon drives. All of us children were loaded up in the car and driven to the beach, to Isle of Hope, or to other island destinations like White Bluff, Coffee Bluff, or Montgomery, where Uncle Windell was eventually to live. We twisted down DesLesseps Avenue, the long curvy road which had served as a race track in the years just before World War I. For a short period of time we drove to Gordonston, an upscale neighborhood, where our parents had bought a lot on which their never-to-be-realized dream home was to be built. We gathered pecans from the magnificent tree, but soon enough, or too soon, we stopped going. There was no explanation. I realized years later that the lot had to be sold, as we had fallen on hard times. So it was necessary for my parents to leave the pecans to rot, along with their hopes and expectations.

The main emphasis on these lazy Sunday afternoons was more on the drive than the destination. We admired the ocean without really playing in it or, if we were lucky, walked out to the end of the pier. We visited the terrapin farm at Barbee's Pavilion, where hundreds of huge turtles sloshed lazily around in the gray, sticky mud until they were hoisted up, washed, then made into turtle soup and exported round the world. Ignoring the fishy-smelling air, we walked out on the pier there, where in the Big Band Era notable name bands, like Tommy Dorsey's, used to play on the long, humid summer evenings. I could envision not only the dancers swaying to the band, but also the old pier swaying to the rhythms of the tide. We usually bought an ice cream, in the at-that-time rare waffle cones. Although the rest of us enjoyed the break from the weekly tedium, Windell was in agony. Being closed in the confines of the car was torture for him, and he used to beg our parents to let him out of the car so that he could run alongside, in the fresh air, in the open spaces, He promised that he would run fast enough to keep up.

We were allowed enormous freedom when we were children, something that children these days rarely experience. Windell spent hours a day with his best friend, Bobby Berry, roaming up and down the streets of Savannah, sometimes on bikes, sometimes on foot. I occasionally played with Windell and Bobby, and Bobby's older sister, whose name I've forgotten. One long sultry summer afternoon, we made up a game in the Berrys' backyard, desperate to allay the long day's boredom. Each of us claimed ourselves masters of some aspect of nature. Ownership was fast, and trespassing was illegal. Others had to barter for permission to use our territory. Bobby claimed "grass," and no one could walk on the grass without either a toll or a trade. Windell claimed "concrete," and no one could walk on the sidewalk, and Bobby's sister claimed "dirt." I was the youngest, and my turn came last. I was flummoxed, as the important things had already been chosen. But I got a bright idea. I claimed "air," and no one could breathe without a say-so from me. The youngest of all, and usually the loser in their games, I won resoundingly that day.

I'm not sure of all the mischief the boys got in to. Though I was allowed to go somewhere like Bobby's, I wasn't given the liberty of taking off the whole day to explore. And Windell didn't talk too much. He did tell me about his and Bobby's exploits of climbing a tree to peer over the tall fence that surrounded a church which was referred to as a "Holy Roller" church. The boys described in detail how the members of the congregation shouted and danced and rolled on the floor. I didn't believe them, though they swore it was true. Mother found out what they were doing and, fearing the church would call the police, she forbade them to go. But they went, anyway. She may not have known, but I did. Nowhere in my starkest imagination would I have believed that I would one day actually teach in a Holiness college and discover exactly what Windell and Bobby were talking about. It was all true: shouting, physical expressions of ecstasy, like "speaking in tongues," and praying "in concert," (with everyone simultaneously praying aloud, ignoring the prayers of others). The services were noisy and lively, yet, despite all this (or because of it?), the people were kind and supportive!

Windell was always a hard worker. For years, before he was old enough to drive, he had a paper route and made daily deliveries on his bike. The paper truck would arrive at the appointed time, at the appointed place, and a man would swing a rectangular bundle of newly printed newspapers onto the sidewalk. Windell then took his bundle and rolled up the papers, tucking the ends in just tight enough so that the papers wouldn't fall apart when he threw them on people's front porches. There were no leash laws back then, and more than once Windell came home with ripped trousers and, occasionally, with actual fang marks, where a dog had not only gnawed his pants, but his leg as well. He also had to collect the money, and collection day was once a month. He hated the money part; apparently some people were no kinder than their dogs, though their fangs were verbal, not physical. He delivered his papers day in and day out for years, just like the proverbial postman, through rain, sleet, and, rarely if ever in Savannah, snow.

When Windell was in high school, Mother's good friend, Louise McLeod, got him a summer job at the CDC laboratory. It was the middle to late fifties, with World War II still an echo. Progress was emerging, and improvements, including new insecticides, were being developed. The Centers for Disease Control (and Prevention), now world famous, had a lab just outside Savannah, which was specifically dedicated to malaria control. It was on Oatland Island, one of the several islands dotted along Highway 80 on the way to the beach. Mostly the lab dealt with mosquito control, but Windell and his group worked with flies. He claims that the fly workers were a bit lower on the hierarchy, and he was always a little envious of the mosquito people.

The job was to study the efficacy of various insecticides, as DDT was being replaced with something a little, hopefully, more people friendly. He and his buddy Belton Dykes, a fullback for the Citadel, began the experiments by anesthetizing a group of flies, and, after the flies were asleep, dividing them up into equal numbers of males and females. (My brother is one of the few people I know who has learned the art of telling the sex of flies! He claims that it's easy once you learn how to do it. There is a telltale difference in the eyes, and the female, alas, has a bigger abdomen.) Anyway, they placed an equal number of males and females in a cylinder, hung the cylinders at a specified distance on a dirt road, and sprayed. Then, they gathered up the cylinders, and counted their dead.

Earnest and idealistic, Windell flirted with becoming a minister. He was elected chaplain of everything, including the Beta Club and the senior class, passionately pursuing his life's career. As president of the youth group, he even preached a sermon or two during the informal Sunday night services at Wesley Monumental, our big, uptown church. Even my father uncomfortably endured a church service – the only time I remember my father in church.

On one notable occasion, the youth held an Easter sunrise service on one of the nearby brackish rivers. The little choir joined "Preacher-Boy Bradford" on the bateau, a square-backed little row boat. They drifted a short distance from the dock where the communicants had gathered. It must have been a moving, impressive sight. The *a cappella* notes of the choir wafted, sweetly breaking the silence of the dawn, as the sun rose peacefully over the marsh grass. Windell intoned a prayer and began his Eastertide homily. Unfortunately the rope securing the small boat gave way, and Windell's words of hope trailed off in the early morning mist, as the boat caught the tide and wended its way downstream. There were no oars on board, and nobody was able to walk on water, so they slowly, yet helplessly, drifted farther and farther away. Finally they were able to catch on to a dock. They tied up the boat with the trailing rope and scrambled to dry land. The proprietor, shocked to see a group of teenagers emerge on his private dock in the early dawn, began shaking his fist and cursing. Windell and the group ran quickly away, though they did shout, "Happy Easter" as they made their escape. Later that afternoon they sheepishly returned with a set of oars and reclaimed their bateau.

Despite the experience, he kept the faith, for a while longer, at least. He did stray, though, for several years. He was unable to accept the sermons and the spirit (or lack thereof) of our minister at

Wesley Monumental who justified segregation on Biblical grounds. It was a painful breach, as we had all grown up in that church and had been faithful attendees, morning, noon, or night. Besides, one of the board members had subsidized both Ranny and Windell in college. But Windell's faith was shaken. Ironically, Windell regained his temporarily lost path through the influence of the existential theologians at Emory, notable among whom was Dr. Altizer of the "God is dead" philosophy.

While Ranny pontificated his liberal opinions, expert with the shock effect, and always baited people into an argument, Windell kept his own counsel. It was he, though, who was a quiet activist. After he graduated from Emory, he again worked at the CDC, this time as a public health advisor, a sort of lay epidemiologist. I remember being chased around the house as he, armed with a syringe, begged for live practice at drawing blood. I made him stick to his orange. A specialist in syphilis, as he wryly referred to himself, he was transferred to New York City. His responsibility was to trace down the sexual partners of the STD patients, to be sure that they knew they had been exposed to disease and could receive proper treatment. As he knocked on doors in the slums in Harlem, he learned to call out "Health Service" instead of "Health Department," so that his clients would not make a mistake of hearing only "Department," and fire guns through the door.

He regularly ate lunch at the same café as Malcolm X. Malcolm X's name was well known by then, and he was much feared in the white community, though he has largely been forgotten by now. (A friend of my brother Neil's once asked him, in all seriousness, "Who in the world is Malcolm the tenth, anyway?") Windell had an abrupt shock one day, as Malcolm X failed to show up for lunch. He had been assassinated.

As a young man, Windell became truly color-blind. He had to stop and think when someone asked what race one of his colleagues was. He had stopped thinking in terms of skin color, quite unusual for a Southern boy. He was one of the few, as race relations brought out passions of every sort, and the unrest and tension were rampant in our country. Thanks to people like Martin Luther King Jr., there was surprisingly little violence. In the 1960s the federal government started to enforce the integration laws, not only in schools, but also in all public places. Windell was an utter idealist and intensely committed to civil rights, but he resented "Yankees" picking up their modern carpet bags, the judges donning their black robes (not certainly the white robes of the Klan, but robes nonetheless) and telling us poor ignorant Southerners what to do. They were color-blind, too, in a strange way, unaware of any of the subtlety of shading, any understanding of tradition and nuance. Windell "heard the call" just as certainly as he had heard the call to the ministry when he was a teen. And he answered it. He was a son of the South, and it was up to idealists like him. So, in the volatile race relations atmosphere of the sixties, when the CDC was asked for help in enforcing non-discrimination in hospitals, he volunteered. He headed South again, to take up the cause below the Mason-Dixon line, with his young family in tow.

It was a very sensitive situation, as he had gone to college with some of the physicians and hospital officials, but enforcing the federal mandate was necessary. Windell laughed, as he discovered that a great deal of the untidiness of the restrooms resulted, not from the inclusion of blacks, but from the reams of toilet paper that the white patrons used to protect their pink bottoms from the recently integrated toilet seats.

It was dangerous, too. He once received an anonymous call to meet down a remote dirt road. He headed out, armed only with his tape recorder, to hear the confession of a white whistle-blower, who, if discovered, was at risk of losing his job, or even his life, because of the information he told my brother. And, of course, Windell had no assurance at all who the furtive, whispered call was actually from, no indication whether it was a sympathizer or an ambush. It was too dangerous a job to keep for long, especially for the father of two young daughters, and he didn't renew the assignment after his two years were up.

Windell continued his career at the CDC, staying in Atlanta. While primarily focusing on his duties in sexually transmitted disease prevention, he was also traveling the globe and dealing with sensitive situations. He didn't talk much about his specific assignments, of course, but he hinted at several things in a general way. His team was involved with the resolution of the lawsuits waged by the victims or the families of the victims of the Tuskegee Experiment. Back in the 1930s, the United States government had used four hundred syphilitic black men (in Macon County, Alabama) as human guinea pigs. Pretending to treat these men, the doctors, instead, studied the ongoing effects of the disease if left untreated. The outrageous abuse was divulged fifty years later, and Windell's team was sent to "trouble shoot" the damage to the CDC and to the government, in general. The "patients" or their descendants were "adequately" recompensed, and the lawsuits were settled. The government provided financial compensation and free health care for life to the litigants, as if money could replace shame, indignity, and suffering.

Windell's professional low point came in the 1980s. There erupted an epidemic of an unusual strain of carcinoma in the San Francisco gay community. Hundreds of people were infected, and the CDC was supposed to investigate all such outbreaks, to come up with a plan for prevention. But the Reagan Administration refused to fund any investigation, viewing AIDS (and the cancer) as a well-deserved punishment for homosexual behavior. Abstinence was the only official government policy. It took the death of a film celebrity, Rock Hudson, to get national attention and to provoke President Reagan to address the issue with information and funding. Those years of having their hands tied when hundreds of people were dying were maddeningly frustrating. Hitting the brick wall of presidential and national non-support was physically and emotionally, not to mention morally, exhausting.

This mild-mannered, yet strong, brother of mine retired from the CDC in 1995. He feels that he had some part in making the world just a little bit better, and he still has a soft place in his heart for the disadvantaged. He has maintained a firm resolve about progressive politics, especially where the needy are concerned. I am extraordinarily proud of him.

NEIL: THE COMIC

Neil was the funniest person I have ever met. He was the third son, the fourth child. He was born with a quick wit and a natural sense of humor. His name was Neil Andress after my paternal grandmother's father. Neil always despised his name, which I couldn't understand, because I think it has a resounding, dignified ring, but when he was little, he later explained, all he heard was the "dress" aspect of his middle name Andress. He took it personally and resented it greatly.

Neil didn't live the life of "The Beaver," and his parents weren't June and Ward Cleaver, the ideal television family in the 1950s. Far from it. He was a whimperer and sucked his thumb. I'm pretty sure now that he was a great deal like my father, though I certainly had no perspective then. That was undoubtedly why my mother never "took" to him, and, frankly, neither did many other adults. After all, it was easier to direct one's displeasure toward a young child than to a grown man. It probably didn't help, either, that Neil was born just at the time that our parents' lives began to fall apart. He was a constant reminder of the reversal of their fortune.

Sallie Krickel

Neil was four years younger than I, and I confess that I regarded him as a typical pesky little brother. He was always hanging about when my girlfriends and I twitted our inane, mindless conversations, which we considered of utmost importance and secrecy. Not only that, he repeated them! My Uncle Claude, my father's younger brother, was the only one in the whole family who took a special interest in Neil. My acerbic Aunt Billie, mother's sister, introduced him, to his face, as the "black sheep of the family."

Windell and I spent many an afternoon watching our younger brother play ball with the Panthers. We'd take the back seat out of our old, old car and prop it up on the ground, leaning it against the trunk of a tree. Mother, busy with two jobs, was never able to go to the games, and we were often the surrogate parents to our younger brothers, especially Neil.

Many comedians claim that humor is born out of adversity, and Neil certainly had a far from pleasant childhood. But even when he was a toddler, Neil was funny. One day he and my father were walking down the beach. Neil was dragging his feet and kicking up the sand. My father said, "Neil, pick up your feet," and Neil immediately plopped down and lifted first one foot and then the other. It's true that toddlers, like new speakers of a foreign language, take everything literally, but with my brother it was something more. He was just born funny. Another time, a few years later, my father threatened: "Neil, if you don't stop that I'm going to take off my belt, and you know what that means." Without missing a beat, Neil replied, "Yes, sir, your pants will fall down."

Neil was nine years old when our father died. By this time, our Great Aunt Sarah had died of cancer and both of my grandmothers had succumbed to strokes. Mother became a single parent, and life was hard for everybody. Suddenly there was no structure in a home where "structure" had been the very essence of our lives. Mother taught middle-school science and also usually moonlighted to keep us fed and clothed, so that my two younger brothers, Neil and John, were left pretty much on their own. We three older children were either off at college or working afternoon jobs. I was at home for a year and tended to my little brothers, but then, when I turned fourteen, I got an after-school part-time job at the Savannah Public library as a student "page."

Mother enrolled the younger boys in the Panthers program, an after-school football camp, not because she was interested in grooming them to be athletes, but because she felt, quite rightfully, that they needed some sort of afternoon supervision. Neil took to football, and played in middle school and high school until Mother made him quit because of his grades. Until the day he died, he reveled in his past football glory and knew everything there was to know about the game, all the plays, the players, the history of each game and each coach, especially of his beloved Georgia Bulldogs.

Neil was "invited not to return" to Armstrong, the local junior college that we three older children had graduated from, even though Ranny was on the faculty. Mother was understandably furious, and she gave up on Neil's academic future. I helped him apply to Brewton Parker, a Baptist junior college in middle Georgia. He was accepted, and I sat up sewing name tags on his clothes and linens. We left early the next morning, just the two of us. Such a conservative fundamentalist college was an unlikely fit for him, but he adjusted—or probably they adjusted to him. After getting an AA degree, he was accepted to the University of Georgia. Though he didn't last but one quarter, explaining that the Baxter Street hill was just too steep a climb and the alarm clock was too unfriendly, he qualified as a bona fide alumnus, a Georgia Bulldog. That's all he really cared about.

Just because he had a less than impressive academic record in high school and didn't finish his bachelor's degree, that had nothing to do with Neil's innate intelligence. Neil was a genius, literally. By the time he reached middle school, he had become a discipline problem and an academic underachiever. He was tested, and the results were that his IQ hit the genius mark. His teachers told him that he was so brilliant that he was bored in school, which accounted for his poor performance and disruptive behavior. (Neil charmed all ladies, young and old!) That was all Neil needed. He had found an excuse to slack off and to misbehave. Whenever he got into trouble, failed to turn in his homework, or made a bad mark on a test, he'd just sigh, like his mother, and exclaim: "I'm just soooo bored."

Lila Varnedoe, our neighbor on 46th Street, encouraged Mother to send Neil to Philips Exeter Academy, the prestigious prep school that her son Kirk (who became the head curator of MOMA, The Museum of Modern Art in New York) attended. Neil had interviews and took entrance exams, and he impressed the socks off everyone. But, of course, he needed financial aid. So they set him up with special tests for a scholarship. He bombed out. There was no doubt about his intelligence, but I think that Neil felt that he was not ready to go so far away from home. Subconsciously, or consciously, that was the way he worked it out so that he would not have to leave family and friends. I, similarly, remember that I was glad that I was too poor to leave home at age thirteen for finishing school as some of our neighbors did. I couldn't have coped. Our father's early death probably left us all a bit insecure. We needed to cling to each other, even if our grasp was intermittent and tentative.

When John and Neil were in their teens, mother was struggling, not only with us difficult children, but with her expanding waist line. Neil had started smoking and Mother was far from pleased. To thwart his newly acquired habit, she proclaimed that he would "not smoke in her house." She insisted that he sit on the back steps to have a cigarette, rain or shine, hot or cold. Neil complied.

Then the inevitable happened, the inevitable when Neil was around. One evening as we sat down to dinner, Mother announced that she was cutting down on calories and would eat only one biscuit. She ate her biscuit, but as the meal progressed, she asked for another. We all sat still. She asked a second time: "Please pass the biscuits." We remained immobile. A third time she asked, her tone getting more and more tense, "*Please* pass the biscuits." Neil, with an exaggerated sigh and a shrug of his shoulders, answered, "Well, yes ma'am, but you'll have to sit on the back steps to eat it."

With little emotional support at home, Neil's friends became a surrogate family. He remained friends with his buddies all his life, just as if they were brothers. And he always had a string of girls at his beck and call. They fawned over him. When I mentioned in Danielsville that I was from Savannah and that my maiden name was Bradford, a couple of my friends, Sharon Varn and Carole Henry, were astonished. They had both dated Neil…only once, the most any self-respecting girl would have done. But they all loved him anyway, largely because of his wit.

Neil laughed a nice deep down, authentic laugh. He had a whole spate of jokes, and he greeted everyone, not with "Hello," but with "Have you heard the one about…." All his intelligence was devoted to the remembering and telling of jokes. He could never tell one, even an old one, without punctuating the story with a laugh, which made it all the funnier. Knowing that I play bridge every Tuesday night, he used to call me on those afternoons, saying, "I've got a good one for the girls tonight."

He didn't spare himself as the object of humor. One of his favorite stories was the tale of his college fraternity initiation. He had learned that the "brothers" took the initiates to a particular place in the marsh, stripped them, and left them to make it back home. Neil and his buddy made plans to outsmart them. Neil arranged for a girlfriend to park on the sandy road and pick them up, bringing some extra clothes along. The adventure began.

Sure enough, Neil and his fellow inductee were taken to the lonely road, divested of their clothes, and left on their own. After a few minutes, they spotted the girlfriend's car. She blinked the headlights. At this provocation Neil began to prance down the road in the direction of her car, buck naked mind you, doing something like a rooster strut. She blinked again. He stepped up his pace. She began to blink furiously, which egged him on. When he reached the car, he shouted out "Showwww time!" But the surprise was on him! She was blinking the lights, not as a come-on, but as a signal that her mother was sitting in the passenger seat. When I told this story as part of my eulogy at Neil's funeral, a woman came up laughing, telling me that she had been that very same girl.

As we grew older, Neil and I became close. He and Laurie lived at the bottom of a narrow sandy lane, in a cottage on Oglesby Pond near Portal, Georgia. By this time we had become best of friends and confidants. After Edward died, whenever I felt discouraged, I'd drive to Neil's. When I turned off the highway, an enormous weight was lifted from my shoulders, and I'd breathe a down-to-the-depths sigh. Neil would welcome me and mix me a "brown," his signature drink of diet Sprite and Lord Calvert Canadian Whiskey, and then we'd settle in. Neil not only made me feel at home, he *listened* to me. What's more he *heard* what I said. How many card games we played, how many hours we laughed away, how many hundreds of jokes we told and retold. We talked seriously sometimes, I confess, but I felt comfortable enough with Neil to tell him anything. A night or two with Neil and Laurie was the balm of Gilead, and I returned home restored. One of the great things about Neil was that he was absolutely accepting, never judgmental.

He cultivated delicious blueberries. He'd call me early every summer and say: "I have one word—blueberries," whereupon I'd throw some clothes in the car and head to Bulloch County. He was famous for his "Low Country Boils," which we enjoyed time and time again, not only at his house, but at Tybee and at Mary's rehearsal party in Danielsville.

We talked about old times. Accepting that we were not our mother's favorite child, either one of us, led to funny anecdotes and plentiful memories. The best example was a time of family gathering in Danielsville. Mother, bless her heart, for years knitted caps for the homeless in Savannah. She did excellent handwork and combined interesting colors. Occasionally we'd spot with delight someone on the street who was wearing one of Mother's distinctive watch caps, pulled down for warmth over his ears. She generously gave all the children and grandchildren a hat, too. One Thanksgiving when all the family gathered at Booger Hill, she spread an abundance of caps out on my kitchen table and invited Neil to choose one. He replied, "Mother they are all so beautiful, why don't you just choose one for me?" She insisted that he pick one, any one of his choice. He repeated his protest, and she further insisted. Finally, he chose a pretty blue one. She quickly announced, "Any one except the blue one." He and I exchanged a private glance and grin and later did a thumbs up. What might well have hurt someone's feelings, Neil was able to laugh at. It helped, I think, that he had me as a cohort in mischief.

We shared a moment of uncontrollable giggling, when, at Mother's 80th birthday party, our brother Ranny got us to hold hands and lift them together to feel, as he called it, communal "synergy." Quite an experience, to Neil and me, an hysterical experience, coming from our aggressively atheist brother. We snickered uncontrollably, even under the admonishing glances of my well-behaved daughters.

Mary pointed out that Neil was always able to turn some uncomfortable or even disastrous scene into something funny. He had the wonderful capacity for self-effacement. He never ridiculed others. He laughed at a dinner scene at the Varnadoe's, one of Savannah's most elite families. One night as the cook was formally serving plates on fine china, she spooned a serving of peas onto Neil's plate. Neil paused and requested a little bit more "pot likker." The Varnedoes collectively looked up perplexed, yet polite as always. But the cook knew exactly what he wanted, and she complied. What would have sent the likes of Woody Allen to the therapist's couch, Neil just tucked away for a future story.

He told about the time he was going to save on the plumber's fee by unstopping the toilet line. In a way that only Neil could tell, he dug up the pipe, jammed a "snake" up the line, all to no avail. Finally, he put his face down to see what was keeping the sewage from draining. At that very moment, the obstruction gave way, and, as he told it, he got a face full of poop.

When Neil was young and still at home, Mother needed him to go to Uncle Windell's and get some horse manure for her flowers. It was an unpleasant task. He not only had to muck out the stable, but he had to load the manure onto the truck, drive to Mother's, shovel off the trailer and put the "guano," as our grandmother Sissy would have said, around the plants. It was a very hot day, which made the task even more unpleasant. He was in a grumble. Anna Bruce, the girl next door, came over to bolster his mood. Dear, naïve Anna exclaimed: "I didn't know your uncle had horses," to which Neil, knee deep in horse droppings, replied: "Not horses. White mice."

Everyone who knew Neil was touched by his wit, his kindness, his interest in and love for his family and friends. I was devastated when Laurie called late one night to tell me that he had inexplicably collapsed in the front yard and had been taken by ambulance to the Bullock County Hospital. I packed my car and waited through the hot, sticky night for the first rays of daylight to drive down. Neil died before I could get there.

Later that night, a somber night indeed, I caught an image of Neil calling to St. Peter, "Hey, Pete, did you hear the one about..." as he looked over his shoulder, gave us a grin and a wave, and danced through the Pearly Gates. I trust that the dance was a bit more dignified and subdued than his earlier one at the fraternity initiation. If not, heaven had better watch out!

Neil died in July 2008, and, Lordy, how much I miss him!

John: The Serious

John was the fifth and last child born to my parents. He was a beautiful baby, with olive skin, like my father's youngest brother, Henri. He had lovely brown curls, too. Mother was reluctant to cut his hair, and I imagine that part of the reason is that she was sure (or she hoped!) that John would be her last child, and she wanted to preserve his babyhood. There was certainly a strong bond between the two, which lasted all of Mother's life. John was the fourth son, and, therefore named after the fourth and last side of the family. He was christened John Ingram Bradford, the namesake of John Mason Ingram, our "Uncle Jack" who lived with us.

I don't think that any of us were aware of how confusing and unsettling young John's life was. To begin with, Ranny was twelve when the youngest sibling was born, and he felt, as the oldest, some sort of adult relationship to us younger children. He had rummaged around a bit in family genealogy and thought that John should be named for some obscure ancestor, Stephen Decatur. I thought that an ever-so-romantic name, and I cast my vote with Ranny. So, even though our parents held fast to naming him after my great uncle, Ranny and I referred to him, for a couple of months at least, as "Stephen Decatur."

To add to the confusion, since there were already so many "Johns" in our family, he was called by his middle name, "Ingram." We older children transformed such a stiff, formal name into numerous nicknames, all of which infuriated our littlest brother. Showing early the strong resolve that he has had all his life, John announced, on the first day of first grade, that his name was "John" and that was the only name he would answer to. That pretty much settled that, except for my grandmother's numerous Ingram cousins, who persisted in calling him by his middle name, their family name, which always in their estimation implied near nobility. I might add here that they were highly provincial.

As a little boy John had many masters, or mistresses or madams, whatever. Because of our father's ill health, Mother had begun teaching. Our grandmother Sissy became, thus, the main disciplinarian in the house. She was to me, unwaveringly strict and stern, but maybe even she had a tender place in her heart for this little one, surely to be the final child. With the rest of us in school and our father at work when his health would allow, Sissy and John were left home together. She walked him to kindergarten every day, to a Methodist church about four or five blocks from our house, retrieving him at noon.

In the spring, before the year was up, Sissy suddenly died. I'm not certain whether John finished out the year from her death in March to the end of the program, but I somehow doubt that he did. His care was haphazard after that, with his going on business trips with our father from time to time. Mother always claimed that our father was particularly smitten with babies, but lost interest as we children grew older. So, doubtless, our father doted on John, at least the year after Sissy died. But then our father, himself, died suddenly. What a disastrous series of deaths and disappointment for a young boy to cope with. We were all so busy licking our own wounds that I doubt any of us had time or energy enough to be of much succor for him. It's particularly wrenching for me to learn that John has no memories whatsoever of our Aunt Sarah, of either of our grandmothers, or even of our father. Perhaps he just closed himself down emotionally.

After Sissy and our father both died within a year of each other, our beloved collie "Lassie" became terribly debilitated. Mother had to "put her down." Not long afterwards, John was given a beagle puppy, whom he named "Albert." There were no leash laws back then, and Albert, like all the other dogs in the neighborhood, was free to wander the streets. We didn't know it then, and it seems like we usually had to learn things through experience, or, more expressly through error, but owners of hunting dogs need to be vigilant right before hunting season begins. People drive around and steal them. That was surely the fate of poor Albert, who abruptly disappeared and was never seen again, either by us or by any of the other families in the neighborhood. John was heartbroken. He stood by his window every evening, just as the sun was setting, and called plaintively, over and over again: "Albert, come home."

The truth is that just because we were never allowed to talk about my father after he died, that didn't mean that we didn't grieve. We buried our grief in the isolation of our separate hearts. Doubtless, and I think that we knew it even then, John was calling out for more than his beagle, but for the thing that could not be spoken nor ever again found. Those were hard days for everyone.

Since Mother was busy at work, I became a mother substitute for the younger boys. I was shamefully partial to John, mostly, I think because the seven years between us gave me maternal feelings for him. Neil was only four years younger, and I considered him a pest. John was much easier to get along with, and I played with him for hours and hours. He did have a temper, though, which he seemed to have been born with. Whenever he had a bad tantrum, Mother picked him up, took him into the bathroom and put his head underneath the spigot of the tub, then turned the water on. The technique was very effective, perhaps an inspiration to Dick Cheney.

When we lived on White Bluff Road, my grandmother often sent me to play outside with John, who was but a toddler. At the end of a long hedge was a tree whose trunk had grown in a twist, making a 90-degree angle. I fashioned a saddle, and John spent hours riding his horse, with makeshift reins, me holding him on. We also had a pool with standing water in the deep end. I was supposed to keep a vigilant eye on my little brother. One day, I apparently got distracted, though I can't now remember how, some eight-year-old preoccupation, and John disappeared. Frantically I searched for him. I found him inside the concrete pool, not crying, just there in the shallow end, walking around, babbling. I quickly scooped him up to the grass and failed, for the obvious reason, to mention the incident to my parents or my grandmother. I was grateful that he was not yet talking, himself. To this day, I don't know how he got there. He was too small to walk down the steps, and there was no sign of tears, so he surely didn't fall in.

When we moved to 46th Street, Sissy turned me out day after day with both brothers, Neil walking and John in his stroller. The roofline of the nearby Presbyterian church was long and straight, with decorative spires at each end. We could see only the roof, not the church, itself, on the horizon, as I pushed the stroller down Washington Avenue with one hand and clutched Neil with the other. I told Neil, John being too young to understand, that that was the city wall and that we all had to be careful not to breach the gate, whereupon we'd be shot on sight. I was convincing--and naughty--as

I highly traumatized the five-year-old Neil, who constantly asked if we had strayed near the walls yet.

I was in charge of dressing John when he was a little boy. Being an older (and wiser!) sister, I had definite notions about what he was to wear. Often he resisted. I assured him that I knew more about boys than he did, because I had more brothers. Very seriously, as John was a serious child, he'd stop and count my brothers, then his own. I had four, whereas he had only three. He always acquiesced. After some time, he clued in. He told me that he knew more about girls than I did, as he had more sisters than I. I merely replied that such a notion was ridiculous, as I was, after all, a girl. That ended the discussion. And John has never forgiven me.

I spent hours upon hours with him playing with his "men," little plastic cowboys and Indians or army men. We'd build a fort in the corner of the dining room and were even allowed to keep it up during the weekly cleaning of the house. We'd saddle up the horses and plan attacks, mostly ambushes. When Santa brought me a "Baby Coo" doll one Christmas, Neil had to have the next year what he called his own "Doo Doll." I'd never been interested in playing with dolls, not much at least, so Neil's doll games didn't appeal to me, but I was quite comfortable with forts, Indians, cowboys, and army men.

When John was a teenager, he contracted measles. He was confined to his bed in a darkened room. He was miserable. I spent time reading to him, and then got the bright idea that I would teach him to play chess. I did. Naturally I let him win the first half-dozen games. He, after all, was my baby brother, seven years my junior. I then decided that he would have to lose a game or two, also. Well, the upshot was that I couldn't win! My little brother, a total novice who had played only a few games, was unbeatable. I was chagrined. He recovered, and we never met over the chess board again.

John continued to be a handsome lad into his teens. He, too, tried his hand at football, if that's not mixing a metaphor too greatly. Like Neil, he started off as a Panther, then moved on to play on the middle-school team. But he broke a front tooth in one game and injured his knee in another, an injury which has plagued him for life. Dr. Peterson, our family doctor, pointed out to Mother that John was not built for such brutal physical contact, and John's athletic aspirations were cut short early, just as Neil's had been. Fortunately, he was a pretty good student.

John was as serious as Neil was funny. Once when he, Ranny, and I were on a nostalgic trip through Alabama, I asked, in Neil-fashion: "Have you heard the one about…" John replied tersely, "No. And I don't want to," as resolutely as he had proclaimed in first grade that he would answer to no name except "John." My youngest brother had no room in his life for levity. He was born with a no-nonsense attitude.

The two younger boys always shared a room, except for the brief time that Neil moved a sleeping bag into the attic, retreating back down to his bedroom only when his asthma flared up. Life was not easy for either of them. Whereas Ranny and Windell had never fought, John and Neil were "at each other" with frequency. Part of this was due to their diverse personalities, but part, I think, was due to the fact that there were no checks and balances. Not only was the older generation gone, but Mother worked long hours, so the younger two boys had little supervision. I can't imagine daring to fight in front of Sissy, who was not too old to impose the punishment she gave her own two sons when they scuffled. She forced them to fight on.

John became a committed and very successful businessman, and his consuming work left little time for anybody in his own family, but, after he retired, he and Mother resumed their former closeness. It was particularly touching to see and feel their devotion to each other during the last several years of Mother's life. John caressed her and held her hand when they walked down the hall of the hospital. He poured all of his attention to her well-being. When she died, I told John that I loved him, not only because he was my brother, but also because of his tenderness toward our mother. He had given her something that the rest of us weren't able to.

Neil worked for Unijax Paper Company, and he got John a job there shortly after John and Julia were married. Neil's approach was always with an eye for the humorous, and, when he visited the men's room in every establishment for miles around, he reported with great gusto and some irony which bathrooms had two-ply toilet tissue and which had scrimped by using only one ply. It was surprising how some top-end restaurants and stores economized by allowing their patrons to have scratchy bottoms.

John took his job much more seriously. When it came time to advance, which meant moving to Atlanta, Neil chose to live a low-key, modest life, enjoying the slow pace of the rural area and the companionship of his friends and established clients. John moved to the big city, and his career was remarkable. He was the top national salesman in the entire company year after year. His rewards took him to vacations all over the globe, from Morocco to China. In every promotional video to inspire salesmen, John Bradford was the star. Neil took some razzing from his colleagues, but was always proud of his accomplished little brother.

My youngest brother became so successful in his job that the whole company was restructured, with the comment by the CEO, "that nobody will ever be able to make as much money here as John Bradford has." On his own, John retired early, still in his early fifties.

He began another business, renovating old houses, again with a Midas touch, and has gone on to other entrepreneurial enterprises. He lives in an authentic antebellum home in the city of Marietta, Georgia. He is a man of purpose and has enjoyed a great deal of financial success.

However old we get, John will always remain my baby brother, the one with the serious blue eyes and light brown curls dancing in the breeze, a handsome and resolute little boy who took charge of his uncertain life and became the master of it.

SISSY: CAPTAIN OF OUR SHIP

We called our mother's mother "Sissy," Ranny's childhood mispronunciation of "Sister," which is what her five younger brothers and sisters (two of whom lived with us) had always called her. Sissy was born in 1880 and was christened Ethel Viola Ingram. Her mother was a Newton, who shared a common ancestor with Sir Isaac, and the Ingrams and the Newtons never forgot "who they were." She was nineteen years older than the youngest child, Julian, and she tended to her younger siblings as if they were her own. They were devoted to her for the rest of their lives, and she must have had a sweet, soft side in her younger days.

Sissy and I knew each other well, though we didn't really know each other at all. She and I shared a bedroom after Aunt Sarah died, but we didn't share anything other than our twin beds side by side, iron beds which were painted black and which had been part of her "married furnishings." Like her iron beds, she was cold, stern, and unrelenting. Not too long after she died, I read "A Rose for Emily" and would have sworn that Faulkner had known my grandmother. Sissy and Miss Emily had the same stiff torso, silhouetted in the shadows of the closed window. I watched every morning, summer and winter, as Sissy laced up her corset as tightly as she laced up her emotions, yanking the strings from bottom to top, one by one, with great resolution. Thus body and soul were fortified to meet the challenges that the day would inevitably bring.

I thumb through photographs of Sissy on the beach with us grandchildren. She was dressed in an amazingly skimpy bathing suit, nearly as small as the corset she wore under her dresses. I also see the photos of her standing in an old bateau (pronounced "bad-o," in corrupted French fashion) wearing a broad-brimmed straw hat and long sleeves, both to protect her from the sun and salt which would have weathered her skin as gray and cracked as the surface of the little boat. She taught us how to drop our thick-stained lines weighted down with sinkers and saggy chicken necks over the side of the boat. If we were lucky, we pulled up unsuspecting crabs clinging complacently with their pinchers to their chicken-neck lunch, numbed in their gluttony. Just before they reached the surface and were startled by the air, before they were able to drop back into the soft, warm mud, Sissy scooped them up in a crab net. She shook them into a bucket to join their equally ill-fated sons and brothers, but not daughters and sisters, as it was illegal to keep females, especially the females with masses of yellow eggs. No one in the boat knew how to swim back then, as we were small children, not even Sissy, but she stood guard over the murky brackish water and balanced the boat as deftly as if she were the captain of a yacht. With her at the helm, our little rowboat never capsized, though it surely swayed with the tides and lurched with the sudden movements of us children. I know that these things happened because of the photographs, and we must have had fun, but the pleasure has life only in snapshots, not in my memories.

I vaguely remember the summer that Sissy, Aunt Sarah, and I took the Pullman train to Florida to visit their sister, my Great Aunt Pearla, but even that trip doesn't conjure up pleasant memories. The extended cousins were ill-mannered and unfriendly, and I recall the name of only one of them, Norman, who was being groomed as a concert pianist. We were allowed nowhere in the vicinity of his grand piano, making a wide circle when we walked through the living room. Norman was spoiled and much doted on, though the dreams for the young prodigy never materialized. So I guess he just grew up fractious, rather than famous. I was surprised on the trip down that my puritanical grandmother actually walked down the aisle of the train in her dressing gown and slippers, all in front of utter strangers. What a shock. That night she and I were stuffed together into the top Pullman compartment, and Aunt Sarah got the lower berth, a concession, rightly so, to her blindness. The noise and motion of the train offered neither sleep nor pleasure.

My happy memories of Sissy are bound inextricably with food, especially the glorious Sunday dinners. We came home after Sunday school and church to a big platter of fried chicken, rice and gravy, peas or butter beans, sliced tomatoes in season, and biscuits. She specialized in what we called "blackened squash." She sliced squash and onions and sautéed them long and slow, turning them over frequently so as not to burn, until both the squash and onions caramelized. They were sweet and delicious, and her technique remains a favorite of all my children. Her chicken was lightly dusted with flour, seasoned mildly with salt and pepper, and fried golden brown in bacon grease, a tin of which always stood on the top of the stove between the two back burners. Her biscuits were small, thin and "short," which refers more to the texture and fat content than to the size, though they were, indeed, small, small and flat, and absolutely delicious.

We ate rice with almost every evening meal. In fact, after tucking away her handwork in the sewing basket or setting aside her huge black magnifying glass and newspaper, she'd say, "I guess it's time to put on the rice," and head to the kitchen. We coastal people, with our sandy soil, rarely ate potatoes. I only discovered baked potatoes and tossed salad at my friend Elizabeth Allen's house, and I attributed the exotic food to the fact that her mother was a "Yankee." All our greens were cooked, except for an occasion or two when we ate raw cabbage in coleslaw.

I loved stewed tomatoes, made with a pinch of sugar and a dash of salt, and served with rice and streak-o-lean, strips of pork which were first boiled in water, then fried crisp, with lovely crunchy edges. Sissy cooked greens and succotash, scalloped tomatoes and fried okra. She made delicious vegetable gumbo, which we in North Georgia refer to as "soup mix." But best of all were her hoe cakes, the size of crepes or tortillas, but made with only cornmeal and water with a pinch of salt and drizzled into very hot bacon grease, cooked crisp with crunchy lacy edges. The taste was a little bitter-sweet, but absolutely delicious.

All these dishes were typical Southern fare at everyone's dinner table, but now they are found exclusively in soul food restaurants. Given our current society's fast pace and commitment to consumerism, nowadays most people do little more than slit a vent in the cellophane before closing the door to the microwave. The timer dings, announcing that the bland rubber-like vegetables are, loosely speaking, "cooked." Sissy would be aghast, rightfully so.

The warmest memory I do have is the afternoon snack that was waiting for me when I came home from school. I don't actually remember her at snack time or even the snacks, themselves, but just the pleasure I felt that someone took the time to do something special for me. I missed that terribly after she died. For weeks after her death, although I practiced every step on the way home from school, reminding myself that she was dead, the touch of the knob as I opened the door affected me in some Pavlovian fashion and I'd call out, "Sissy, I'm home." The house was empty. And I felt doubly dejected, with the forgetting that she had died and the stillness in the kitchen.

Sallie Krickel

But my most vivid memories of her are unpleasant. She was ever so strict and unwavering. My Aunt Madeline, my father's youngest sister, confided that she had never really cared for my grandmother, finding her rigid and distant. Even mother told me on several occasions that Sissy had a "nervous disposition," never explaining exactly what that meant. (Mother had the habit of saying, "Well, you know..." and trailing off without telling us anything!) Under Sissy's vigilant and critical eye I suffered as dramatically as only a pre-teen girl can. The Sissy I remember was a difficult and unhappy person. She tore up and threw away any comic books left lying about. She scolded us constantly. Nothing I did measured up to her expectations. I didn't dry the dishes well enough; I swept the floor either too hard or not hard enough; I never stood up straight.

As one of her two lone granddaughters and the one she lived with, I was expected to be prim and proper. She tried hard, and I'm often mindful of her efforts. She wouldn't let me play hopscotch in the dirt, but insisted that I play on the grass. She tore up long strips of old sheets and laid out my hopscotch design. Of course that didn't work at all. For one thing, the "lines" didn't stay in place. What was worse, though, was that we could never tell who stepped on the line, as there was no smudging of the earth. Pretty dresses didn't stop me from climbing trees; they merely made the effort less decent.

On the cusp of adolescence (I was twelve when she died), I resented her and chafed under her strict and unrelenting requirements. I even one time had the temerity to complain to my mother. Children back then didn't talk back to their elders or, if they did, they were roundly punished. In terrible frustration, I told my mother that she was going to have to choose either Sissy or me because we could no longer live in the same house. What a thing to say, and the surprising thing is that I had been bold enough to speak so disrespectfully. Even more surprising is that I was not punished.

The most vivid memory that both Neil and I had of Sissy is her shaking her finger in our face, firmly insisting: "Don't you dispute my word." And I didn't. Sometimes the boys did, and their mouths were washed out with soap. I can't remember her smiling at us, cuddling us, or being in any way intimate. Particularly crushing were the times that I broke, absentmindedly, into song as we were doing the dishes. She'd scold me, saying that if I couldn't sing on key, not to sing at all. I rarely do, even after all these years. One of the cardinal rules was that we couldn't sing or even laugh at the dinner table. I can understand her fussing if we had our elbows on the table, but the not singing or laughing seems to me now merely a stifling of happy thoughts and impulses.

I wonder how long it took for her to cultivate such bitterness. She was such a contrast to the young woman in her family photograph, the one who seems so pleased with her life and her four young children, who has an almost pleasant half-smile on her face and an air of contentment. I think that she might have been capable of humming, if not outright laughing, back in her younger days. But those days had long ended. As long as I knew her, she laced her corset tight.

Sissy and her children (from left) John and Windell, Mother and Aunt Billie

Even the stories about her as a young mother were uncomplimentary, though not intentionally so. It was my mother, a great admirer of my grandmother, who told me about Sissy's efforts to break her sons from fighting by whipping them if they stopped. It reminds me of Livia in *I, Claudius*, who insisted that the slaves in the arena fight to their death. If not, they would be killed! Livia wanted no theatrics, no sham pigs' bladders full of blood; she demanded real brutality and real blood. Judging by my uncles' strained relationship when they were adults, Sissy's tactics had not worked.

Whenever her own children displeased her, she sent them to bed without any dinner, solitary confinement without even bread and water. When our grandfather was out on his railroad "run" and Sissy was left alone with the children, she brandished her dainty pearl-handled revolver and fired shots in the air if the "negroes" across the railroad tracks got too rowdy. She was a veritable "pistol-packing lady" not a "mama," as she certainly felt herself too dignified to be called that.

Mother told a story about our grandfather's short tenure as a Klansman. A group of the townsmen donned white sheets and "visited" en masse the home of one of their neighbors. The husband, it was discovered, was being unfaithful to his wife, and the Klansmen meant to set him straight. It was not a racial matter, as both the husband and wife were white, but a moral matter, at least a different kind of "moral" issue. Mother proudly used this story as an illustration of the virtues of the Klan. That aside, and that would be another story, what was important was my grandmother's reaction to his midnight ride. She met him at the door when he returned and told him quite emphatically that if he ever rode with the Klan again, she would leave him. He didn't and she didn't. That was quite a bold assertion for a woman of her era, but I'm sure she meant it, even though she had no other place to go.

My husband Edward always maintained that "there was not a kitchen in the whole world large enough to accommodate two women," and, late in her life, I asked mother if she and Sissy had ever had any discord. They had never shown any in front of the children. She replied instantly and firmly, "Yes, we certainly had." But she never elaborated; it was a plain, direct statement. I wanted to hear more, but nothing else was forthcoming. I remained curious, but mother shared her own mother's reticence about discussing feelings.

As I've aged, though, and have become a grandmother myself, I am seized with overwhelming regret about my grandmother's state. She had spent her childhood and married life in comfort and security, if modest security, but in her last years she was dependent on the charity of others. She lost her money in poor investments (a failed business venture of my father's, according to Ranny) and was reduced to living on a small pension. She lived in a household fraught with the cold tension of her daughter's loveless marriage, inhabited by five active (to put it kindly) grandchildren, destined to share her room with an ungrateful granddaughter, and inhibited by her inability to ever, ever give or receive confidences.

When I was very young, probably around five or six, our parents suffered their personal financial depression. My father became ill and lost his business. Our nursemaids disappeared to tend to other people's children, the cook prepared another family's dinner, and the gardener's trowel dug flower beds across town. After several years of my father's declining health, our situation was near desperate. Mother began teaching school, and Sissy became our unpaid servant, consigned to cleaning and cooking. How terribly cruel. Her impatience and her cruelty to us children provided the only outlet for her inner rage, even if subconsciously. No wonder she was so cold, distant, and strict.

Neil tells a story about her in a way that only Neil could tell. One day a mouse (though, for narrative purposes, Neil always referred to it as "the rat") had the temerity to invade our kitchen. Our dignified grandmother got the broom and cornered the rat in the pantry, whereupon she lost all sense of dignity and propriety and pounded the unfortunate thing to death. Neil described the scene of Sissy delivering blow after blow on the hapless creature, with blood spurting everywhere. My grandmother raged with increasing ferocity. Neil said that, after a while, he began "pulling for the rat."

To all appearances she was an extraordinarily puritan lady, one who would never have stepped out of the house without gloves and a hat, however strained her circumstances or anguished her heart. She saw to it that we, her five charges, watched our manners at the dinner table and everywhere else. She was as guarded in her speech as she was in her appearance. The subject of sex was not only unmentionable, but unthinkable. Too "refined" to speak of anatomy, she not only referred to the thigh of the chicken as the "second joint" but to the breast of a chicken as "white meat." Suggestive, sexually charged vocabulary could never have passed her lips.

On the fourth anniversary of her sister's death, the ominous Ides of March, 1955, Sissy and Uncle Jack, along with their double first cousins, Claudia and Annie Ruth Ingram, went to Bonaventure Cemetery to lay commemorative flowers on Aunt Sarah's grave. Sissy suffered a stroke. Uncle Jack and the two elderly cousins managed to get her into the car, to the floor of the back seat. They drove to the hospital, but she died that afternoon. Ranny came to Charles Ellis School to get me and told me that she was ill and in the hospital. He gave me the option of going to see her or of taking John and Neil to the park for the afternoon. I chose the latter. To be utterly honest, I preferred to go see her, but, I, too, had my grandmother's strong sense of duty, and I knew that my younger brothers needed seeing after. Besides that, it never occurred to me that she, Sissy, the strongest and most monumental person I'd ever known, could actually die. She had always looked adversity straight in the eye. She was unconquerable. I would think that she could have warded off Emily Dickenson's "Mr. Death" with a shake of her finger in his face, a defiant stare, or, if that didn't work, a bloody broom handle.

The news of her death was crushing. My failure to go to her bedside was devastating. Though we were never what one would call close, we were important to each other. My recent resentments of her assailed me, and my self-incriminations were intense. I heard Uncle Jack say that she had prayed on the way to the hospital for God to "take her" so that she would not "be a burden to anyone." I was horrified that she seemed to have abandoned me so willingly. I took her death as a personal betrayal.

I have always been a little disappointed that, as much time as we spent together, Sissy never told me stories of her childhood or even of my mother's. She never left me with words of wisdom. The only things that she might say that were not totally utilitarian, were exhortations like, "Don't carry a lazy man's load." I can't remember a single present she gave me other than a book, *Nico's Mountains*. I still have her bedroom suite and her engagement ring, and a few other things like her seal coat, but Mother saw to it that I have them. They were not from my grandmother per se. The main thing she left me are restless thoughts of disappointment and the awareness that I could never "measure up."

AUNT SARAH AND UNCLE JACK: OUR UNCLAIMED TREASURES

In addition to my parents, my four brothers, my grandmother, and me, our household also consisted of my grandmother Sissy's unmarried sister and brother, Aunt Sarah and Uncle Jack. It was understood that widows and spinster children (male and female) would be taken care of by relatives. We took our responsibilities seriously.

My Great Aunt Sarah (after whom both my mother and I are named) was a patient and gentle soul. Everybody loved her. She had

become blind in her early fifties and had had to take early retirement from the Central of Georgia Railway. She and Sissy roomed together at our house, wherever we lived. Most every morning we children would begin our day "looking for Aunt Sarah's cane," which she would have leaned against a piece of furniture the night before and which had subsequently fallen behind it. We actually, for the most part, conducted our daily chore without too much of a grumble, partly because of the break from our boredom and partly because Aunt Sarah was a sympathetic pres-

Sissy and Aunt Sarah

ence. Unlike most of the dour Ingrams, she had a wry sense of humor. She had been an avid reader when she was "sighted" and even tried to teach herself Braille when her impairment worsened. When we lived on White Bluff Road (not long before her death), she entered a jingle contest for which the prize was a newfangled contraption called a clothes dryer. I can't remember the entire jingle, but it had the lines about the difficulty of "hanging clothes on a tree" because she was "blind as blind can be."

Although she was blind, Aunt Sarah made herself useful. She still dried dishes every night and she helped with folding the laundry. In the afternoons, when she would formerly have sat down to needle-point, she learned to cover coat hangers, using a special technique of knotting the yarn. It always amazed me to see her. Yet, she and I had some tense moments.

She was the first person I knew who used Recordings for the Blind, and back in the late 1940s only the Bible had been record-ed. She would describe the Braille characters for me, asking me to find a particular passage on the old, brittle 78 records. I couldn't decipher the "letters" and we would both end up frustrated. I was sorry to let her down. She, also from time to time, would ask me to check her handwriting to be sure that she had not written a word which ran off the page. I didn't know cursive and all the words ran together to me. Again I disappointed her. Worst of all, I couldn't comprehend her blindness. Sometimes I tested her. While she sat on the sofa, I tried to sneak across the room without her knowing. She always, alarmed, cried out: "Who's there?" I was intrigued. If she couldn't see me and I sneaked by without making a sound, even holding my breath, how did she know I was there? Now I realize that she could perceive a shadow moving between her and the windows on the other side of the living room.

Aunt Sarah contracted cancer. Of course, as children, we were told merely that she was sick. I knew all about sickness, as I had had measles and mumps. After the pain advanced, she went to the hospital. I overheard Mother or Sissy telling someone that Aunt Sarah was too weak to turn over, and I was baffled. I practiced turn-ing over time after time, sometimes using only arms, sometimes only legs, sometimes just my torso. It was effortless. I concluded that this was another adult hyperbole, though I didn't know that word yet, and I dismissed it from my mind.

Aunt Sarah never came home. I'll never forget her death when I was seven. One spring afternoon, arriving home from school, I was excited to see the driveway lined with cars. With such a large family, someone was always visiting, and I entered the door with enthusiastic anticipation. There was a collection of relatives, surely enough, but no one talked in a normal voice. Aunt Sarah had died. I had never even thought of death. I could hardly comprehend the finality of it all. That's surely the worst thing, the finality. I had a lot to learn, and I did learn as Mr. Death was to become a frequent visitor.

Sissy and Aunt Sarah's brother, my Great Uncle Jack, was a bachelor, too, though he seemed, honestly, more like an old maid, a needy, querulous "unclaimed treasure." Uncle Jack "came home" to live with us after his retirement. Poor thing, he was a fussy old man, easily startled and jumpy, which probably had a lot to do with a whole shelf of medicine bottles on his bedside table. He had to have his food prepared separately, as he couldn't eat what the rest of us did. Well, actually, he did eat some of the same food, but he had to have it cooked specially, like taking a serving of cornbread stuffing, flattening it out like a pancake, and frying it crispy, which, by the way, I've learned is delicious.

There had never been any question of Uncle Jack's post-retirement plans; it was always certain that he would move in with his sister (Sissy) and her daughter. It must have been awful for him to have to room with Ranny and Windell, after having quarters of his own, but, as usual, we all coped.

Uncle Jack was still alive the summer of 1960, the year I graduated from high school and mother finished up her master's degree. She decided to live on campus in Statesboro, and both of the older boys were at summer school at Emory. Since, in addition to my part-time job at the library, I, a teenager myself, had charge of the household and the care of my two younger brothers, Mother decided that Uncle Jack, who always required extra attention, should "visit" someone else for those six weeks. She called his sister Pearla and his brothers Julian and Lafayette, but it suited no one for him to visit. So, he went to live on a temporary basis in a facility in Thunderbolt, near where Windell lives now. It was not a typical nursing home, but rather a nice, old house with bedrooms rented out and meals furnished.

Uncle Jack felt abandoned and was dreadfully unhappy. I felt guilty, knowing that I, basically, was the reason he was there. I went to visit nearly every day to assuage the pangs of my conscience. One blistering afternoon, as I arrived, the staff told me that he had taken a grave turn and probably should go to the hospital. I called Mother, but she was on an overnight field trip to Sapelo Island and couldn't be reached. I could find neither of my older brothers. So it was up to me to make all the decisions. I was worried that Uncle Jack couldn't afford a hospital, and I wondered if it were really necessary for him to go, but I got them to call the ambulance.

As soon as he was settled, I went home. I recognized the ominous thud in my chest and realized that Uncle Jack would not be coming home. By then I had become wise to dying and the trappings of a funeral. I had learned the drill, and I set about tidying up the house, getting ready for the onslaught of relatives, the few great uncles and great aunts who had survived and the whole, then decrepit, army of cousins who were limping along, out of formation, in the certain march toward their own destiny, pausing at our house on the way.

My Mother Sarah

My parents were the foundation of the whole group. Their disparate personalities were an enormous (the most enormous?) influence of my life. They met when my father was a young businessman and my mother worked in a lab, as she was a certified phlebotomist. He came in for some lab work after he had broken his arm and, after some mutual flirting and conversation, asked her for a date. Even though she was a college graduate and a member of the workforce (unpaid, as she was a woman and salaried jobs were reserved for the men during the Depression), she told him that she would have to ask her mother first. Sissy must have given her nod of approval, and after a short courtship, the couple were married in 1935.

Little Sarah Georgia

Little Sarah Georgia was the fourth and last child of my Robertson grandparents, Ethel (Sissy) and Arthur. She was an adorable little child, with platinum blond hair and a fetching smile, a little bit shy, judging by her childhood pictures. Living in the shadow of her two older brothers and her willful sister, her demeanor was calmer and more compliant. But she certainly showed her true mettle when time and circumstances required. All I know about her childhood are the few, sketchy stories she told me. Whenever her rowdy older brothers were punished by being sent to bed without supper, Mother always sneaked a biscuit or two from the supper table and surreptitiously slipped them into the miscreants' room. Though she doted on her brothers, she smarted even into adulthood about the injustices of her sister, five years her senior, with whom she shared a bedroom and who made her life miserable. By her own admission, Mother was the angel of the whole group; and, judging from what I knew of her siblings, she was right.

Mother virtually worshipped her father. Though without any advanced education himself, my grandfather had served as the local teacher for a couple of years before he took a job with the railroad. His great dream was for all his children to go to college. When Mother started elementary school, he relocated the family from rural Dover in Screven County to Macon because he felt that she was too young to ride the train to school, which her older brothers and sister had done. The schools in Macon were better, and he had high aspirations for his brood. His hopes were not realized, as not only did the boys not go to college, Mother thinks that they never even finished high school.

Grandfather Robertson

Grandfather was in despair, but his hopes were renewed, when Billie, who was very bright and a good student, graduated from high school and enrolled at Wesleyan, the women's college in Macon. Unfortunately, in her junior year, she secretly married, and her father found out. It must have been quite a dilemma for my grandfather, but puritan propriety outweighed education, and he made her quit school to go live with her new husband. Her entire life she regretted that she never finished college, but Grandfather stood his ground.

He must have been pleased, indeed, when Mother enrolled in GSCW, Georgia State College for Women, now called Georgia College at Milledgeville. Poor little freshman, she was terribly homesick. We have letters she wrote my grandmother, entreating her to write permission for mother to go out on a date. (GSCW during the 1930s required the girls to have written permission for every single date.) Mother explained to Sissy that she didn't know who she would go out with or where they would go. She would work out the specific details if only Sissy would grant her permission. Once she wrote, very apologetically, asking for an extra seventy cents, so that she could buy two new uniform blouses at thirty-five cents each. Mother's solution to being homesick was not to quit and go home, but to graduate in three years. My grandfather was justly proud. Because he lived in Savannah now and had to catch his railroad "run" in Macon, he couldn't attend her graduation. But he went early, the Saturday before the ceremony, and took Mother, Sissy, and Aunt Sarah to lunch. It was a joyous occasion. It was also a humbling occasion, as he had to ride the Greyhound Bus from Milledgeville to Macon, and, for a railroad man, riding the bus was a shameful thing. On the return trip, he suffered a stroke. I don't think that Mother's graduation, as thrilling as it was, caused his stroke, nor the abasement of riding the bus, but he never fully recovered. Mother, Sissy and Aunt Sarah returned to Savannah with sadness, rather than elation.

The nation's economy declined, recession hit full force. The Great Depression soon brought many family members to Perry Street, where my grandparents had set up housekeeping. Their grown sons, Windell and John, were both out of work, and they came home to live, too. My Aunt Sarah moved in, as well as Sissy's double first cousins, Claudia and Annie Ruth Ingram. So my mother, as a new college graduate returned home, home to this large conglomeration of people.

House on Perry Street

Her father recovered physically from his stroke, but he remained confused. His behavior became more and more erratic. Sissy was not able to care for him, so my Uncle John, his second son, was given the duty of handling his father. That didn't work out. My poor grandfather deteriorated at a fast pace, and one morning, my once dignified and gentle grandfather actually appeared in Chippewa Square, in front of the house, not only confused, but completely naked. What a terrible thing for him and what a shameful thing for my straight-laced grandmother. Neither her white gloves nor her black veil could conceal this great humiliation, and Grandfather was taken to the Georgia asylum, where he lived the last few years of his life in a state of utter oblivion. His brother and sisters never forgave Sissy for having him confined, though I don't think that anyone offered to help out. Irony of ironies, the Georgia State Hospital for the Insane was also located in Milledgeville, Georgia, the same town in which his daughter had graduated from college. So the town symbolized his greatest achievement and his greatest ignominy.

As I said, my own mother worshipped her father, and she used to tell me how wonderful he was, how loving and accepting of everyone, except, using her own terms, "Jews, Catholics, and Blacks." And, I never pointed out, except also for his own children. It was mother who told me that, when Uncle John got married at fifteen, my grandfather was so upset that he locked his son up in his bedroom to keep him apart from his dearly beloved new wife. John broke out a window and escaped.

My grandfather also refused to allow Uncle Tommy ever to set foot inside his house, as Uncle Tommy, a divorced man, had seduced and eloped with his elder daughter, my Aunt Billie. He refused even to visit Billie, though Sissy didn't forsake their daughter and boldly visited on her own. I'll accept my mother's assertion of grandfather's all-embracing kindness and acceptance, with a smile on my face. After all, the only way

I have even really known him is a gray headstone, chiseled sharply with his name and the years of his birth and death. That doesn't reveal much—or maybe that reveals everything.

Uncle Windell, my parents, Aunt Billie, Grandfather Bradford

Mother had earned a degree with a double major in physics and English, with a minor in chemistry. She graduated in June 1933, and she married on June 27, 1935. The ceremony was held at home, as was the custom of the time, in the large parlor on Perry Street.

My father was a successful businessman, and the future promised nothing but the best of all that life could bring. My older brothers, Ranny and Windell, were born. Then I came along. Unfortunately my father began to have a succession of serious health problems, heart disease, tuberculosis, and serious esophageal dysfunction, while still in his thirties. His business ventures failed as surely as his health. The situation became more and more desperate. Even though Mother was qualified to teach or to work again in a lab, my father held to the old-fashioned notion that it wasn't appropriate for a wife to work "outside the home." A working wife upset the normal balance and emasculated a man. It was a strange position for him to hold, as his own mother had had to work after Grandfather Bradford died. After several years of downward spiraling, mother was forced to get a job. My father reluctantly allowed her to teach school, one of the few "acceptable" professions for women. Philosophical ideas aside, we were hungry.

When my father died, mother was left, not only with the care of her five children and her unmarried uncle, but with mountains of debt from my father's illnesses. She had had no idea how things stood, as it was also part of the code that women didn't meddle in family finances, even if it was she who provided them. Our father's body had long since been broken by heart disease and his spirit by disappointments. He had lost his health insurance because of illness (the pre-existing disease con-

Our family before John was born

dition) and had long since cashed in his life insurance to meet the family's immediate needs. Mother stacked up the bills, one time laughing that she was beholden to doctors with names of every letter of the alphabet.

The stack of my mother's debts was nearly as tall as the stack of her shattered dreams, but she was not one to sit around and bemoan her fate. She enrolled in a master's degree program, not particularly to learn anything, but merely to enhance her salary. She had to drive to Statesboro, fifty-five miles away, every day during the summers and every Saturday during the school year. Even though she taught an occasional course at Savannah State, the black college just a couple of miles from our house, white people were not allowed to take classes there. We even spent one desperate summer in Tuscaloosa when she won a fellowship to the University of Alabama.

Mother had part-time jobs, too. She worked as a telemarketer for *World Book Encyclopedia* in order to earn enough points for us to receive our own set. She felt mortified and hated it. In those days, before telemarketing became widespread, one was required to reveal his or her name, first and last. I remember her slurring over "Srrr Bbbbfd," in a desperate hope of anonymity.

She taught in the early years of the Head Start Program and had wrenching stories to tell of her little charges who slipped their afternoon snacks into their pockets so that they would have some supper in the evening. Many of them had no real home, but "stayed with" various people at night. At the end of one year the poverty-stricken little children threw her a going away party. They surprised her with a table full of every kind of Twinkies, Little Debbies, and other delectable convenience-store sweets. She looked into their malnourished faces and eager eyes and told them that she wanted to share the delicious abundance with the whole class. They refused a single bite, saying that they had brought it all to her. One boy bragged that he had hocked his high school ring for the money, but he was only in the fourth grade. If he had hocked anything, it certainly hadn't been his. It was a terrible dilemma, but there was nothing for mother to do except reach down into the depths of her moral courage and thank them. She gathered up the probably shoplifted loot and headed to her little white bungalow in Wymberly, just before suppertime, wondering what her destitute little students would find to eat that night.

Like her father, she valued education, and all five of us children attended the local college, Armstrong, and then Ranny and Windell headed off to Emory and I to Wesleyan. A fellow communicant at Wesley Monumental helped subsidize the boys, and we all had academic scholarships, the only way we could have attended expensive private colleges. In fact, when I used to fill out applications, I would get the awards back in the return mail. Not exactly, of course, but when anyone found out that my mother was a widowed schoolteacher with five children, people would almost take the shirts off their backs. It was kind of amusing to me, because I didn't feel at all pathetic. Quite the contrary, I had a strange sort of confidence and a serious commitment to making good grades, actually more like an obsession, and I had scored pretty well on the SATs. Like my Grandfather Robertson and my mother, too, I still value education, and I love to learn, though I'm a dabbler in lots and an expert in nothing.

Mother paid off all the debts and other bills. Somehow, someway, with strong resolution and deep faith, she got on her feet. But it was not easy. After my father died, Mother went to the bank to borrow some money. The loan officer laughed her out of his office. Not only did she not have any collateral, she was a woman. And even though she was expected to rear and provide for her five children, she was not allowed the means to do it. Her resolve didn't buckle, however, and her determination was struck.

Within five years after my father's death, Mother decided that it was time to buy a house. She again hit the wall of resistance, the forerunner to the great glass ceiling. Insistently, she told the bank to call her references. Judge Oliver, our lifelong friend who presided over the trial in *Midnight in the Garden...* told the banker that he would never make a more secure loan or a better investment. The loan officer relented, and again she prevailed.

Mother bought the house in Wymberly, on the Isle of Hope. She was prouder of her little house than she could ever have been of any of the fine homes she and our father had dreamed of and designed. Furthermore, it was *hers,* an outside acknowledgement of her inner strength and courage. With the younger boys in high school, the end of her maternal responsibilities was in sight.

She transferred her church membership from the huge downtown Wesley Monumental to the more casual Isle of Hope Methodist. She remade her image into someone that she should have been all along. She resumed her social life, which had been sacrificed to the cares and burdens of rearing a family single-handedly. She bought some bridge cards. She renewed her DAR participation. She became active in her professional sorority and joined a book club. She eagerly resumed her participation in church, serving on the board, joining a "circle," and singing with the Sparklers, a senior citizen choir. She baked pounds of "brittle bread" for the bazaar. She knitted watch caps for the homeless. She was loyal to her tithing and managed a little philanthropy. Washing her china and crystal and polishing her silver, she entertained graciously, just like in the early days.

Nothing has pleased me more than to see my mother, who in our darkest days had alternated the only three "work" dresses that she owned, able to shop at any store she wanted to, to buy not only whatever she needed but whatever she wanted. She once apologized when she came to visit me for a week that she couldn't decide what she should wear and ended up bringing thirteen pairs of shoes. I was thrilled.

She knew and loved all fourteen of her grandchildren, always mentioning their little individual traits and accomplishments. She was strict with them, just as she had been with us. But they accepted that and admired her and loved her dearly. We've laughed away all the Meema-isms, including the embarrassment of being hosed down nude in the backyard on Colonel Estill Drive after a visit to the beach. Just as Sissy had kept us steady on the little crabbing bateau, not letting us lean too far over the side of the boat and

(From left, back) Neil, Ranny, Windell; (front) John, Mother, and I

plunge into the murky water, Mother helped us all and chartered

our courses, her children and their children and theirs, too. More than seventy-five family members attended my mother's funeral, including all the grandchildren, all but one of the great-grandchildren, many nieces and nephews, despite the fact that she had outlived all the relatives of her generation, on the Robertson and Bradford sides.

I have a few regrets, of course. I assume that's natural. I must admit that I wish she had bequeathed to me her lovely singing voice, her beautiful penmanship and her extraordinary sense of direction, rather than her knobby knees and her sagging wattle. I guess I'll have to settle for what I've got and be grateful for it.

My Father Brad: "The heart has its reasons...."

My father, a young businessman

My father was a cad. So everyone said. Everyone except me. To me, he was the only adult who gave me open, genuine affection. Even though I was thirteen when he died, I still sometimes snuggled with him as we watched TV. I don't ever remember any other adult hugging or kissing me except for what Ranny and I refer to as the "Judas kiss." Mother would wait up for us when we returned home at night, and actually kiss us on the lips. In that way, she could determine if we had been smoking or, God forbid, drinking. (To my memory "Preacher Boy" Windell was exempt from the ritual.) Then she'd sit me down and stare, waiting for me to confess to something that she only imagined or feared, something that wasn't, in fact, true. These scenes hardly qualified as affection, and I don't remember her hugging or kissing me otherwise. My father, on the other hand, often gave me either a light squeeze or a glancing kiss on the cheek, spontaneous and natural. I loved him with all my heart. He was the most important person in my early life.

It's hard for me to write about him, because the person that everyone talks about is not the same person that I knew. I called him "Daddy" when he was alive, but I've always referred to him as "my father" after he died. The two were not the same, and I think that I've wanted to keep the intimate and personal man separate from the one who supposedly committed dastardly deeds and was someone that everybody, or nearly everybody, disapproved of. All these years after his death I've had to listen to how much of a blackguard he was. Even though he was part of my life for only thirteen years, I've defended him for more than half a century, though silently, as it was never a family dynamic to talk freely or to think kindly about him.

My Aunt Madeline, his youngest sister, once told me that I would hear lots of negative things about my father, but that there was another side of him, too. I did hear the seething disapprovals from my oldest brother, from my mother, from my mother's sister, from my Uncle Windell, even from some of my cousins. These were not really conversations, merely muffled, disparaging contempt. After he died, we did not talk about him at all, save for one outburst by Ranny, who with great vitriol (and maybe with a sense of grief that even he did not understand) shouted that he was glad that our father was dead and that we were better off without him. I felt my heart rip open.

It was years later that my mother, usually when we traveled, would try to justify her antipathy for my father, but I didn't want to hear and I tried to tune her out. One time I asked her why she had married him in the first place, and she, shocked, told me that she had loved him. She sure had me fooled. Adult relationships are too complex for a child to

My father relaxing with Lord Calvert

comprehend. When Mary asked Madeline to tell her about my father, Mary's grandfather, Madeline clammed up. I think it was out of loyalty to my mother, but I surely would like to have known something concrete and positive about him. I do know that he came to Madeline's rescue during a difficult time in her life. Apparently, she and her first husband, Dan Locklin, decided to divorce. I was not privy to that information, as things like that were not mentioned to children. I overheard my father talking to a lawyer, saying that "she" had definitely decided to proceed with the divorce, and that "she had made up her mind." Devastated, I thought that the "she" was my mother. By the time Mother got back home, I was inconsolable. When pressed, I told her what was wrong, and she was absolutely furious that I would think such a thing. The truth is, I'd been thinking about it for years, in a quandary about which parent I would live with if I had a choice: My mother would take better care of me, I knew, but my father would love me.

Like the rest of us, my father was complicated. He showed definite favoritism to me as the only girl out of five children. Mother said that when I was a toddler, I padded along behind him whenever he was home, reluctant to let him out of my sight. It was shameless the way he showed me preferential treatment, and my brothers learned to get me to ask him for a favor, as he always told me "yes," and always told them "no." Even I knew it wasn't fair.

My older brothers, Ranny and Windell, remember him as an inconsistent authoritarian, ready with a belt at the slightest annoyance. I can remember hearing the spankings and cries of my brothers, which made me feel awful, kind of sick inside. I don't remember what caused the punishment, not a single time. He never, not once, spanked me, and I remember his reprimanding me only once when I held my milk glass up to my mouth without actually drinking the milk. I do remember that my brothers felt grateful that they got only "spankings," not "whippings," and certainly not "beatings." It was as if they softened the reality of the sometimes rather brutal punishment by using milder euphemisms.

My father turned forty-six on the twenty-sixth day of May 1956, and he died one week later. It's ironic that, after my father's death, the only reminder that was left behind was the unopened belt that we had given him for his recent birthday. It stayed on the dresser, the one that had been Sissy's, gathering dust, a grim reminder of the relentless, unhappy punishment of my brothers. After a week or two the belt disappeared, too. Poof, just like my father. Neither was alluded to again.

I have tried to reason it out, to explain away my older brothers' continued strong antipathy toward him. They were teenagers when he died, and adolescent males, testosterone coursing through their veins, are most often resentful of their fathers. We can only look to the prototype of Oedipus who, in a state of sudden, unnecessary rage, killed his own father, Laius, who was in an equally sudden, unnecessary rage. I like to think that my brothers would have come to some sort of reconciliation if my father had lived longer. I don't know. Windell doesn't think so, though he's not sure. When I mentioned it to Ranny, he responded with a thoughtful pause.

Our father was brutal to my little brother Neil, but then so was my mother. Neil's thumb sucking enraged them. I still don't understand why. Frankly Liz sucked her thumb, too, and I can't see that it did her a great deal of harm, except that she sucked in too many germs. My parents spanked Neil soundly, and their treatment of him fell just short of sadism. They bought metal braces and attached them to his thumbs. They painted his nails with a foul-tasting chemical named "Thumb," and they bound his hands with socks. The braces were easy for him to untape, he developed a tolerance for the peppery nail polish, and he managed to work holes through the socks by repeatedly rubbing his thumb along the inside. But, alas, none of our parents' schemes worked, and Neil persisted in sucking his thumb until he began to smoke. God only knows what would have happened if he had been a bed wetter!

I think that Neil must have been a great deal like my father, which explains my mother's aversion to him, and might explain my father's, too. Neil was sort of squeezed out, with my being just older and the only daughter and John, just younger, privileged as the baby.

After Sissy died, since Mother had started teaching, our father sometimes took little John with him on business trips. It was necessary, but I got the impression that he didn't mind in the least. One such time, when I was in the sixth grade, our father had a heart attack in South Georgia and had to be hospitalized. They put a crib in my father's room for John, and there was a local interest story in the Savannah *Morning News* about the incident, complete with pictures of my father in his hospital bed and John beside him in his crib. I was completely mortified. I dislike illness of all kinds, both then and now, and consider it a very private matter, certainly not one to be plastered all over the newspaper.

My father grew up in as much privilege as rural Alabama could supply. His father was a physician, who doubled as the school superintendent and a councilman, among other things. My father and his brothers, born in quick succession, were prone to mischief, especially since there were enough of them to form a pack. One of the stories our father told us was about the pot-bellied stove in the one-room schoolhouse. Centered in the middle of the room, it was the only source of heat. A pan of water on top provided moisture in the room, as wood-burning stoves tend to dry out the air. One morning my father and his brothers arrived early to school, even before the teacher. Instead of filling the pot with water, they peed in it. When the teacher arrived and started up the fire, a putrid odor settled on the room. Aghast, she was afraid to turn the Bradford boys in because their father was her boss, so to speak. They got away with lots of other misbehavior, too, for the same reason.

I remember some of the other tales my father told us. For instance, he had to walk five miles, uphill, barefooted, in the snow, to get to school every day. I knew that snow was rare in middle Alabama, and I asked his mother, my grandmother Bradford, about it. She just laughed and told me that a servant had driven him to school every day of his life on a covered buckboard. He told me about his school lunches, every day, the same menu. He'd take a couple of cold biscuits left over from breakfast, poke a hole in the sides with his thumb, and then fill them up with sorghum. They were wrapped in a cloth, and put in a tin pail, the lunchbox of the day. Our grandmother confirmed this.

After their family home burned, my grandparents and their children moved into one of the wings of my grandfather's clinic in Birmingham, though it's not clear to me when they lived in Birmingham and when they lived in Linden. But, at any rate, every day when our father, a young boy, returned home from school, a nurse would cry, "Get out the bedpan! Mr. B.R. is coming." He'd throw up on cue as he crossed the threshold. That's one sure thing that I inherited from him, in addition to a flat behind and long, bony fingers, as I, too, get nauseated at the antiseptic hospital smell.

My father claimed that he had broken every bone in his body when he was little, which is such an obvious exaggeration that I didn't believe him even then. Later, I was not so convinced. When seven-month-old Mary broke her leg and was diagnosed with "brittle bone disease," I realized that Ed had had the same thing, which accounted for his breaking his arms five times, and I did some research. It turns out that *osteogenesis imperfecta*, the technical name, is inherited and that it typically skips a generation. I wish I had more details about my father's childhood, like whether or not his siblings broke their bones, too, but all their history is buried now, along with the people who lived it.

Neil must have inherited his sense of humor from our father. It certainly did not come from the dour Robertson uncles. Along with the tall tales about his childhood, our father delighted in vexing Uncle Jack, who was a sissified bachelor. Even before Uncle Jack retired and moved in with us, he visited often. As we were wont to do, we said a blessing before every meal, with my father in charge of asking someone to pray. Nearly every time Uncle Jack was there, my father would say, in a solemn tone, "Jack-ass the blessing, please," with just the right cadence and emphasis. Uncle Jack would audibly crumple his napkin, and Sissy, his sister and my father's mother-in-law, whom he referred to always as "Miss Ethel," would gasp. The rest of us would quietly giggle, the same mini-drama acted out time after time. The crumpling of the napkin, the gasp, and the muted giggles. Of course, we didn't dare laugh out loud.

Neil told me about riding around with our father as he conducted business. He left Neil in the car, saying that he'd be back in only a few minutes. Returning much later, he'd always apologize and say that "he got tied up." Neil could only envision our father roped to a chair, for some unknown reason, then escaping and beating a hasty retreat back to the car. Ranny also remembers our father's standard response to the dinner bell: "You can call me Bill or call me Sam, but don't call me late to dinner." He was known to twirl his hat around if a black cat crossed his path and to throw salt over his left shoulder to ward off evil spirits, so he, at least, had something of the playful about him.

According to Ranny, our father would disappear, sometimes for weeks at a time. Our mother didn't know where he had gone or when he would come home. I don't remember any of that at all. If it's true, it surely not was a frequent habit. (Ranny, my source for my parents' relationship, was a fanciful narrator.) Nonetheless, it must have been awkward, to say the least, with Mother's own mother, Sissy, living with us, too. I know that my father was divorced and had another child a few years older than Ranny. Divorce was rare in the early 1930s, and it still amuses me to think that both my mother and my Aunt Billie, though uptight and prim, had married divorced men.

It has been suggested that my mother was kept ignorant of the previous marriage until after her own wedding. Again, I'm repeating Ranny, as I personally was never told such things. Nonetheless, our half-sister, Catherine Lee, did visit us once at the beach, but I don't have any clear memory of her. When Windell, quite naively and with the best of intentions, contacted her several years ago, it was obvious that she was not interested in meeting with us, the second family, much less in having any relationship.

I know these things, too. When our grandfather died in Linden, Alabama, in 1938, our father fetched his mother and the younger siblings, Henri and Madeline, and situated them in a two-story house on Henry Street, not far from our own. He took care of Grandfather's servants, too, and found jobs for them in Savannah. One was named Green and the other one George Washington Abraham Lincoln Hazard, nicknamed "Abe." They remained devoted to my father all his life and, though Green moved on to Detroit, he always called us when he visited "South." Abe worked part time at my father's business and part time as a driver for my mother and grandmother.

So, even though he was but in his thirties, our father assumed the responsibilities of seeing after us, his own family, as well as his mother and siblings, and his wife's extended family. Ranny even has a negative twist on this, too, but I think that I got his attention when I pointed out that when our sons, Ed and Alfred, were that same age, it was unimaginable to think of them saddled with the care of so many people. What I said sank in, I think, because Ranny rather reluctantly admitted that he could always depend on our father to supply a truck and driver for anything at school which required moving or delivering. That's the only positive thing he has ever said about our father, and this after decades of verbal patricide, or "daddy-bashing."

My memories were much more positive, of course, but they were clouded by my father's illnesses. I last remember him as a healthy man when I was about eight. He was tussling on the floor with Neil and me, and it is a warm happy memory. He began having serious health problems while still in his thirties. He smoked and drank more than he should have. I remember coming home after school one afternoon, happy to have him back from the hospital, and dashing into his room. I was horrified. There he lay, propped up in bed with a lighted cigarette dangling from his lips, hooked up to an oxygen tank which had the warning emblazoned on it: "Flammable. Do not smoke."

I worried about him constantly. One summer afternoon, at a canasta luncheon which Louise McLeod hosted for her niece Peggy, a sudden summer storm blew in. All the other girls were positively titillated about the lightning and thunder, hoping for the excitement of a power outage. My only thought was that my father's oxygen would be cut off. I was miserable all afternoon and relieved to get back home.

Despite his poor health, he tried to keep working. After he cashed in his life insurance, apparently he borrowed money shamelessly. Ranny still chafes about the whole situation, and life must have been especially bitter for him as a teenager in the face of total social disgrace. As the crowning degradation, somewhere along the way, our father embezzled funds from his employer. All of this was hidden from me, and I have only found out about it in my adult life. This was the time that Ranny woke up one morning and picked up the morning paper. There were gaping holes on the back page, as articles were cut out which told of our father's disgrace.

Ranny also said that our father had borrowed a large sum from his first cousin, Elizabeth Mashburn, Melanie's mother. A couple of years ago, I asked Melanie about it, and she doubted that it was true. Her mother had been tight as a steel drum about finances, and Melanie, as the only child, would certainly have heard about it. I had laughingly offered to take her out to lunch to recover my family's honor, but, happily, we were able to go Dutch. My youngest brother John pointed out that, undoubtedly, our father was desperate, ill, unable to work for long periods of time. With a wife and five children to support, he had resorted to extreme, though unwise and less than honorable, measures. What a Romantic idea, our very own Jean Valjean, living in our very own home.

Then the late-night phone call. When my mother woke me up, my aunts Anne and Madeline were already there. Uncannily I knew what Mother was going to say. (Had I heard, half-asleep, their anguished whisperings?) I remember resenting having an audience at my most vulnerable time and feeling emotionally naked. I wanted to be "shut of them all."

The circumstances of our father's death were, like his life, shrouded in mystery. Was it a heart attack that caused the accident? Was it a car accident that caused the heart attack? Cautioned not to look at his battered and distorted body but to remember him as he was before the wreck, I never looked at his face. I steeled my determination not to cry in front of my mother. My grief turned into hatred between my mother and me. It makes one wonder if, maybe,

God has a mean streak, God who turns trusting, innocent babies into resentful teenaged monsters.

I grieved for his death, but, most of all, I grieved that his life had turned out so badly. I knew that he had to have been desperate, as he was surely aware that he had dissipated the family coffers and shamed the family name. My fertile imagination took over. His life was wretched and hopeless. Perhaps he was in such anguish that he deliberately pulled his car into oncoming traffic. Perhaps, on the other hand, he had just had enough of failure and disappointment and had run away, faking the accident. I scanned crowds for years, hoping to find him, especially in every new town I visited, knowing that if he had, indeed, escaped his life, he would not be in Savannah. I even fantasized a life with him still around, and he became as real to me as he had been before he died. What's more, now he was perfect.

I try to direct my thoughts away from such matters, but I find myself still, after all these years, sighing deeply whenever I think of my father. I know that I need to put the matter to rest. After all, he'd have been 103 by now and would be so very weary. I'm glad he's at peace. I think, more than anything else, that despite the disappointments and embarrassment, I needed to love him and that, somewhere deep inside me, I still do. "The heart has its reasons which reason does not know." (*"Le cœur a ses raisons que la raison ne connaît point...."* Blaise Pascal, *Pensées*)

* * *

The door to the Bradford house has long ago creaked shut. As Sartre observed: From each individual's existence there is "no exit." Like everyone else our hell *was* "other people." Our house, which should have been our refuge, offered little real protection. Our parents glared at each other with a soundlessness that deafened us all. Sissy tore up our comic books with a vengeance, then laced her corset a notch tighter; Aunt Sarah and Uncle Jack endured their indignities wordlessly, and we children were "seen but not heard."

Each of us was in the clutches of our individual, unspoken misery, misery that could not be escaped. The hopelessness, the sadness, the frustration grew and grew and grew. Since we could not speak of it, it was the house, itself, that trembled with all the pent-up, gut-wrenching misery and gave out a long, low, agonizing groan.

Other Important Adults, Relatively Speaking

AUNT BILLIE: THE LEGEND OF THE LONG UPPER LIP

I never wanted a sister. Everyone assumed otherwise when Mother was pregnant with my little brothers. I may have been young, but I was not stupid. Being the only daughter granted me certain rights and distinction. I was not about to jeopardize my position, as if I had any choice. Besides that, Billie was my mother's older sister, and no one in her right mind would choose a sibling like her. Sisterhood had, for me, an extraordinarily pejorative connotation.

Sissy, my grandmother Robertson, after producing two sons in the two years after her marriage, gave birth to a daughter in 1908. Three children in three years put her on the verge of being "common." The newest baby was a beautiful little girl who was, unfortunately, christened "Willie Ethel." She was named after her mother, Ethel Viola, and her grandmother, Willie Tallulah. The name, alone, was enough to make any person angry for the rest of her life. She was.

Willie Ethel burst defiant from her mother's womb in full armor like Athena ready for a fight, except that Athena sprang forth, not from her mother's womb, but from her father's head. This much doted on little girl was pampered and indulged. She was, also, from the very beginning, willful and demanding. She ruled the roost. So, five years later, in 1913, her world was turned upside down when another baby girl was born. To rub salt in the already festering wound, the baby was named "Sarah," a name that was not only euphonious but which carried with it the aura of the Biblical. Her sister's name, alone, was doubtless one of the many reasons that Billie resented Mother all their lives. But then Billie resented everything, and she rarely resented in silence. It was just part of her nature.

Mother was named after my grandmother's unmarried sister, my Great Aunt Sarah, who lived with us and is also my namesake. It was the ultimate confusion when, after I was born, there were three "Sarahs" living in the same house. The solution was for Mother to maintain her name intact and for Aunt Sarah to become "Sadie," though we children actually continued to call her "Aunt Sarah." I was nicknamed and always called "Sallie."

Our society reveled not only in patronymics – Ranny was Brazil Ransom IV – but in matronymics, too. An interesting trend when I was young was to name the first daughter entirely after her mother, and she was called by her mother's maiden name. This explains the unusual designation of my cousin "Stratton" named Adela Stratton Ingram after her mother, and my neighbor called "Comer," born Lila Comer Varnedoe, named after hers. At least there was not as much confusion as having three "Sarahs" in the same household.

Back to the point of my unfortunate aunt. Some time or other, probably in high school, Willie Ethel deemed herself "Billie," a name that had greater resonance for a flapper, a liberated young woman of the 1920s. Her aunts and cousins persisted in calling her "Willie Ethel," however, when they perfunctorily asked after her health. They had to ask my own mother, as Billie had long since alienated all of them, the firsts on a long,

long list of people she fell out with. She didn't even get along with her two brothers, at least as far as I can remember. Her brother Windell was as intractable as she, and there was no love lost between the hypercritical and domineering two. She felt that John, although milder by temperament, was a social embarrassment.

One time when Billie was invited to a dance in high school, she asked her father for a new dress. He said he couldn't afford it. The next day, she defiantly went to the nicest department store in Macon and purchased not only a dress, but an entire new wardrobe, putting the charges on my grandfather's account. Mother said that Grandfather never made her take anything back, his pride was so strong, and that he paid the bill off by bits for several months. I hasten to remind myself that my source of information about their childhood comes from my mother exclusively and that she was certainly not an impartial narrator. But, if later years mirror the earlier ones at all, the stories ring true.

There's no doubt that Billie was smart, excelling particularly in math. The teachers at Miller School for Girls (The public schools in Macon were not coeducational until many, many years later.) always compared Mother to Billie, saying things like, "Your sister would certainly have known that," or "You're not the student your sister was." This is not a rare situation in most siblings' lives, but Mother smarted painfully over such thoughtless, if not cruel, remarks. So the girls' resentment toward each other was mutual.

My grandfather felt that education was of utmost importance, and he must have been proud when Billie enrolled at Wesleyan. She spent two years there and excelled in her classes. When she was a junior, she was devastated that Grandfather made her quit. He found out that she had recently eloped with my Uncle Tommy, an older man who drove a flashy sports coupe. (A professional salesman, he sold himself in the bargain.) Billie had tried to keep her marriage secret and continue on with her classes. But my grandfather got wind of her elopement anyway, and he forced her to leave school, on the grounds that a married woman should live with her husband. Now one might say that she had "made her bed and must lie in it," but such an allusion was far too graphic for my straight-laced grandfather.

After her abrupt departure from Wesleyan, Billie moved to Tennessee to her new husband's home, becoming a stepmother to his two children, one not much younger than she. They all lived in the house with her mother-in-law, a short, plump, fractious woman, according to Mother's account. So Billie's flapper wings flapped no more. She felt herself terribly abused, and she wore the heavy mantle of bitterness until her death. The fact that Mother did graduate from college six years later didn't exactly assuage her hurt and disappointment. After our father died, Mother even went back and got her master's degree, but Billie pretty much ignored that.

Billie's bouquet at Mother's wedding

Of course, there had been no bridal gown or formal wedding party for Billie, and she must have been jealous of Mother when she got married. But Billie had her way after all, because her bouquet as Matron of Honor was huge and far outshone Mother's modest gathering of bridal flowers. Billie was not to be denied again. Her smile in the pictures of Mother's wedding reflects her smug victory. I might note, that when Billie, as a widow in her mid-fifties, married for a second time, she had a huge wedding with three hundred invited guests and a lovely seated dinner. I don't remember her bridal bouquet, but I'm sure it was grand.

The sisters' relationship was a love-hate affair, to the outside observer lighter on the love aspect than the on the hate. Though they sometimes giggled like teenagers when they were together, they mostly argued and took their rivalry to an absurd degree, but then all such rivalries seem absurd from the outside. They have to do with feelings, building on decades of injustices and slights, both real and imagined. Even the tiniest of nuances gain gigantic proportions. I can't think of a nice thing Mother ever said about her sister, though surely she must have. When Mary, Mother, and I visited Billie for what we knew was the last time, Billie was lying serenely in a hospital bed, in a coma, wearing a lovely pink dressing gown. She looked peaceful, and it was a sober and touching scene. Walking back to the car, Mother shed some quiet tears. Mary asked why she was crying, and Mother explained that Billie was her sister and she loved her. Mary was dumbstruck, incredulous, as she had never heard her grandmother say anything at all that might be construed of as nice about her. That's another part of the "sister mystique."

One of Mother's pet peeves was Billie's use of the term "irregardless." Billie used the word often, and, testily, Mother would correct her. But Billie stood her ground. She never let Mother get the satisfaction of being right. The closest thing to "nice" that Billie ever said about Mother was "Poor Sarah," as she shook her head in a combination of dismay and disdain. "Poor Sarah" referred, in Mother's mind at least, to Billie's disapproval of Mother's marriage, her current weight gain, her meager wardrobe, her repeated production of babies, or her unfortunate resemblance to the Robertson side of the family, whatever the current conversation was about.

The Brits pride themselves in having a "stiff upper lip," but they can't compete, believe me, with my mother and her sister. They battled over not who had the stiffest but who had the *longest* upper lip. Sissy, their mother, was an Ingram by birth, a Robertson by marriage. The Ingrams felt themselves far superior to my grandfather's family, far superior, probably, to everyone else. A distinguishing feature of the Ingrams was the unusually short space between the bottom of their nostrils and the line of their top lip. The socially inferior Robertsons, on the other hand, had a longish space. Of course, what Mother and Aunt Billie were really arguing about had little or nothing to do with facial design. It was more profound than that, a matter of pedigree. They stopped short of actually getting out a ruler and measuring, but they, instead, measured their upper-lip length by holding up two horizontal fingers just under their noses. (In my opinion Billie's upper lip was shorter, as she looked much like an "Ingram," but I would never have admitted it to Mother out of a sense of loyalty.) In a twist of irony, the "two-fingered measurement" was just the gesture that their husbands, much to the sisters' dismay, used in measuring out their whiskey. Mary discovered when she was in college, that prospective adopters of children from Russia were cautioned about adopting a baby with a short upper lip. It was a sure sign of fetal alcohol syndrome. Mary never told Mother, and Billie had already died, so it was a moot point. But we enjoy the irony.

The constant, heated rivalry acquired obsessive proportions. It extended to every aspect of their lives, including their physical aches, pains, and maladies. (A friend of mine refers to the litany of women discussing their aches and pains as an "organ recital.") They boasted about their arthritis, each convinced that she suffered more. Billie played the trump card when she went to a special clinic in Florida and had gold injections, literally injections of real gold. They didn't help much. The sisters also competed to see who would win the distinction of qualifying first for a handicap sticker. Billie won, but Mother hurried behind.

By far their greatest contention was over who was blinder. Like all the women in our family, and not a few of the men, they suffered from some form of macular degeneration. Mother and Billie actually came to verbal blows over who could see the worst. Mother scrutinized every word of print that Billie read and every object on the horizon that she noticed, noting its size and distance, remarking that, if Billie could have seen such and such, her eyesight was certainly better than Mother's. It's always seemed to me particularly pitiful to vie for the greatest disability, to relish one's maladies, simply to have "a one up" on one's sister, but then sibling rivalry knows no bounds and has no logic. Their "blindness" extended far beyond their lack of visual acuity!

Perhaps as protection against Billie's overbearing personality, Mother assumed a passive-aggressive role, which she played throughout all her life. In my later years, I realized that Mother, in some strange way, enjoyed the role of the abused little sister. She was, in her mind, at least, a real Cinderella character, except that this Cinderella's Prince Charming fell dreadfully short of her dreams. She wore the mantle of martyrdom well, which I think made her feel a little smug, and, in an almost perverse way, a little superior. Mother didn't confront, but perfected the teeth-clenching, soul-numbing glare to express her disapproval of almost everything and everybody. Though silent, the potency was heavy, except that one was never quite sure what the offense was, a sharp contrast to Billie, who had no subtlety at all about voicing her opinions. Her mode was attack, full steam ahead.

Billie was, too, one of the pioneers of road rage. She'd blow the horn, roll down the window and lambaste fellow drivers, shaking her closed fist and yelling at them about their impaired mental faculties and inept driving ability. She didn't even shy away from burly truck drivers, and they would shrink from this diminutive, gray-haired harridan. To her credit, I doubt if she ever cursed or gave herself over to hand gestures. She was, strangely enough, too "genteel" for either. She had her own warped personal code of propriety.

Not content with yelling at fellow drivers, Billie even argued with her car. She and her second husband, John Mountney, sported a very expensive, state-of-the-art automobile. It was supposed to impress us all, and she would be deflated if she knew that I don't remember the make or model, but, it was, as one says, "loaded." Even thirty or so years ago, it had a talking computer. If she opened the door while the keys were still in the ignition, the car would announce: "Your keys are in the ignition." She'd snap back impatiently, saying that she knew they were and that she'd take them out only when she was good and ready. If one of the car doors was not closed securely when she started off, the computer, in that robotic voice computers use, would point out: "Your door is ajar," to which she would reply: "The door is a door; the door is not a jar." Coming from anyone else that would have implied some sort of wit, but Billie had no sense of humor. She just specialized in arguing.

She harangued her boss, as well, when she went to work after the boys left home. If half of her stories were true, it is not only amazing that she kept her job, it's astonishing that he didn't disembowel her. She took on the manager of the local television station, the minister, her congressman, and whoever else happened to come her way. There were no limits to her wrath, and her most venomous behavior was reserved for her husband, our Uncle Tommy. She was a legend.

Aunt Billie argued with Elizabeth, my little daughter. When Billie quizzed her about Biblical characters, Elizabeth dutifully answered, quickly and correctly, much to Billie's dismay. Finally Billie asked her something absurd, like the size of Joseph's sixth molar and was visibly elated when Elizabeth didn't know the answer. She made some inane remark about the fact that Elizabeth might learn such things when she grew older. Another time, when Elizabeth was about three, she came in to play a surprise game with us, and said, "All right, everybody, please close your eyes," to which Billie replied that she had no intention of closing her eyes and that Elizabeth couldn't make her.

How unpleasant to have to boost her ego at the expense of a toddler, but that was my dear old aunt.

Mother and Billie shared their children and treated us all the same. Billie took us in summer after summer and Mother pitched in when she could. When we rented a beach house one summer, Billie and the boys spent the season with us. My cousin Joe, who thinks that my mother was a fully beatified saint, remembers fondly their visits to Savannah, which I don't recall at all. I can't imagine how mother stretched our apartment out to accommodate three others.

Billie was a combination of Robertson inflexibility and Ingram snobbery. She was an unmitigated social climber, à la Hyacinth Bucket, and her letters to Mother were filled with all the details of her social calendar, including names of people Mother was supposed to be impressed with. Mother had never heard of them. Billie spoke in near reverential awe about the stores she shopped at, the restaurants she frequented, and the people she knew. One summer when Ranny, Windell, and I visited, she had an Asheville society reporter come and take a picture of one of our backyard barbeques, (similar to Hyacinth's candlelight suppers). We found our pictures the next morning plastered all over the society section, drinking lemonade and roasting hot dogs over Uncle Tommy's brick barbeque "pit" which was so fancy that it even had a chimney like a fireplace in the house.

When we went to Asheville for Billie's funeral, I was impressed by the lengthy, two-columned article in the local newspaper, head-lined in bold font: "Important Social and Civic Leader Dies." It was an astonishing article, and I thought to myself that Billie had, indeed, been as remarkable as she claimed. Perhaps we'd not been appreciative enough. Mother set me straight in short shrift, as she said that Billie had written her own obituary several years before she died.

I hope that Aunt Billie was successful in climbing that ultimate social ladder and that St. Peter was appropriately aware of how graced heaven was to have someone of Willie Ethel Robertson Hiles Mountney's stature. As the ultimate irony, although Billie had willed her impressive, important body to Duke University Medical School to be used in medical research, they rejected her when the time came. She was too old and debilitated to be of any use.

Like my mother, Billie was devoted to her church, becoming even the first woman of her Presbyterian congregation to be elected an elder, a fact of which she was justifiably proud. Both enjoyed a wide circle of friends. Mother seemed a little more genuine to me, but then she was my mother. Billie was aggressively friendly, when she felt it necessary, and I've heard such treacle ooze from her lips to require an injection of insulin. But I heard the other things, too.

I'm convinced that Billie must have had a metabolic imbalance or something, as no one would have wanted to humiliate and alienate everyone whom she loved and who loved her. The sisters struggled with their human condition, their unique personalities and accident of birth order. I continue to feel a great deal of affection for them, mixed with a heavy dose of amusement, and not a little self-awareness of similar qualities in myself.

THE ROBERTSON BROTHERS: WINDELL AND JOHN

My uncles Windell and John, just one year apart in age, fought as children and resented each other as adults. Their disparate personalities made it impossible for them ever to be truly good friends. They both doted on my mother, their baby sister, and were barely able to sit in the same room with their aggressive sister Billie.

Uncle Windell was a bully. I knew him well because he lived in Savannah and we saw each other often, even during those years when he and my father didn't speak. Mother claims that he had been a real "ladies' man" when he was young, but it was hard for me believe that my unpleasant, bald old uncle could even have been appealing. In his adult life, he was the building inspector/tax assessor for the city of Savannah, and Mother claimed that he had lied about having a high school diploma. She also claimed that he made a good part of his income from the "contributions" of his clients, the kind of contributions given in advance and not written down in the books. After he retired he moved to a big, sprawling clapboard house, which had originally been the schoolhouse at Montgomery, a community near Savannah, the kind of suburb which has a little settlement of blacks and large "white" homes on the river. The Montgomery Road was narrow and quaint, shaded by enormous oaks, whose limbs were laden with Spanish moss trailing haphazardly like unkempt tresses caught in the breeze.

Uncle Windell finally had plenty of room for his horses, which he had previously had to board. His pride was his golden Palomino stallion, Comanche, who was a magnificent creature with a long beautiful blond mane and tail. He was tall, proud, and big boned with taut muscles tensing in his sleek thighs and flank, and he held his head so erect that he appeared to look down his regal nose at the rest of the world. Though aloof and spirited, Comanche was not a problem. Uncle Windell was. My cousin Joe witnessed Uncle Windell in a wild rage, slugging this beautiful, huge horse on the side of his head so hard that Comanche was knocked to the ground.

Childless himself, my uncle felt the need to turn his fatherless nephews into "real men," which meant baptism by saddle. My older brothers had already reached maturity before our father died, but Neil's account of his initiation rite still brought a tone of controlled, yet unmistakable, anger even fifty years later. I'm not sure exactly what transpired, but the experience was belittling and humiliating. Ironically enough, Neil went on to sire four sons, a reputed test of manhood, whereas my uncle remained childless. Virility, apparently, is not measured by riding a horse.

The Lady of Booger Hill

Uncle Windell pelted my mother with advice on childrearing, and he was offended when she didn't jump every time he spoke. I was grateful that he pampered me when I was little, and there were definite privileges in being the only girl. He made a big deal about Easter, sending me a corsage every year to match my new Easter dress. One Easter morning he even brought me a soft Angora rabbit who had long, silky white fur, timorous little pink eyes, and a nose which twitched constantly, as if he smelled something mysterious that the rest of us couldn't detect. The new bunny lived in a pen near the chicken yard, fairly far from the house. Occasionally we let him out to play, chasing him down if he hopped too near the varmint-laden woods. One morning we discovered that the cage was empty. The door was supposedly left open and the bunny escaped. He was absolutely vulnerable and probably didn't survive many hops into his much coveted exploration of the woods. Other than speed, rabbits have no means of protection. I've even read that mother rabbits will kill their young if danger lies nearby, as they would rather kill the babies instantly than have them become victims of predators and teased to death, like a cat teases a mouse in its deadly game. Nature never ceases to amaze me.

Uncle Windell took special interest in my brother Windell, his namesake. Windell said that our uncle, after our father died, told him that he wanted to be a surrogate father and encouraged him to come to him if he needed anything. The only problem was, according to Windell, that he was never available. Windell called, but the calls weren't returned. It turned out to be merely bluster. When Uncle Windell's wife, our Aunt Thetis, died, not long after our father's death, Uncle Windell started coming to our house for breakfast. He always put an eggshell in the percolator when he brewed coffee, the reason for which I don't remember. He also had a habit of sprinkling salt in his coffee, which he claimed enhanced the flavor.

The worst habit he had on those mornings was to cool his coffee down with tears, literally. Sitting forlornly at the kitchen table, he sobbed and sobbed while mother stood at the stove cooking his bacon and eggs. She was a recent widow, herself, struggling to survive, and more specifically struggling to get herself and her five children off to school every morning. She was too busy to moan and groan, but we all listened to his mawkish sighs of self-pity. Ranny got exasperated one morning and pointed all this out in not-so-gentle words, and after that Uncle Windell stopped coming over, at least before school.

Mother let my brother Windell move in with our uncle to assuage his loneliness after Thetis's death. Before long Mother heard through the grapevine that Uncle Windell was tomcatting around, that he wasn't quite as lonely as he made out. My brother was the one home alone. He moved back in with us, and Uncle Windell soon remarried. His second wife, Inez, a brave and accepting soul who had two daughters, brought along a ready-made family, and their life together was good. She was non-threatening and non-assertive, which was essential to their relationship, though, much to the delight of Mother and Aunt Billie, her English grammar was atrocious.

Though my uncle went out of his way to be thoughtful of me, the lone girl, I was not oblivious to his disgusting brutality. He delighted in braggadocios stories about his merciless treatment of blacks. The highlight of his prowess was the time when he, in pure Abner Snopes tradition, rode his motorcycle through the middle of a group of black men. One of them cursed him. He got off his bike, took a chain and beat the whole group bloody. He felt quite heroic in telling the story, which Ranny pointed out was certainly not true. Even though it was fictitious, the narrative speaks not only to his character, or lack thereof, but to his pathetic idea of what the heroic was. Along with his gun-stuffed cabinet, he kept a glass-covered display case with rattlesnake rattlers mounted, a testimony to his expertise with a rifle, as well as his puffed up vainglory.

My favorite story is the one he told about his dog. One night the dog started barking and wouldn't stop. Uncle Windell yelled and threatened, but the dog ignored him and continued to bark on. In rage, and it didn't take long for my uncle to get really, really angry, Uncle Windell dashed out of the back door. He saw the shadow of the dog curled up at the edge of the patio, and he mustered up all his strength and kicked him as hard as he could. Only it wasn't the dog. In the dark of the night he had kicked a cement block. He was "laid up" for three days, missing work for the first time in his life. Bullies are not my favorite, and we all, quietly of course, cheered for the dog's good luck and good health.

As I said, he was not incapable of generosity. He called my children on Christmas Eve each year (or each year that he was speaking to me), and pretended to be Santa Claus. He was very convincing and they were wide-eyed with amazement and excitement.

Uncle John, who lived in the shadow of his strong older brother, was a ne'er-do-well when he was an adult, and I imagine he was the same as a child. He found his solace outside the home, and Mother told me the story of John's early marriage at age sixteen to a "much older" woman of nineteen. The family had recently moved to Macon from rural Dover so that the children would have better educational advantages. Neither of the boys was much interested in school and actually didn't ever attend after they moved to town. They hung out at a local drugstore, instead. Somehow John became acquainted with Margaret, a nurse, even in the Biblical sense. They eloped and she was soon with child. Grandfather was horrified. He forbade John to see his wife and locked him in his room. But nothing could deter true love and teenage hormones, and Uncle John broke out of the window and rushed to the side of his dearly beloved—or, at least, his dearly beloved for a couple of months more. Not long after their son Jack was born, they divorced. His second marriage to my Aunt Sara was long lasting, and they had three children, Tommy, Jimmy, and Judy, my lone girl cousin, with whom I shared much childhood devotion and many adventures. Although Uncle John was always nice to me, the daughter of his little sister, I remember him as unremarkable and uninspiring, never upholding the many promises he made to us children. Though he would "belt" his son to within an inch of his life (so it seemed to us other children), Tommy, as an adult virtually worshipped him.

RISING UP FROM POOR ROBIN: THE INGRAMS

Sissy's father, James Averette Ingram (1854-1920), my great-grandfather, was known as "Ebb." He owned a mercantile business in Poor Robin, Georgia, a town in Screven County on the banks of the Savannah River, which was a popular crossing spot for people migrating to Georgia from South Carolina. His store housed, in addition to food and supplies, the post office and the train station, so he was the proprietor, the postmaster, and the local depot manager. His business was, I guess, the hub of the tiny town,

James Averette Ingram

which by now has faded from the map, unlike another nondescript little town called Terminus, then Marthasville, which burgeoned into Atlanta. He also farmed on the side, as did most people back then, a rustic jack of all trades, one might say, or, more pretentiously, which he would have appreciated, a rural Renaissance man. All the Ingrams considered themselves very fine, indeed.

Willie Tallulah Newton Ingram

In 1879 he married Willie Tallulah Newton, who shared a common ancestor with Sir Isaac, a fact of which her whole family was keenly aware. From their union issued eight children, six of whom reached adulthood: Ethel Viola, Sarah Savannah, John Mason, LaFayette Newton, James Armond, Pearla Rebecca, Willie Jane, and Julian Averette. Ethel Viola, my grandmother Sissy, the eldest, was born in 1880. She, Aunt Sarah and John (our Uncle Jack) lived with us. LaFayette, Julian, and Pearla settled in Florida.

James and Willie Jane both died a few days after they were born.

Sissy was close to her siblings, and I have a few memories of them stored in my mind. Of course, I knew Aunt Sarah and Uncle Jack intimately, as they lived with us. One time when Uncle Julian was "misbehaving," though I never learned exactly what that referred to, Aunt Louise, his wife, sent him to Savannah to stay with us. Sissy had died by that time, but my mother was given the responsibility of "straightening him out." Whatever the provocation, Mother must have been successful, as Uncle Julian returned to Jacksonville after a couple of weeks. Another time Uncle Julian and Uncle LaFayette, Sissy's other brothers, visited for about a week, and we called them, behind their backs, of course, the "three broken-down musketeers," as they hobbled around poorly and had to take many stops to regain their breath when they walked up the stairs. We visited their sister,

Aunt Pearla, but I don't remember that she ever visited us. She was unlucky in marriage and progeny, though I don't know specific details. I remember Mother and Sissy whispering words like "alcoholic," "abusive," and "nervous breakdown," terms which meant nothing to me as a child.

In addition to brothers and sisters, Sissy didn't lack for cousins! Among the many, I recall Ingrams, Shuptrines, Saffolds, Newtons, Berrys, LaFars, whom I heard Sissy and Mother talk about but whom I didn't really know. They hinted that these cousins "put on airs," which I assume meant that they were more prosperous than we. There were cousins Ila and Eula, who lived in nursing homes (distant from Savannah and from each other). I positively hated the nursing home visits, where most of the patients were lined up in the halls, strapped to their wheelchairs, and sat slumped over as inert and formless as giant sacks of flour, not really alert enough to show their desperation. The air was suffused with a combination of uric acid, marinating the mattresses and chairs, and the antiseptic used to disguise it. In the great battle of smells, the urine won out. After saying hello to them and holding our breaths while they hugged us with cold, wrinkled arms and bony fingers, we went outside to play. I remember sand and sand gnats, oppressive heat, and waiting impatiently for my mother and grandmother for an interminable time, and that's about all. I regret that I was too young to be interested in them or in how they were related to me; I was merely struck with how extraordinarily old they were and how bored I was.

Two of the staff members at the Savannah Public Library, where I worked in high school, were cousins and exactly one-half of my elementary teachers were cousins of some degree. It seemed that they were hiding behind every bush.

Of all Sissy's first cousins, I remember best Cousins Claudia and Annie Ruth Ingram, my grandmother's double first cousins, offspring of siblings of one family who had married siblings from another. They were among the abundance of "unclaimed treasures," and they had always lived together. In fact, they both had actually lived with my parents in the big house on Perry Street during the Depression when everyone was out of work. They had a room in the third story. Back then, the situation was so grave that lots of the family moved in. The ones who had jobs pooled their money, and the others took care of the cooking and the housework. My mother always remembered the outrage when they discovered that Claudia and Annie Ruth were sneaking food to their brother, Ike, through the back door. Ike was not a supporting member of the household and had no rights, not even to food if he were hungry. The rules were strict.

Claudia and Annie Ruth looked nothing alike. Claudia was large, with thinning gray hair, a round face, a little pink pig nose, and a huge double, or maybe even triple, wattle. It looked like a big sausage roll which hung from ear to ear and rested on her chest. She had a long stray hair or two on her face which escaped the tweezers, increasingly as her eyes dimmed. Nearly blind when I knew her, she was extremely unpleasant; not deliberately so, she was merely one of those people who are born with a sour disposition. She was a good deal larger than her petite, rather pretty little sister, who was thin and sprightly and had a pleasant disposition. Claudia, as the older sister, assumed the role of surrogate mother and dominated Annie Ruth all their lives. I remember that Claudia would spank Annie Ruth's hands if the latter said anything that Claudia disagreed with. And this went on in front of company. I wonder what went on behind closed and very securely locked doors.

The sisters lived in a third-floor walk-up on Perry Street, next door to where the family had lived during the Depression. The house was on Chippewa Square, across from the Savannah Theater, and I sometimes dropped by for a visit to kill time until the city bus arrived. There were no cell phones, and no other way for me to warn them. They were such hysterical birds, a wattle-faced turkey and a flittering little sparrow, that they were afraid of their own shadows. Besides that, they were hearing impaired. As I climbed the narrow winding steps up to the third-floor flat, I stomped loudly to warn them of my arrival. I could hear them bustling around their apartment. When I knocked on the door, I could literally hear them inside, shutting the doors and scraping the furniture to barricade themselves in, admonishing each other to be quiet, with terrified whispers which were louder than shouts. Sometimes I would call out loud enough for them to hear and recognize my voice, and they'd open up the door, but mostly I just had to turn around and make my way to the bus stop.

As Ingrams, they were very pretentious. But they were also very poor. Of course they didn't drive, not many ladies of their generation did, and I often drove them to the grocery store. Out the door they'd come with their white gloves and dark hats with veils, and we'd head off. By necessity they had to shop in the "colored" section of town, which was far cheaper, but they did so with self-appointed dignity, decked out in their formal attire and proudly proclaiming that they "didn't buy meat there," an important distinction, which, in their minds, separated them from the dark-skinned, shabby clientele. As my reward, they'd take me to Taylor's on Abercorn Street for a nice vegetable lunch. Even as a teen, I hated the Southern overcooked veggies, the culinary equivalent of beating a dead horse, with all the nutrition leached into the water and replaced with greasy bacon drippings or other fat. They were soggy and lifeless. I always tried to talk them out of lunch, but the truth, I now realize, was that they wanted to have a nice vegetable lunch themselves, and Taylor's was too far for them to walk. Might as well kill two birds with one stone, no disrespect to them.

The Lady of Booger Hill

I used to take them and Uncle Jack on long drives. My usual destination was the family plot at Bonaventure Cemetery, the Christian part, of course, not the Jewish, which had a separate entrance. It's a beautiful place and I thought they'd want to visit the graves of most of their contemporaries. Uncle Jack finally, quite testily, told me they didn't want to visit the cemetery anymore, for me to think up something else. Claudia and Annie Ruth had been with Uncle Jack and my grandmother the day that my grandmother had collapsed from a fatal stroke, so no wonder they preferred to drive elsewhere.

The steps at Claudia and Annie Ruth's were narrow and winding, precarious, especially to the visually impaired Claudia. But they had lived there so long that they stubbornly refused to move, until their house was sold and they, as renters, had to relocate. They moved into a first-floor flat on East Broad Street, a low rent racially mixed neighborhood, quite a comedown for an Ingram. Claudia died shortly thereafter, and everyone was happy that Annie Ruth would finally, for the first time in her life, be free from her domineering, grouchy older sister. But Annie Ruth shortly "took up residence" in the cemetery plot next to Claudia, to use an Emily Dickinson allusion. Strange creatures as they were, they were a significant part of my childhood, and thinking of them brings back warm, if funny, memories.

Sissy's cousin that I most admired was Daisy Cooper. She was a cut above the rest of them intellectually, and she was a social progressive. She had been married at an early age to a much older man, the mayor of Sylvania, and she became a widow while she was quite young. She always referred to her late husband as "Mr. Cooper," and she told me that she addressed him that way when he was alive. That all seemed so strange to me, being intimate enough with a man to bear his children, but not intimate enough to call him by his first name. We called this cousin "Cousin Daisy," until, one day, she informed us that she didn't like the sound of that name. From then on, we called her "Aunt Daisy," though she was my first cousin twice removed, not my aunt.

Aunt Daisy held none of the prejudices that others in her generation and subsequent ones held. She was intellectually independent, if not socially. Her lot in life was to keep house for her daughter Marian, a wonderful lady who was my sixth-grade teacher (and my second cousin once removed) and her family. Marian was an accomplished pianist, who taught music lessons at home in the afternoons after school. Marian's husband was a huge blustering Baptist preacher, nicknamed "Crook." He claimed that he got the nickname when, as a football player at Mercer, he was expert in stealing the ball, forcing turnovers. But one wonders, because he was a shady, shady character, and he had lots more money than one would expect of an ordinary Baptist preacher. He was very kind to me.

Growing up with an extended family didn't seem unusual to me as a child. Knowing the difference between a second cousin and a first cousin once removed was just part of our knowledge and conversation. Southerners, traditionally, maintain close family ties, kind of like the ancients: "I am Aeneas, son of Anchises," "I am Odysseus, son of Laertes," and all the Biblical begats. Such information isn't superficial. Defining our heritage and our ancestors helps us to define ourselves. I guess that's what a memoir is all about.

However valuable and important, knowing second and third generations of relatives has its drawbacks, too. We children faced death early and often. In the space of five or so years, four of our immediate family members died, and our once large household dwindled to six people. Living with death is far different from hearing about it. I was saddened that my other grandmother "Granky," who also lived in Savannah, died, but Sissy's death had a powerful immediacy. Her shadow and memory still lived in the room we'd shared and in the kitchen which had been her domain. She had done handwork in the easy chair in the dining room. Her presence, if not her body, was everywhere, every day, something almost palpable.

From Bethesda to the Battlefield: The Robertsons

Mother talked little about her own Robertson grandfather, who was my Great-Grandfather Robertson, and I think that she may not have actually known him. His name was John Lewis Robertson, and I got the impression that he died before she was born. I'm not even sure of his exact birth date, but he was born sometime in either 1847 or 1848. His mother, Susannah, was widowed early and felt that she was not able to care for her three young sons, so she gave them over to the charge of The Bethesda Home for Boys, just outside of Savannah. Mother confided to my son, Ed, that Susannah had dropped the boys off on her way to Florida to meet her lover, who was a cousin of hers. She never told me that, but I always had the impression that there was something amiss, if not downright shameful, about the story she did tell.

John Lewis was the youngest of the three, and none of them adjusted to life in the orphanage. The two older boys ran away and joined the Confederate Army. John Lewis was so lonely that he ran off, too, to join his brothers. He was only thirteen years old. Mother told me that he served as a bugler, or flag bearer, or something that sheltered him from the carnage of the front lines. Both of his brothers were killed, the older one (named George?) at Gettysburg. The middle boy (named Andrew?) was wounded and spent some time recuperating in Savannah. When he recovered he was sent to Atlanta and died in the Atlanta Campaign. So it was left up to John Lewis to preserve the family line, as he was bereft of brothers and male cousins.

He married and settled in Irwinton, near Macon. Mother did remember her Grandmother Robertson, Georgia Anne Maria Strong, but again the details are sketchy. Mother visited her occasionally during the summer and said that her grandmother was little more than a plain country woman who owned a little store. Frankly, mother, who adored her own father, was rather embarrassed about his forebears. They didn't quite come "up to snuff," or rather they did dip *into* snuff, which was highly unacceptable and embarrassing.

My great-grandparents, John Lewis and Georgia, had five children: Mattie, Edna, Windell Arthur, Herman, and DeeDee, the latter surely a nickname. They all five settled in Macon or the greater Atlanta area. Windell Arthur, my grandfather, was always referred to as "Arthur" and was born in 1877. He married my grandmother, Ethel Viola Ingram ("Sissy") in 1905, and they had four children: Windell Arthur Jr., John Averette, Willie Ethel, and mother, Sarah Georgia.

Railway travel predominated in the early part of the twentieth century. My grandfather, Arthur, after a brief stint as a country schoolteacher, spent most of his life as a railroad conductor. My uncle Herman, his brother, was a railroad man, too, as were other relatives. They lived in little towns dotted along the railroad tracks between Macon and Savannah, wherever their "run" took them. Apparently there was a little job-related strife between the two men, competition as to who would get the most favorable "run": Zeus and Poseidon, Cain and Abel, the same old story. Also my grandfather's siblings never forgave my grandmother Sissy for sending him to Milledgeville after he lost his mind, so there was always tension between us and the rest of the Robertsons.

For years, the Central of Georgia Railway had its own hospital, which was located in Savannah, on Bull Street, about twelve blocks from our house. Since so many of our Robertson relatives were railroad people, whenever there was anyone in the hospital, we were the home base for the family caregivers, and for that reason I got to know my extended Robertson relatives. Despite our cramped quarters, Mother somehow always found a little nook to house one more visiting body.

Grandfather's younger brother, Herman, had two sons, Frank and George. Frank, who received his master's degree from the Yale School of Divinity, became a Methodist Bishop of Kentucky. His brother George was the head of the South Georgia Methodist Children's Home in Macon. Both were extremely jealous of each other, and I trust that these two self-professed religious men spoke to God more often than they spoke to each other.

Grandfather's eldest sister, Aunt Mattie, lived in Macon in a stuffy, closed-up house, which smelled sour and musty. She was always confined to her bed, propped up on a dozen pillows. She kept her snuff in a red silk-lined box in the top draw of her dresser. She could not reach it herself and had to suffer the indignity of asking somebody to bring her the red china box, closed tightly with a delicate clasp. She never referred to it as her snuff, though everyone knew that's what it was, and she doubtless knew that we knew. Mother even hinted that her own grandmother, Georgia Strong, had been a snuff user, too, though such things were never uttered out loud.

Mattie had three children, Sue, Bonnie, and Robert Roy. Robert Roy was a small wiry man who pretty much stayed away from family, and Sue, as long as I knew her, was bedridden, propped up on pillows like her mother had been. Mattie's daughter Bonnie was the daughter I remember best. She was a little bird-like creature who wore bright red lipstick smeared across the lower part of her face, with the creative indifference of a five-year-old child or a beagle puppy. As a young woman, she had fallen in love with a medical student and had supported him throughout medical school. Promises were made, and she visited him in Augusta as soon as her work week was over, bringing him solace for the weekend and cooking food for the next week. He was too poor to consider marriage, so that is how the situation stood.

As soon as he graduated, the wedding bells rang, as everyone expected. Unfortunately they rang, not for Bonnie but for someone else "more suitable." She was left with their love child to rear on her own, and, in my imagination, she wore her scarlet letter smeared across her face, with its flaming red swipe, rather than stitched on her bodice. We were always told that Bonnie was divorced, scandal enough for the first part of the twentieth century, but in adult life Mother admitted the truth. Bonnie couldn't have been divorced, since she had never married.

When I was a student at Wesleyan, Bonnie tried in her pitiful way to repay all of our hospitality for the days that she stayed with us when her father had been in the Central of Georgia Hospital. She called me from time to time and invited me to dinner at the Woolworth's lunch counter. I was mortified, first for my friends to see this ridiculous creature with bright red lipstick smeared from ear to ear, poorly dyed thinning pink hair, and coke-bottle glasses. I was fearful, too, that I might be seen eating at the local dime store. I am, after all, my mother's daughter.

Among other memorable characters was my Great Aunt DeeDee, the youngest of Grandfather Robertson's sisters. She had disgraced the family when she married an "Indian," as we called a Native American, a shameful thing for the last century. They had a daughter, Charlie Fox, whom we knew and adored. Aunt DeeDee was a weeper, a religious weeper. She stayed with us, too, when her father was a patient in the Central of Georgia Hospital, and she clasped us children to her copious bosom with her voice tremulous and her eyes filling with unrestrained tears making rivulets down her wrinkled cheeks. Her only other child, Johnnie Maude, inherited her mother's tearful bent, but not in my opinion, her genuine sweetness.

All these things must have been an anathema to Sissy, as the Ingrams would never have let themselves give over to emotion. They stood erect and strong through happiness, sadness, and adversity alike.

My Aunt Edna was my Grandfather Robertson's second oldest sister and was quite respectable. Left a widow at an early age, she educated her daughter Frances and was a notable enough benefactress of the Macon Public Library that her portrait was hung in the foyer.

THE BRADFORDS: ANOTHER STORY ALTOGETHER

"GRANKY"

Granky as a young girl

I never knew either of my grandfathers, one who died in his mistress's arms and the other in an insane asylum. My grandmother Sissy was a dominant figure in my life, but I wish I could have spent more time with my other grandmother, my father's mother.

We called her "Granky." It is such an inelegant name for such a kind, gentle, soft-spoken soul, and her other grandchildren merely referred to her as "Grandmother." I wish we had, too. I don't know how or why we came up with such a nickname, a combination of "grumpy" and "cranky," for she was neither. Quite the opposite, she was pleasant and easy going, or seemed to me when I was little. She had snow-white hair, exceedingly soft hands and an ample bosom. Whereas hugging Sissy had been like cozying up to a stainless steel pole in February, being hugged by Granky was as pleasurable as nestling down in a bowl of marshmallows.

Sallie Krickel

She was born and christened as Jennie Lee Andress. Her father, Neil Andress, was a prosperous landowner. Granky's mother had died young, and I can't even remember her name, so Granky's upbringing was entrusted to the care of a maiden aunt, Minnie Robbins. For some reason, another cousin grew up under Aunt Minnie's care, and Granky, according to family legend, lived in the shadow of her older, much prettier, much doted-on cousin. Her childhood slights, either true or imagined, might have been foreshadowing of her life to come. As Flannery O'Connor wrote, "Anybody who has survived childhood has enough information about life to last…the rest of his days."

Her early life, if not totally happy and secure, was privileged. After high school, she attended Judson, a women's college in central Alabama, quite impressive for a young woman at the turn of the twentieth century, when only two percent of the entire population attended college, much less a woman from rural Alabama. She spent a year as a music major, which implies that she had already had private piano lessons as a child.

Grandfather Bradford
at medical school graduation

After only one year, she returned to Beatrice, Alabama, where she met and married our grandfather, Brazil Ransom Bradford II, a physician recently graduated from medical school in Mobile. Her father had a beautiful Victorian house built for them as a wedding present. The house still stands, and is charming, if not downright elegant, with the lacy gingerbread trim both on the porches and the graceful gables of the gently sloping roof. My grandparents settled down to starting a family and embarking on a promising future.

But it was not to be. Although he was known to be a fine doctor, my grandfather was unreliable as a husband, father, and provider. I don't know what their early life together was like, but I do know that they moved around several times and finally settled in Linden, Alabama, right on the Mississippi line.

Rural Alabama was nearly frontier country back then, civility having been left on the East coast. I saw the tombstone of my father's Uncle Luke, which states his name, then only his birth date followed by the words: "Murdered 1902." He was a wealthy miser who kept his money under his mattress, but his homestead had not proven to be a very secure bank, and one dark night he was tortured, robbed and shot. The only remnants of his fortune were a few mattress feathers which had wafted through the air and settled on the floor.

My grandfather, according to colorful legend, was prone to strong drink and womanizing, in addition to poor money management. Ranny told me stories of our grandfather sitting on his back porch, drinking and shooting his rifle at any blacks who walked by. (The story is outlandish, of course, but it was told to me as truth.) In the telling of it, there is no suggestion that he, as the town doctor, was merely drumming up business; he was just a volatile man, with a sense of humor, like many of the Bradford males.

I was told that my grandfather had a long-time affair with his nurse, Miss McMinn, whose family gave the name to McMinnville, Tennessee. Once, just after my parents had married, Granky, put out by her husband's shenanigans, arranged for him to visit my parents in Savannah. Miss McMinn came along, too, and my parents moved from their first-floor suite on Perry Street to rooms upstairs for the duration of the visit. Mother, who had not much love for the Bradfords, told me this story. When I asked if my grandfather and his nurse had shared a bedroom, Mother became so flustered that she couldn't answer. But, after all, that's what one's mistress does, no matter what century or what address. Since the Perry Street house was home to various relatives, mostly middle-aged puritan cousins, I can imagine what a scandal the doctor and Nurse McMinn caused. Miss McMinn was at his bedside a couple of years later when he died. It's interesting that when Lucy Mercer was at President Roosevelt's bedside as he drew his last breath in Warm Springs, it was viewed as romantic, but my family, at least on my mother's puritan side, considered my grandfather a hopeless reprobate.

My grandfather and grandmother Bradford reared eight children into adulthood. Several other children died in infancy or early childhood. One daughter was named Madeline, and she was the darling of her older brothers. She died as a toddler, and when another daughter was born, she was considered a replacement and was named Madeline, too. Uncle John Neil, the oldest of the children, came home and was startled to find that his sister Madeline was not the same beloved child he had doted on, but a different girl altogether. This is a strange, but not unknown, phenomenon, necronymics, the practice of naming a second sibling after a deceased one. (Our father actually had two first cousins, sole brothers in their family, with the *same name*, Henri Andrew, to be sure that their father would have a namesake.)

When our grandfather died in Linden, Alabama in 1938, Granky was left impoverished and was reduced from being the wife of the local doctor to a state of financial destitution. In addition to her own children, Granky had undertaken the rearing of two of her grandchildren, our cousins Claude and Beverly. Their mother, Fannie Ruth, had died in childbirth, whereupon my uncle Claude took to the bottle, a close companion and great solace to most of the Bradford men and not a few of the women. He couldn't drink away his grief, so his two children were, for all intents and purposes, orphans when Granky took them in.

With no other means of support, Granky rented a house on the corner of Reynolds and 49th Street, where she eked out a modest living cooking breakfast and dinner for working men, and occasionally letting out an overnight room. These were the years during World War II when many men left home and worked at the shipyard in Savannah, "helping out in the war effort." Some were not draftable for any number or reasons. As there were virtually no hotels or motels, some women, including my grandmother, provided the workers with home-cooked meals. Ranny remembers that she fed ten to twelve men a day, with the assistance of two black women helpers.

I visited her, probably more times than I can recall, but my personal memories are blurred. Only a few details of those times are etched in my mind. Granky kept her money in her brassiere, left cup, which she laughingly referred to as the First National Bank, and she always had a clean cotton handkerchief pinned to her dress at the shoulder. She wore an immense diamond ring, the sole relic of, if not happier, surely more prosperous days.

When World War II ended, Granky lost her clientele. Since she had spent her life as a wife and mother, caring for others was the only skill she knew. She was a splendid cook, or supervisor of cooks, as I don't know how much of the actual work she did. After the boardinghouse, she became the dietician for Pape School, an exclusive private girls' school in Savannah, long since co-ed, now called Savannah Country Day. She suffered indignities from the spoiled young girls who complained about the meals, in addition to the shame of having to work in the first place. This was the only grousing that I remember her doing.

Sallie Krickel

I'm not sure how long she stayed at Pape, time is relative to age, but a family crisis arose when Pape contracted out to Morrison's Cafeteria, and my grandmother's services were no longer needed. Her children gathered to decide her fate. Since Granky was not financially able to maintain her own household, she went to live with her daughter, my Aunt Anne Inglesby and her family on 53rd Street, about seven "short" blocks from our house. No one else could provide for her, and we certainly couldn't either. Our family was already smushed in like raisins, with my parents, five children, Sissy, and my Great Uncle Jack all living in a moderate-sized apartment.

Granky was to share a room with Jennie, Anne's four-year-old daughter. That was all the room they had. Claude Jr. was sent to Birmingham to live with one of his mother's sisters, and Beverly to Columbia to live with my uncle Henri and his family. When Beverly graduated from high school a few years later, Granky went to Columbia for the ceremony. She planned to return for Ranny's graduation at the end of that same week, but she suffered a stroke and died. She was only sixty-nine.

I wish that I had known my grandmother better. I was twelve when she died, only a few months after the death of my other grandmother, Sissy. Mother claims that Granky, her mother-in-law, was a wishy-washy woman who always agreed with whoever was present, opting for keeping the peace and smoothing out anything rough or unpleasant. She might have been right, of course, as I wouldn't have known about such adult matters. All I know is that that wasn't the way she made me feel.

One night when the Inglesbys were out of town, Granky invited me to spend the night with her. I think that it was right after Sissy died, and, therefore, a short time before she, herself, suffered a fatal stroke. I slept in Jennie's bed in their shared bedroom. I can't remember what we talked about, probably nothing particular, but I fell asleep easily and slept well. It is a happy memory.

THE OTHERS....

Brazil Ransom I

The first Bradford I remember hearing of was Brazil Ransom I (1794-1884). His name stuck with me because he was the first in a long line of Brazil Ransoms, the fourth and last of whom was my brother Ranny. Brazil Ransom I had thirteen children: Thomas, Mary, Matthew, Arthur, Luke, Christopher Columbus, Minerva, Mark, Richard, John, Harry, Alice, and Nathaniel. I remember my relatives laughing that old Brazil Ransom had named his children "Matthew, Mark, Luke, John, Tom, Dick, and Harry," though not in that order and not intentionally. There were just so many of them. His oldest son, Thomas, was my great-grandfather and he had thirteen children, as well: sons Brazil Andrew, John Peru, Adolph Luke, Brazil Ransom II, Norbourne, and Henri; and daughters Toinette, Tolitha, Azaline (who was the first nurse graduate in Mobile), Lodie, Madeline, Hortense, and Phala.

Both my great-great-grandfather and his son Thomas were pioneers and became wealthy landowners. They had both received large land grants in Marengo and Clarke Counties, Alabama, for their service in the Revolutionary War and the War of 1812. Though they enjoyed substantial means, they were a rowdy bunch. Family legend tells that they stole horses from the Rebels and then sold to the Yankees, or vice versa, something like that. I surely don't know, but that sounds an awful lot like Rhett Butler, Scarlett O'Hara's true love. I guess there is a lot of the fanciful included in most family lore. On the other hand, there is such a plethora of stories about the reprobate Bradfords, anything could be true. There surely is something behind such strange names as Brazil Ransom and Peru.

Brazil Ransom II was my grandfather. He attended Tulane Medical School and graduated from Mobile Medical School in 1904. He practiced medicine in the small towns around Linden, the county seat of Marengo County, and reared his children there. He was also on the staff at Doctor's Hospital in Birmingham. He married Jennie Lee Andress, whose father, John Neil Andress, was also a prominent local landowner. I know nothing about the Andress branch of the family.

My paternal grandparents sired eight children who lived into adulthood: John Neil, our father Brazil Ransom III, William Claude, Daniel, and Henri Brown, and my three aunts, Lauralie, Lillian Anne, and Madeline Niolon. They were all born in the first quarter of the twentieth century. My father, the second child, was born in May 1910.

My father claimed to have had over one hundred first cousins. I always thought that was a playful exaggeration, like his walking barefoot uphill in the snow (in flat middle Alabama) to school every day, so I didn't take him seriously. But he may have had a point here. Families were large, purposefully, to provide help on the farm. There were no radios back then, not to mention television, computers, or any of the modern electronics, the names of which change too frequently to mention. Added to that, there was no birth control. Since life had little in the way of entertainment, the obvious result was that most women had babies every year or so. In my opinion, birth control was one of the greatest inventions in the world, ranking right up there with the harnessing of fire and the invention of the wheel, maybe even at the top of the list.

The succeeding generations became smaller and there were only sixteen grandchildren, the exact replacement number of the eight children and their spouses. If one counts my half-sister Catherine Lee, my father provided nearly half of the entire number. People were scandalized when my mother gave birth to her fifth child. Her friend Myrtle Wynn, who, by the way, was childless, rudely pointed out that mother was either careless or Catholic. Since we were all members of the same Methodist church, there could have been but the one conclusion. So, from a very large family of aunts and uncles I had but ten Bradford first cousins. I didn't know any of them well, not nearly so well as my Robertson cousins. We didn't share childhood adventures, so almost all I know about them, other than the Biblical "begats," are a few memories and the stories told to me.

Mother's family felt superior to the Bradfords, and we were not encouraged to see each other. I now realize that it was a classic case of reverse snobbery, as the Bradfords were certainly a rung or two higher on the social ladder and many rungs higher on the economic scale than Mother's family. I honestly think that her disapproval was due to the fact that the Bradfords drank from time to time, like every day, and my grandmother Robertson was a puritan and an emphatic teetotaler, except for eggnog at Christmas. She was also narrow-minded and extremely judgmental.

My father's sister Anne lived about seven blocks from us. She had married Tom Inglesby, who was from a rather prominent family in Savannah, and Mother claimed that Anne soon forgot she was a Bradford. That may have been true, but if so, no one could have blamed her for distancing herself from the rowdy group of hard drinkers and rabble-rousers who brought their rough frontier ways from Alabama to Savannah. I always liked Anne a lot.

She was the prettiest of the Bradford girls, and she didn't really distance herself from the Bradfords, hardly so, since she "took in" Granky the last years of her life.

Anne and Madeline, the youngest sister, were devoted to each other and shared a nanny when their children were young. In my mind Madeline and she were extremely sophisticated. They both enjoyed a cocktail at night and both smoked cigarettes, which seemed to me exceedingly glamorous. Anne certainly had some of that Bradford spunk. I recall that, when she lay in bed literally dying of lung cancer, too weak to lift her arm, she had someone, anyone who happened to be around, to hold a cigarette to her lips. She would enjoy only a shallow draw, for her breathing was laborious. I know that most people would find that horrific, but somehow to me it has a tinge of the admirable, a courageous sense of defiance at the certainty of approaching death, a "rage against the dying of the light," both the light of life and the light of the cigarette. Anne's children, Tommy, Henry, and Jennie, were younger than I, and age differences were significant when we were young. Of course, Mother didn't encourage our association either.

Our father's brother, Claude, lived in Savannah for a while, and I knew his two children, Claude Jr. and Beverly. Poor Uncle Claude always seemed down on his luck. Unable to care for his children, they lived with Grandmother Bradford (Granky) and even occasionally stayed with us. Claude Jr. was a wild teenager who was blind in one eye because he had run into a clothesline and caught his eye on a clothespin while he was out "prowling" one night. His disability didn't prevent him from being drafted, for some crazy reason, and he served in the Korean War as an infantryman even though he was totally blind in his shooting eye. Like his father, good luck was always elusive, and he died some years ago in a veterans' home from advanced alcoholism. His sister, Beverly, just older than Ranny, was very beautiful, and she was a secret role model for me as a child.

I saw my cousin, Connie, Uncle Henri's only child, very rarely, but we've had several long conversations as adults. She told me that the only time she saw her father cry was when he learned of my father's death. She was just a little girl when she walked into the bathroom and discovered her father broken and sobbing. It was a terribly distressing scene for her, but I was touched to find that someone besides me had cared about my father and had grieved at his death. We were among the few.

I was closest to my Aunt Madeline, my father's youngest sister. She was always easy for me to talk to. She was very pretty and stylish, and was the first woman I ever knew to have manicures. She was an executive secretary at Savannah Electric and Power Company, and she dressed in glamorous clothes. After an unhappy first marriage, she married Felix Caldwell, a prosperous Jew who owned chic dress shops in Savannah. His family embraced her and her two children, Stephanie and Bill, though some members of Madeline's own family, specifically Uncle John Neil, her oldest brother, expressed their anti-Semitism in disgusting terms. Felix was devoted to her and the children, and he delighted in buying beautiful dresses and in spoiling them all. Felix was always kind to me, and he was one of my favorite family members.

Their daughter, Stephanie, was an adorable little girl. Somehow she got it into her mind that pretty girls weren't supposed to be smart. So she played the role of a dumb blond, though she was not blond and certainly not dumb. Her parents enrolled her in Columbia College, a small women's college in South Carolina, where she surprised everyone, mostly herself, when she thrived in academics, making the Dean's List time after time.

Her brother Bill, though he's now a school principal (and a member of MENSA), did his share and more of mischief when he was little. He always had a wry sense of humor. One day when Madeline was visiting us, Bill got tired of waiting, so he made the best of his time by decorating the inside top of the car. He created a symmetrical masterpiece by heating up the cigarette lighter time and time again and burning little miniature round coils on the ceiling upholstery, all perfectly aligned, his own abstract Sistine Chapel. His mother was not appreciative of his artistry. Neither was she pleased when he went through his teenage "Bible-thumping" phase. I can only imagine how his Jewish stepfather felt.

One summer in the late 1950s I spent several weeks with my friend Suzanne Stern, who had moved from Savannah to Birmingham. Her father, Leonard, took us to lunch at "The Club" (pronounced with the stress on *The*). While we were waiting for our order, he went over and spoke to a man across the room, a man who resembled a Weeble, with his wide belly and rather smallish head and legs. His bald head and bulbous nose looked vaguely familiar. I asked Leonard who he was, and he replied "John Neil Bradford." He was my uncle, my father's oldest brother, whom I obviously didn't know well. John Neil came over to our table, and we had a warm exchange. Within the next few days, my Aunt Estelle and her daughter Carolyn Lee, another of my first cousins, paid their obligatory visit. I had known Carolyn Lee mostly through secondhand reports from Ranny, who was much impressed with her extraordinary beauty. He was clearly disappointed that I was not more like her. And he was right: She truly was beautiful. Although not more than a year older than Suzanne and I, she was gorgeous and worldly, with heavy makeup and bleached hair. Suzanne and I sat rapt by her endless stories of boyfriends. When a thunderstorm blew in during the afternoon, Aunt Estelle and Carolyn Lee, both terrified, retreated to the Stern's basement. They stayed there the whole afternoon, venturing out only after the sun broke through the clouds.

I have yet one more cousin, Dan, whom I've never met. His father, Dan Sr., was a younger brother of my father's who moved to California as a young man. He was killed in a freak accident, leaving his widow with a young son. She, and I can't even remember her name, remarried, and they've never, apparently, wanted to keep in touch with us. I don't even know if my cousin was adopted by his stepfather and took another name.

My father's sister Lauralie had no children. Madeline and Anne chafed when Lauralie absconded with Granky's large diamond ring, implying that she had actually removed it from our grandmother's lifeless body as some sort of spoils of war. She had been noticeably absent from the battle, though, and had left the caregiving to others.

Those were my only Bradford first cousins. Of all the wonderful things my mother did and was, I wish she had not felt the need to ridicule, and no one, to my recollection, escaped her jaundiced eye, not to mention her tongue. Envy jumped straight out of Pandora's Box into Aunt Billie's heart and from there rebounded into my mother's. I think that most people who have allowed that insidious trait to consume their every thought do because of an inferiority complex, and Mother certainly had no need to feel inferior. She was attractive, intelligent, accomplished, and devoted to her friends and family – or at least to certain ones, at certain times. But, she was unrelenting in her criticisms of the Bradfords, and her opinions colored my feelings as a child, but certainly not as an adult. I have spent more time with my Bradford cousins as we've grown older, and they are fun and experts in giving fine parties. I like them all.

The summer after our father died, Mother won a scholarship for graduate study at the University of Alabama. We all packed up, and even, if I remember correctly, had items tied to the roof of the car, as we had to take bed linens, pots and pans, and all other kitchen needs.

Mother said that we looked like the *Beverly Hillbillies*, a popular television show in which yokels from the Smoky Mountains strike oil and move to Beverly Hills to live the good life, taking their hillbilly notions with them. The analogy held true only because of our loaded-down car, as we traveled to middle Alabama, not Hollywood, and we hadn't struck it rich. Not by any means. Windell remained in Savannah to take care of Uncle Jack.

Mother had contacted a realtor beforehand to secure us a house, but, when we arrived, the plans had fallen through. Our only alternative was to spend our summer in a housing project in Tuscaloosa, Alabama, the hellhole of the deep South, at least it was during the summer of 1957. Mother and Ranny took classes at the university, and John and Neil were enrolled in the pilot school. That left me home alone, in desperation, with the chores of keeping the house clean and having lunch ready at noon. The temperature was as hot as a summer in Savannah, but there was no ocean breeze. The hot air just settled on everyone and stuck to our skins and our furniture, making us salty and slimy. In the fifties air conditioning didn't exist, at least not in a housing project in Alabama.

The only good thing to come out of that summer, and I mean the *only* good thing, was my meeting my cousins in Linden, Alabama,

Melanie

where my grandfather had been the doctor and my father had grown up. I was introduced as "Dr. Bradford's granddaughter," and people's positive reaction pleased me, as I had never heard anything good about my grandfather, who had died before I was born. My favorite cousin by far was Melanie. I liked her instantly, with her quick wit and her pretty brown curly hair. She had been named Melanie after her father,

Melvin Mashburn. Her mother's friends teased her that she had named Melanie after the sticky sweet Melanie Wilkes in *Gone with the Wind*, the wildly popular Southern saga written by Margaret Mitchell. Finally Aunt Betty, Melanie's grandmother, in a state of pique, said that she was not named for the saintly Melanie Wilkes at all, but, instead, since Melanie's middle name was Belle, she had been named after Belle Watling, the famous madame in the novel! It's easy for me to see where Melanie's wit and spunk came from. Bright and well-read, she is the Bradford cousin that I'm closest to, even though she's a "second cousin," not a "first."

Getting By and Making Do

Sticking Along Summer at the Pace of a Snail

Our family rarely went on vacations, per se, at least in the years that are most vivid to me. Once we rented a cabin on the Ogeechee River. There were a couple of times that we went to Atlanta, and mother bought me a few dresses from Rich's basement. There were afternoons at the beach, after we could no longer afford a cottage for the whole summer. We had occasional picnics, usually with other family members, and some god-awful trips to the Okefenokee Swamp. Since Mother was a science teacher, she was much interested in the ecology of the swamp, but I loathed these trips. In my opinion, if I had seen one rattlesnake milked,

At Tybee

I'd seen them all. Our trips on a little rowboat with a guide filled me with terror, as he pointed out all the alligators both on the banks and in the water, lurking, in my mind, to gobble up some tender girl flesh.

We children did go to camps. I remember going to various day camps, to summer camp at Epworth

Forsythe Park

by the Sea on Saint Simons Island, and to some Girl Scout overnighters, primarily at the Lowe house in Gordonston. But, those times have not, for some reason I can't explain, left pleasant memories. lthough not particularly so on the outside, I was privately very insecure. The problem with travel is that space is not the point. Wherever I went, my mind went along too, and it brought heavy baggage. The loneliest place in the world, I discovered, is in a room full of girls.

On a picnic

It seemed to me that everyone was talking about the fact that my brothers and I were fatherless, unusual for the time, and I raged with silent grief about my father's death and raged, too, about people's pity, shown through their glances, rather than their words. I've never, ever wanted anyone's pity. Furthermore, camp allowed some downtime, I guess for meditation and introspection, or prayer, at a time that I was trying to escape my painful thoughts and memories of betrayal. I had, by that time, totally despaired of prayer.

We children were shipped off to Aunt Billie's in Asheville for several weeks in the summer whenever there was a crisis at home. We would most often come back home to a new house, well, not exactly a new one, just a different one. One summer our father was in a tuberculosis sanatorium. We were told nothing, but we heard the hushed, ominous whispers of Aunt Billie on the phone to our mother. There were always such secrets, such foreboding uncertainty in our young lives. I'm sure it was regarded as "protection," but if children have any imagination at all, the truth would have less damage than the desperate fantasies of the mind. We felt battered about, without any tangible thing to hold on to.

Aunt Billie did an amazing job during those summers we spent at her house. I don't see how she was able to pull it all off. She was very high strung by nature, and unbearably strict by inclination. But, nonetheless, she took us in. Billie had two sons of her own, Joe, about a year older than I, and Richard, about a year younger. Even as children, the two boys were disparate. Richard was tall and lanky, and, though not much given to talk, had a pleasant, handsome face and a twinkle in his eye. Joe was on the small side, but his height belied his incredible strength. Joe was the strongest person I knew, and he was strong without the ugly bulges of the muscle bound. Richard was laid back, and Joe was always in motion.

Aunt Billie was most certainly the daughter of my stern Robertson grandmother, Sissy, in both looks and temperament. The main difference is that she had more energy to devote to scolding and a voice ten or so decibels louder and about an octave higher. I learned the meaning of "shrill" from her. I can remember the high-pitched scolding for submerging her percolator in the dishwater, an awful, but unintentional, mistake. My chore for the day was to dry the dishes; and she was the dishwasher. When she got tied up in a lengthy telephone conversation, I decided to surprise her by both washing and drying the dishes. Only thing was, I washed the percolator too. She was understandably livid, and I felt terrible, but we all survived, even the coffee pot. I made it a point not to cry.

Yet, she put up with us, usually four of us plus the two of her own, for weeks. She had her rules, who wouldn't with six children running around, and she "must be obeyed," echoes of Sissy's admonition: "Don't you dispute my word." We were not allowed to set foot in her living room, ever. (My children remember that, after Billie married John Mountney, her living room was furnished totally in white—white draperies, upholstery and carpet, and they were forbidden entry.) Of course, I surreptitiously crept through the room a couple of times, just to prove that I could, and I imagine my brothers and cousins did, too. If we were playing outside and needed to use the bathroom, we had to use the one in the basement, rather than tracking in the house. The problem was that the basement toilet was not in a "water closet," but stood naked in the vast concrete room, out in the open. Most often I was the only girl, not able to relieve myself in the outdoors, and I developed a very strong bladder during the summers. I hated the snickering as I was being spied on by the boys.

Every week, whether needed or not, she lined all us children up and gave us a tablespoon of cod liver oil and one of milk of magnesia. What a Draconian tactic. We dreaded that Friday night ritual. And the ritual which followed the next day.

One summer she devised a plan that we were to do "table topics." We took turns studying a subject, which we reported at lunch. Joe, always needling the rest of us, most particularly his mother, chose one day the topic of "worms." We were all aghast, especially Aunt Billie, but he had been given free choice, so we had nothing to do except let him at it. He described with great enthusiasm the mating habits of earthworms, which resulted in a sticky ring of mucus around the female's bellies, where they kept their unborn babies. We all choked. The funny thing is that "worms" is the only table topic that I have remembered all these years, more than sixty of them, with not even a vague hint of anyone else's report.

My most vivid memory of those summers is the way Aunt Billie demeaned her husband, Uncle Tommy. I have never, ever seen anybody treated so foully as he. I can to this day recall the tirades of her high-pitched shrieks, calling him stupid right in front of all us children. When he opened the front door after work, she'd leave the kitchen and meet him in the walk-through den. And she'd begin her daily rant. He merely stood there with his head lowered, studying his shoes until she stopped. He'd then reply, "Yes, Billie" and shuffle away down the steps to the basement. His only sign of spunk was to walk away mid-tirade and close the door to the basement, whereupon she'd just ratchet up her voice an octave or two, as the sound of his steps grew fainter.

Uncle Tommy was a proficient amateur photographer, which is one of the reasons we have lots of photos from our childhood. He developed his own pictures in his darkroom in the basement. It was a mysterious place, where children weren't allowed, and he had rigged a light bulb outside his darkroom door. When the red light was glowing, the developing process was underway, and we were told that even the least shard of light would spoil the entire procedure. He spent endless evenings in his darkroom, protected by the closed door and the forbidding red light. When he wasn't in there, the door was kept securely locked. It was a puzzlement to me as a child that he didn't develop *that* many pictures, especially considering the amount of time he spent there.

One day he forgot to lock the door, and the boys crept in. They announced, "No girls allowed," even though my cousin Judy and I threatened to tell Aunt Billie. What the boys had discovered, I learned many years later, was Uncle Tommy's cache of "girlie" magazines and whiskey. Nobody could blame him for seeking his solace elsewhere, considering the way Aunt Billie treated him. A nip or two of whiskey must have been warm and soothing, and the "girlies" (as he called women of all ages) in magazines had inviting lips and smooth bodies. Their smiles never cracked into taunts and insults.

*Ranny, Windell, Sallie,
Neil in Asheville*

Uncle Tommy and his boys went camping as their way of escape. Those were their only carefree, stress-free days, and Joe and Richard have always referred to these trips with fondness. After the family bought the cabin on Lake Lure, Uncle Tommy virtually moved there, allowing him a few years of peace before he died of cancer. Joe married early and left home, too, and Richard strung up some sheets and blankets, cordoning a private little nook, and moved into the basement.

We played outside a whole lot during those summers, a healthy and usually happy way to pass the time. The Hiles' back lawn (Billie would never have used the term "yard") was terraced and spacious, with stone steps going from the upper to the lower level. She had lovely flower gardens, and there was a pasture of horses just beyond the back fence. Uncle Tommy had built a brick barbeque pit at the edge of the grass, and we had outdoor suppers, usually hot dogs or hamburgers. We captured fireflies, carefully poking holes in the top of the fruit jars with an ice pick, fantasizing that they would serve as a lantern in the darkness. But when we woke up the next morning, the fireflies were always dead, all of them. We must have decimated half the population of lightning bugs in western North Carolina.

There was a vacant lot next door with tall trees and wild grapevines, which we referred to as "monkey vines" trailing off haphazardly from the tops of the trees down to the ground. The boys scaled the trees and, com-

(From left, back) Ranny, Joe, Windell, (front) Sallie, Neil, Richard in Aunt Billie's backyard

plete with Tarzan yells, vied with each other to see who could swing out and jump the farthest. I was never bold enough to try. One summer Joe and Richard talked Neil into trapping yellow jackets by holding a jar over the entrance to their underground nest. Neil put a fruit jar over the hole as instructed, and the yellow jackets became furious, as Joe and Richard had predicted. What they had failed to mention to my little four-year-old brother was that yellow jackets always had a back door, another hole not far away. The infuriated insects literally bombarded Neil from behind and sent him shrieking into the house.

Beaver Dam Lake was just downhill, well within

Backyard Barbeque in Asheville

walking distance, and my favorite activity was swimming, which we did from time to time, not as often as I wished. The lake had a roped-off place for children, and there was a wonderful fountain whose water cascaded out so that I could go underwater and come up on the inside, hidden away like under a waterfall. That was my favorite place, in the wonderful, cold water, all alone, obscured from view. I think I could have lived there full time. It alarmed Aunt Billie if she didn't see me, so she'd send someone in to call me out. But I'd sneak back in when I could. The water, as cool as it was, was far warmer and more inviting than her forbidden formal living room.

The weekends were full of adventure. We'd often go to the park for picnics, over to nearby mountains to climb and splash around in the deliciously cool mountain streams, to Cherokee to have our pictures taken with the "Indians," who had hidden out in the mountains rather than being force marched to Oklahoma. We camped out several times a summer, always fun, despite the kamikaze-like assaults of raging yellow jackets. We even sat around the campfire at night, crooning "On Top of Old Smoky," changing the original lyrics to something less appropriate. Understanding that in our coastal brogue, s-o-o-t was pronounced "sut" we sang, "On top of old Smoky, all covered in "sut" I lost my true lover, who fell on his ...." What's interesting now is not the lame childish obscenity (and that was the worst "cuss word" that I knew), but the peculiar Savannah accent.

There was a cluster of us. Windell, Joe (or "Joe Bob" as we called him then), my girl cousin, Judy (who went with me one year), Richard and I were all within four years of each other. Ranny, a bit older, began working part time as soon as he was old enough, so he stopped making the annual treks. Neil, four years younger than I, accompanied us only the last year. By the time John was old enough to vacation, we others were teenagers and our summers were occupied elsewhere, so he never went. Windell remembers our summers there as the only, not the best but the only, happy memory of his childhood.

The summers that I didn't go to Asheville, I visited Judy, my only Robertson girl cousin, who was two years older than I. She usually came to my house in Savannah, too, but I have no recollection of her visits with me, only mine with her. Again, it seems that we spent a lot of time together, though it was probably only two or three summers and only for a few weeks at a time. Judy was plump, even as a little girl. She had a round pinkish face, not ruddy but pretty pink,

Judy and I with Christmas dolls

with naturally curly blond hair, a few shades lighter than my own. Her eyes literally twinkled. She was jolly, and our "tickle boxes" were often turned over.

Those early years were extremely long, just as long as these later years are short. Whoever says that time is constant is certainly wrong. The summer days we spent at Judy's were endless, hot and boring. With her parents working, we stayed home all day, under the indifferent eye of her Grandmother James, who spent most of her days in her dimly lighted room sipping from a Mogen David bottle that she only half stashed away. Ranny says that she, Mrs. James, even smoked a corncob pipe.

Judy's brothers, Tommy and Jimmy, approximately Neil and John's ages, were home, too. We whiled away the relentless days lazing around. We'd lie on the yard swings, belly down, with arms and head hanging over the front and feet dragging the parched sandy soil.

Sallie Krickel

We talked endlessly, but God only knows what we had to talk about. We were too young for boyfriends, too ill-informed for serious discussions. We talked, that is, except for the days when, in typical girl fashion, we didn't speak to each other! We even accompanied each other to the bathroom, one perched on the toilet and the other on the edge of the tub. I later read that Louis XIV held court, too, with his minions while sitting on the toilet, though we didn't feel especially royal. Even unregal Lyndon Johnson had groups gather in his "throne room."

Uncle John was known to promise us frequent trips to the swimming pool, but they never materialized. On the weekends he set us to shelling peas and beans, bushels at the time. We children sat around in a circle, heaping up the pea hulls in the center, and sneaking in sometimes a handful of unshelled peas, trying to finish early so we could go on the promised swimming trip. We got caught, of course. I don't think I ever went swimming when I visited them. Well, only once, in a pond nearby, but only briefly after we realized that the cows used it as a latrine and the neighbors as a dump.

Judy and I found ways to break the boredom. We played cards. We fought a battle of several hours' duration with an enraged sow who had escaped a neighbor's pen. She chased us around the yard, we convincing ourselves that she was mad with rabies. We dashed across the yard (yes, they had a "yard") and took refuge in the back of a pick-up truck. Once I nearly didn't make it. Pigs, even overweight ones, move deceptively fast. We gathered all the spoiled canned tomatoes in the shed and hurled them at her. The jars broke, and she was covered with the red slimy mess. After several tense, exciting hours, she shrugged her fat pork shoulders and gave up the chase. She lumbered on back home. We retreated, exhausted but triumphant, to the house.

We had water fights in the kitchen with the sprayer hose. They were fun, but it took a long time to clean up, so we abandoned that pastime after a few slippery skirmishes. Judy's parents bought a television in the early years of the 1950s. They lived outside of Jesup, Georgia, however, where there were no nearby towers. It was before the advent of satellites. So they mostly got snow. Honestly. We'd sit in front of this marvelous new invention for hours on end pretending that we actually were seeing something. Occasionally there was a little sound, which was exciting because it interrupted our perennial boredom.

That was the same summer that we got drunk. Uncle John and Aunt Sara had taken a trip to Canada with a group of people. When they came back home, they raved and raved about the new drink they had been served, a "lime rickey." They were pretty laid back about some things and they kept promising us that they would make us one. (My mother would have bust a gusset.) But they never quite got around to it. So one long lazy summer afternoon Judy and I took matters into our own hands. We lacked limeade and limes, so we took the gin bottle and some grape Kool-Aid from the fridge and mixed it up, half and half, our very own grape rickey. It didn't taste very good, but we were not deterred. I can't recall exactly what happened after that, and when, but we ended up locking ourselves out of the house. With the ingeniousness that comes with strong drink, we dragged a couple of chairs up to the two kitchen windows, one window apiece. We tried to pull ourselves through to the double sink. When my aunt and uncle got back home, all they saw were four bare legs flailing out the kitchen windows. We had both gotten stuck, half in and half out. We thought it was uproariously funny. They, however, didn't. We were punished and sent to bed early, and they never left the gin out on the kitchen counter again.

Judy, though too young to have a license, was allowed to drive the car. We spent as many hours as we were allowed cruising the dusty back roads. Once we nearly drove into a ditch when we saw a lonely, love-sick stallion standing in the fields in all his glory. One time we abandoned the car in terror when the radiator overheated and white smoke billowed from under the hood. We bailed out of the car, leaving the doors open in our haste, and dashed into an eerie, leafless Cyprus swamp. After the expected bomb didn't explode and the "smoke" subsided, we cautiously drove back home. Thwarted for the day, our adventures resumed the next day, but the heat continued to drag out the long listless summer days.

A couple of years later, when Judy was old enough to have a learner's permit, but I still thirteen or fourteen, we took the car again. The family lived in town by now, and we were not free to drive the deserted dirt roads anymore. But old habits are not easily broken, and Uncle John found it necessary to start checking the odometer readings on a regular basis. No problem. Judy learned, from God knows where, to reset the odometer, which I found out later is illegal. But the only important thing was that we could resume our adventures.

With the onset of puberty, our attentions were diverted to boyfriends and summer jobs, and so our visits stopped. She became "Judi," instead of "Judy," and I changed my name to "Sallie," with an "ie" rather than a "y." We saw each other briefly at her parents' funerals and at a family reunion. I was always planning to renew our friendship when life settled down a bit, but Judi died in her fifties. She came home from work one day, sat down on a bench in her backyard, lit a cigarette, and dropped dead.

I really wish she hadn't. Judy, who had survived pig assaults, exploding cars, a preteen drunken spree, and illicit driving bouts, shouldn't have died so young. I'd love to recapture some of the long hours that we wished away as girls during those languid summers. Time crept by so slowly then. I'd love to lie belly down on a swing, dragging my feet again in the dust, and spend hours upon hours talking, just the two of us. With the passage of time and most of our lives behind us, we'd really have a lot to say.

Judy actually had three brothers, or to be exact, two and a half. Uncle John fathered a son in his early teenage marriage, our cousin Jack. Jack was not too much younger than my mother, his aunt, and he was a splendid young man. He was a freshman at Mercer University, a football player, when I first remember him, and every time I saw him, he'd swing me around in the air in his strong arms. It was exhilarating. He always treated me as special, and I was a flower girl in his wedding. It seemed strange to me that he would ask me, not Judy, his own sister, to be in his wedding, but I was not wise to divorces and other complexities of the adult world. Sadly, I am now.

Tommy, Judy's older "blood brother" is five years younger than I. When we were growing up, he was a pest, and we girls didn't want anything to do with him. He and I became close as adults. Sometimes I had the uncanny feeling when I looked at him that I was looking at Judy herself, as their physical resemblance was so strong, their round, florid faces and their twinkling eyes. I always got the impression that they were just on the verge of breaking into a grin, barely able to stifle it.

Tommy was always funny as a child, cracking jokes and getting into trouble. Neil told me that one time when he visited, Tommy pulled some prank or other, and Uncle John jerked him inside and took off his belt. (I think that whole generation of adults would be locked up these days, but corporal punishment was the norm back then.) Neil claimed that the most god-awful howls burst from inside the house. He, terrified, stayed quivering outside. A few minutes later, Tommy emerged, with all limbs intact and no obvious bruises. He immediately broke into a big grin and said, "Well, we nearly got away with that one." Apparently he was really good with sound effects.

I never knew Jimmy well. There was a big age gap, for one thing, and Jimmy was always a loner. Although Tommy and Judy remained close until Judy's death, Jimmy was pretty much estranged, by his own choice. Now Jimmy, Tommy, and their half-brother, Jack, have died, too. They succumbed to heart disease while still in their fifties, just like their sister.

JUST OUTSIDE THE GARDEN OF GOOD AND EVIL, JUST BEFORE MIDNIGHT

Having lived a childhood of summers in Savannah, Georgia, I understand the concept of murder. The heat and humidity took on an almost tangible form, morphing into some giant, bloated monster we couldn't fight off, but which seeped into our lungs and pores. Our motion, when not suspended in lethargy, was a feverish movement which was never "toward" anything hopeful, but rather frantically away from everything desperate. Such an oppressive atmosphere suffocated the body, clouded the mind, and brought despair to the soul. Right and wrong be damned. Surviving day to day was all consuming.

I didn't know The Lady Chablis, of course, the outrageous transvestite in John Berendt's scandalous book, *Midnight in the Garden of Good and Evil*, but we did walk the same streets, if not at the same time and not for the same reason. Most of my family, parents, grandparents, aunts and uncles, rest in plots in Bonaventure Cemetery, not far from the famous plot of "The Bird Girl," the statue depicted on *Midnight's* cover. The book, as much as anything, is a commentary on the often depraved life in Savannah, and it is very real to me. When it was published in 1994, *Midnight* both horrified and intrigued its readers, teasing them with lurid details, repulsive and attractive at the same time. Now people in Savannah merely refer to *Midnight* as "the book" with a tilt of the head which indicates some intimate and exclusive understanding. Savannahians don't think that it's quite proper, but it is compelling, and I can't imagine anyone in town who has not read it, once or twice at least.

It reminds me of *Peyton Place*, which "nice" people in the fifties didn't read, but which the Victorian school marms who taught with my mother passed surreptitiously around. The titillating passages were so well worn that the book naturally creased open to them. Like the readers of *Peyton Place*, self-respecting people in Savannah at first wouldn't admit to having read the shocking Berendt "journalistic novel," the genre Truman Capote took claim for in *In Cold Blood*. But the attitudes soon changed when "the book" reached the *New York Times* best seller list and remained there for more than twenty weeks. A movie was soon in the making, with Clint Eastwood as director. The tourism industry boomed in an unprecedented way, so money, in addition to buying politicians, bought, if not respectability, at least acceptance of the lurid story.

I knew a lot of the people in *Midnight*, real, familiar characters. George Oliver, the judge, was my third-grade Sunday school teacher. The Seiler family, whose son Sonny was the prosecutor, and ours grew up together. Even the people I didn't know ring authentic, despite (or maybe because of) their bizarre natures. The town had virtually reeked of unconventionality for as long as I could remember, like my college English teacher who slept with a black garbage man, long before either the races or the homosexuals mingled openly. And, frankly, Savannah was a town ripe for excesses. I think I know the explanation. It was because of the desperation of the hot humid summers, year after year after year.

Savannah was a "wide open" town. It was a port city, with an air force base and an army base nearby, and living was fast. As teenagers our typical date was a movie and a drink. Most of the "cocktail lounges" were crowded with underage patrons, and the police force had contacts who would call whenever there was to be a raid. The proprietor merely announced, "All teens out; the police are coming." We'd leave pell-mell, using the doors as exits and sometimes even the windows. Safe in our cars, we'd circle the block and gleefully watch the raid in progress.

Not a few of my acquaintances committed suicide. One particular girl, Judy, who was beautiful and intelligent, went off to Bryn Mawr and, while just a freshman, lay down on the railroad tracks one dark night and calmly waited for the oncoming train.

During most of my growing-up life, from the second grade through high school, we lived in Ardsley Park, on 46th Street, in an upstairs apartment. Although there was a big oak tree in our front yard, and some smaller ones (the names of which I never learned) along the lane in back, the whole west side of our house stood naked and scorched in the brutal heat of the sun. The concrete sidewalks burned our bare

Upper apartment on 46th Street

feet, and we used to say that they (the sidewalks!) got hot enough to fry an egg. The asphalt streets seemed soft and gooey. There were nights when the temperature still stood at 90 degrees, even after 11:00. There was no air conditioning in those days, and, for some reason, we had few fans, so no air stirred. The stultifying, hot humidity lay heavy on our ever sticky bodies. It was sinister.

My grandmother knew all the tricks, how to open the windows and shades in the early morning, capturing whatever coolness, if any, the night air had brought. Then, about noon, she pulled down the shades, especially on the west side, to block out the furious, unrelenting afternoon sun. The dining room and kitchen were, thus, shrouded in a blanket not only of heat but also darkness. Nobody breathed. Nothing moved, except the mildew in the closet, which crept along silently, persistently, covering our shoes with a film of green dust. It was not a happy time.

Without the lure of television to keep us inside, we children were turned out in the mornings, then summoned for an early lunch about 11:30. After lunch, we were dispatched to our beds to rest. Our rest time lasted for three agonizing hours. The first hour we could listen to the radio, and my grandmother and I became devoted to *Ma Perkins*, *Stella Dallas*, *Young Dr. Malone*, and *Our Miss Brooks*, the fifteen-minute daily soaps. When Goob Snodgrass came on and announced his hillbilly radio show, Sissy instantly turned off the dial. We could then read for an hour. We had a whole series of *Buddy* books and some Nancy Drews. (Before our financial downfall, we subscribed to *Look* and *Life* magazines, too, and I missed them.) And then for the third hour, we had to "lie still." I shared a room with Sissy, and when she said *still*, she meant *still*. An involuntary twitch of the muscle, even a nearly inaudible sigh, brought a harsh reprimand. God help me if I coughed or shifted to my other side. I could hear my brothers in the next bedroom stirring around, even tiptoeing across the room, but, although Sissy might call out to them, she didn't respond all that vigorously. She saved her fussing for me.

We did have fun, too, of course. Not every month was August. Ardsley Park was highly populated, and there were nearly a hundred children within several blocks. We lived in the Blessed Sacrament parish, with the church and school only a couple of blocks away. Our neighborhood was dotted with houses of Catholic families, and then there was our family, with five children, not Catholic, just careless. Even in the heat, there was always a pickup football game going, or a fort-building construction in the "lot" on the corner. There was the Crescent Circle in front of the Varnedoe house, where we could play hide-and-seek in the bushes which grew caves with their over-hanging branches. One of my early boyfriends, with a buddy of his, used to stop by the house, and I'd hop on the fender of his bike as we headed to the "circle" to wrestle. That wasn't quite as bad as it seems, for I was accustomed to brothers and boy cousins, and prided myself on being "one of the boys." The worst taunt, even to me, was to be called "a sissy" (with no reference to my grandmother), and I tried to keep up with the best of them. Mother did put a stop to my wrestling sessions, however, just at the age when they were becom-ing interesting.

We played "kick the can" on long summer evenings, right in the middle of the street. We dashed from "curbing" to "curbing" (our Savannah term for "curb"), a loud shout of "**carrrrr**" interrupting our game occasionally, but the cars were minimal and lazed along in the same hot slow motion as the rest of the world. We were ab-solutely safe. My little brothers and I, along with their friends or cousins their age spent many hours playing "cowboys and Indians" or "cops and robbers," dashing around the neighborhood with our makeshift stick guns. I admit to being the star. Not only did I have the advantage of age and experience, but, as the older sister, street smarts as well. When it was my turn to hide, being either the robber or the Indian, whichever was the game *du jour*, as they were hiding their eyes and counting to ten, I climbed the tree in the lane just outside our back fence. (We had "lanes" back then, not "alleys." In fact, when I first heard or read the word "alley," I had no idea what it was.) From my perch, I watched them for what seemed like hours creeping quietly along, pouncing around garages, investigating the bamboo stand at the Lutheran parsonage across the lane, checking behind trees, peering under bushes, with stick guns drawn and ready to make the kill. I loved it, sitting high in my "cat bird seat," de-tached, with the drama unfolding below.

The Lady of Booger Hill

Neil always told me that when he and John were on opposing sides, Neil would sneak up to John, direct his stick point blank at John's back, and shout, "Bang, I shot you. You're dead." Even though he was just inches away, John would always reply. "You missed. Bang. You're dead." The usual argument then ensued, an early sign of the contentious relationship they maintained throughout their lives.

I watched from the sidelines as the boys played "half rubber," a poor man's version of baseball that was actually created in Savannah. It was played with a 4" diameter (I'm not sure of the size) solid rubber ball cut in half, with a broomstick as a bat. It's a real challenge to hit a ball with a broomstick and an even greater art to throwing a "half" ball, which was sort of like a small, pregnant Frisbee. I was a dud at regular baseball and had no chance at "half rubber." I sat out most games; in fact, I sat out *every* game. Once, decades later, when we all gathered at Neil's house, we got up a half-rubber game. The only successful batters were Alfred's German girlfriend and my son-in-law, Stephen, neither of whom had ever even heard of the game. My family is not notably athletic, so we all, those who played, struck out. That is, until my mother took the broomstick. Neil, who was pitching, edged toward her, giving our eighty-plus-year-old mother an advantage. On the first pitch she walloped the ball so hard that it flew high over Neil's head! Windell got so excited that he crashed into the azalea bushes around Neil's front porch. Then Mother quietly returned to her seat on the porch with a sly, smug smile.

As young children, we were even allowed to walk the two or three blocks, unattended, to nearby Daffin Park. There was a nice playground, and I was, surprisingly enough considering my current girth, very agile on the trapeze, turning flips and hanging from my knees and even from my ankles. Our dog, Lassie, went along and, in her devoted dog-fashion, lugged her four-legged body up the slide steps, a kid like the rest of us. She slid down on all fours. She was so protective, in fact, that she would dash out into Waters Avenue, a busy street, and bark until the traffic stopped. Then she came back and escorted us across to the playground. She was injured several times, unfortunately, but nothing thwarted her natural maternal, even if spayed (or as we said, "spade-did"), instincts. Lassie also accompanied the family to the beach and went swimming along with the rest of us, as there were no rules about dogs at the beach when I was little.

Uncle Windell had given Lassie to Ranny on his birthday when she was a pup, and he told us that she was a "miniature collie." I think that she was not really a special breed, but she was kind, loyal, and extraordinarily devoted to us children. I called her my only sister. She died shortly after my father, not suddenly, but a slow, debilitating death. Mother had her "put to sleep," using the gentle euphemism for extermination.

There was a pool at Daffin Park, too, and we were allowed to go whenever there were enough fifty cents to go around, not nearly often enough. There was also a "sprinkler," which was a huge concrete circle, about a foot deep, in which pipes spewed water out like hundreds of miniature geysers. It was not so much fun as the pool, but it was cool – and free. There was a lake for fishing, but we didn't have poles. Instead we caught "tadpoles" and took them home to watch as they became frogs, but somehow it never turned out like we planned and hoped.

The Salk and Sabin vaccinations had not yet been developed during the early fifties, and polio ravaged the country as surely as Yellow Fever had a century earlier. Children were particularly vulnerable, and we were no longer allowed to go to any public places during the height of the outbreak, not to the movies, or "picture shows" as we called them, and certainly not to a heavily populated swimming pool. In fact the pool actually closed for several seasons. The whole country was paralyzed, figuratively, and some children, unfortunately, literally. The national scare became a reality in our family when my cousin Joe in North Carolina contracted "bulbar" polio. He lay, for weeks or months, I'm not sure which, in an iron lung, his breathing highly compromised. Happily he made a full recovery.

As I grew a little older, my bicycle, whenever I was lucky enough to have one, was my ride to freedom. I was allowed to cycle almost any place, as long as I was home for supper. Danger didn't lurk behind bushes and dark corners back then, and children were safe when turned out of the house. I rode everywhere, even across busy thoroughfares like Waters and Washington Avenues. I traveled miles. I was aware, even then, that if I were to disappear, no one would have any notion where to look. Once my friend Lynn Creamer and I got hopelessly lost in the woods. Heaven only knows where we were, we certainly didn't, but somehow we made our way home. Since I was not late for supper, no one asked questions, and the subject was never brought up. We had utter freedom in the city in those days. Our town was devoid of crime, at least in our middle-class neighborhood. I never even heard of a robbery or murder. Illicit drugs were non-existent.

Savannah had an influx of sand gnats for about two weeks in the spring and then another two weeks in the fall. There was no defense against them. We couldn't close up windows and doors because we would quite literally have suffocated. The screens were penetrable, and the gnats were inescapable. I remember reading Anne Frank's description of the flea-infested concentration camp. Anne's barracks was particularly rife with fleas, which was a blessing in her case, because that made the German soldiers stay away. I thought about Anne and sympathized with her and thought that my gnats were as fearsome as her fleas. They made my life hell, but then I didn't have to worry about German soldiers, except in unhappy dreams.

Sand gnats disappear at dusk, driven away by mosquitoes, their sinister sisters. Hearing the high pitched whine of a mosquito is nothing short of Chinese water torture. These malignant Lilliputian vultures sucked our blood and left our skin itching with sores, adding to the misery of the sweltering heat. There was no respite in sleep.

Mosquitoes didn't live only at our house. The city, surrounded by marshes and bogs of stagnant water, nurtured them. As a defense, a "mosquito-spraying truck" made its way around town at dusk, when the *blitzkrieg* of mosquito assaults was readying its attack, and sprayed a heavy fog of DDT or something equally toxic. We welcomed not only the killing of the insects but the adventure of the truck. Our game was to run along behind the machine, bathing ourselves in the lethal poison, seeing who could last the longest and who would collapse first from coughing. I guess no one realized how dangerous that was, which is strange, especially since Mother was a science teacher, but it surely contributes to the fact that, as adults, all of us have a touch of emphysema.

On a pleasanter note, during the summers we were home for the daily milk delivery. Back in the '50s we still had horse-drawn milk wagons plodding lazily through the streets. We put our empty milk bottles on the front porch, with the order and the cash sticking out the top, and listened for the clop, clop, clop of the horse's hooves as he pulled the wagon from house to house. Well trained, the horse knew which houses to stop at, and did so voluntarily. The milkman was well trained, too, as he hopped off taking his cue from the horse and dashed to front porches. Dry ice steamed like smoke when the milkman unlatched the thick doors to the coolers. It burned like fire, too, if anyone touched it. Of course, living in such a hot climate, we had to hurry the newly delivered milk to the fridge. Though pasteurized, the milk was not homogenized and the thick cream rose to the top, rich and ready for the whipping.

An ice truck still made deliveries to neighborhoods, and we were treated by the driver to shavings of ice to suck on, if we were lucky.

The Lady of Booger Hill

Our family rarely needed a big block of ice, as we had a refrigerator, not an old-fashioned "ice box," though I knew people who had to rely on purchased solid ice to keep their food cool. Occasionally we drove to Drayton Street to the ice house, which was always fun, as it was enticingly cool. We'd then chop up the big block into small pieces, the purpose for which I can't remember, possibly to make ice cream.

Since Savannah was semi-tropical, it rained a lot. Afternoon showers were the norm, rather than the exception. Often it rained hard, especially when we had a "nor'easter," a particularly virulent storm which works its way north up the coast, while a counter wind blows down south from the northeast. The rain comes down in torrents, and, since the town is only six inches above sea level, all the run-off and drainage of every kind pours into the ocean. Or it did in the last century when I lived there. If the tide was high when it rained, the water just sat. The town went underwater until the tide went out again. For the city, emergency measures rushed into play; for the children the fun began.

In some places the water was deep enough for children to dive off an overpass, but they had to be careful. If the water was too deep, there might be an actual drowning. If it were not deep enough, there was the possibility of injury. One year a small black boy broke his neck diving off a viaduct. My brothers and I were allowed to wade through our neighborhood, and we joined all the loose debris floating around. We were warned to be careful of manholes, whose covers might be displaced, which would suck us down. We were cautioned about downed live electric wires, too. But children don't ever truly believe that anything bad might happen to them, so out we went. At the corner of 46th and Paulsen, half a block away, the water was so high that it was up to Ranny's chest, we bragged, and we made a dollar or two pushing cars to higher ground. Then the tide ebbed, the water dissipated, and we were left with the sticky heat of the tropics, and, soon enough, the breeding and influx of a new healthy, vigorous crop of mosquitoes.

The weather, it's true, was oppressive. It affected everyone, not only us. It is a near worldwide experience. The main problem of our childhood, I think, is that our life as a family was equally stifling. It lay as heavy on our bodies as the heat did on the streets. So much was uncertain, so much was troubling, so much was hushed.

Our house on White Bluff Road was dilapidated on the outside and desperate on the inside. Fortunately we lived there only about a year. One warm, summer night, as dusk was turning into darkness, my brothers, boy cousins and I lay in bed listening to the radio. The boys were doubled up in beds, but I, as the only girl, had a bed of my own, the one by the door. Before long my uncle quietly slipped in beside me. After a while, he put his hand in places that he shouldn't have and did things that no one has a right to do to a child. He continued, but at the sound of my aunt's voice, he abruptly left. The radio droned on.

I had always liked my uncle. He was particularly attentive to me, and I could tell that he liked me, too. Over the years, whenever I had cuts or bruises he took especial attention, examining them and suggesting a disinfectant or massaging lotion into my dry, cracked heels. I liked him, but I didn't like what he did. Yet we were taught that grown-ups were always right and never to be questioned. Furthermore, children tattling on each other was forbidden, and tattling on an adult was unthinkable. I was an obedient little girl, and I followed the rules.

It happened the next night, too. I wanted to cry. Something fundamental in me told me it was wrong, and I summoned my courage and told my mother. She was livid, but she was livid with *me*. She told me that I ought to be ashamed and that I was old enough (seven) to know better. She told me, too, not to tell anyone, because, if my father found out, he would kill him. She left it at that, and we never broached the subject again. Such things did not happen in "proper" families, and whatever was unacceptable was quietly, and equally decisively, swept out of sight, recalling my unfortunate grandfather's foray into Chippewa Square completely naked. Appearance was everything. I retreated in shame and guilt—and fear, tightly holding on to my dreadful and potentially murderous secret. It never happened again.

In retrospect I wonder where all the other adults were on those evenings, as our house was as teeming with people as a stirred-up fire-ant mound. But I heard no voices, no voices at all, until the radio's drone was interrupted by my aunt's summons of her husband. He then obediently and quietly left the children's room. I'm sure that my grandmother Sissy was never told, nor my great aunt, nor my brothers, nor, certainly, my father. She did tell my cousin's mother, to put them on their guard, and they confided in me. My mother's burden must have been nearly as heavy as my own. But she carried it, undiscussed and unrelieved, to her grave, if, indeed, she allowed herself to remember. I never forgot, but I was luckier in the long run. I met Edward, and being with him felt safe and secure, like falling back gently into a cocoon. Everything that was bad became increasingly blurred. He was easy to love and trust.

It's easy to explain my unhappiness in childhood, the loss of innocence and the sense of abandonment. But even those things aside, it's hard to understand why we children were all terribly unhappy. When Windell and I talk about this as adults, I ask if, maybe, our experiences were the common ones of any childhood and that we children suffer from an introspective nature, but he says, no, that there is something else altogether. There's something that we can't articulate, probably because it was never given voice even then. None of us, my four brothers and me, think of our childhood as pleasant.

That's the one thing we share, the one thing we're sure of. Behind every can that was kicked, every stick pistol that was cocked, every trip to the park, every summer in the mountains lay tension and uncertainty, the fervent hushing of unpleasant things, the constant pretending, the insistence on propriety at all costs, the disregard of children and the ignoring of their pain.

THE LAND OF COTTON IN THE 1950s

I suppose that most people would think that a white girl growing up in the South in the 1950s would have a story to tell. But, truthfully the term "race," as we now understand it, had little impact on my upbringing, for reasons that I will try to explain. Early on we had black servants, as most Savannahians did, but I had no associations, either negative or positive, about them. We weren't close, like Scarlett and Mammy, but I felt no tension either. They were merely a category of beings who peopled my world, like grandmothers, brothers, aunts, uncles, and cousins.

To most children, I think, the family is not only the microcosm of the whole world, but the whole world, itself. I was aware of little else that went on outside the confines of my house and immediate family. Except for people who worked for us, either at home or at my father's business, blacks were not part of my daily experience. Segregation was in full force, and our communities did not mingle, for the most part, at least. I do remember the old, stooped black woman who shuffled her dilapidated wooden cart down the middle of the street. She wore a doo-rag, with little sprigs of wiry, gray hair peeping out the sides. She pushed her wagon with her forearms, leaving her hands free to shell her produce as she walked. As the wooden wheels bumped along the brick streets, she sang, her voice clear and dignified: "butterbeans, green beans, oh-kra."

There was a little black girl who lived in the lane behind our house on Hall Street. She was named Louella, and her mother called her home in that same lovely cadence that the black woman used when she hawked her wares through town. Louella could play in my yard, but I wasn't allowed to go to hers, and we didn't frequent each other's houses. I was four or five, and it all seemed perfectly natural, just another rule imposed by my elders, like eating my vegetables if I were to have any dessert.

Little by little, as I grew up, I began to be more aware of differences, ever so subtle at first. The cook and maid were required to eat out of a pie tin and drink from a Mason jar, instead of using regular china, not even the everyday dishes. I felt awkward and tried not to look at them when they served their plates. As an adult I've become aware of the irony: They were hired to cook our food and put it into our dishes, but could not eat from the very dishes that they had washed, dried, and served the food into. I became aware that blacks sat in the back of the bus, mainly because our maid, when she took me on excursions, was allowed to sit up front because she was accompanying a white child. An unwanted compromise, certainly, but it was unthinkable that a white child would sit amongst blacks, even if a black woman had recently dressed her and brushed her hair.

That was the only exclusion from the blacks-to-the-back-of-the-bus policy until Rosa Parks sat her exhausted body in the white-only section in a Montgomery, Alabama, bus and refused to relinquish her seat to a white man. "Her feet hurt," she explained. These scenes from my childhood are distinctly vivid. I remember the bus drivers in Savannah reminding his passengers "Negroes move to the back of the bus," as many blacks climbed wearily on to the bus after a long day working in white neighborhoods, standing in the aisles because the "negro section" was full. I was also aware that they had so much more fun back there, relaxed and easy, with friendly, intimate banter. Everybody seemed like lifelong friends.

During the fifties, we referred to blacks as "negroes." We were never in our home allowed to use the pejorative "n" word, as we were "cultured" people, cultured in a funny and equally complicated way. I guess that Sissy was showing her cultural superiority when she upbraided me for referring to a black woman as a "lady." She told me in a very firm voice that there was no such thing as a black lady; black females were "women."

Although my grandfather Bradford's black servants were just one degree short of being actual slaves, the few family pictures that we have left (after fire destroyed their home) included both the black and white children on the home place. More than that, they were all mixed up, not segregated in the least. I wonder at what age it suddenly became unacceptable for the races to fraternize, as these children, except for more ragged clothing, were obviously on equal footing.

When my grandfather died, my father felt a responsibility for the life-long servants and he went to Alabama, bringing back to Savannah not only his mother and his siblings, but also several of my grandfather's servants. All that is true, and undeniably kind, yet my grandfather and my father also had unrelenting and firm racist views. Such a dichotomy. Their attitudes were, at the worst, demeaning and even brutal, and at best, "paternalistic."

We all eschew brutality, but a patronizing attitude might be the most awful, as it is insidious, deeply entrenched, and so god-awful smug. The white Southerner, taking as his example the Christian God, felt himself superior, a higher sort of being. (Even our Constitution originally determined that a black man counted only 3/5 on the census.) The white man made the rules and he exacted the punishment. He was, indeed, the god of his empire. It was pure and simple hubris, assuming the role of God, pure and simple and damnable hubris. We addressed black men that we didn't know as "uncle" and black women as "auntie." Again, the white race could feel smug with terms of seeming intimacy, while at the same time establishing their utter superiority.

It was my grandfather Robertson, a mild man, who claimed to love "everyone except...." (His "except list" was rather long!) Mother told us that it was a widely circulated rumor when she was a little girl that nuns had such large sleeves on their habits so that they could hide away their shoplifted goods, and Sissy, my straightlaced grandmother, as she prepared a chicken to fry, referred to its tail as the "Pope's nose." So, in our household, we spread our prejudices around. Ironically, the only thing that we were inclusive about was our firm belief in our exclusivity. Our snobbery was not limited to blacks, but to Jews, Catholics, fundamentalist Christians, Asians, Latinos (the few we knew), and anybody else who didn't share our background and ethnicity. It even included those who used outhouses.

My father died in 1956 with his old philosophy, contradictory as it was, still intact. I remember his and Ranny's arguments over the dinner table, as Ranny was as progressive as our father was reactionary. Political arguments raged every evening, night after night. Once I quoted something that I had heard Ranny say. Feeling pleased that I could contribute to the discussion, I exclaimed: "Don't get so hot in the trot." I was immediately "excused" from that table in shame. For goodness sake, I naively thought the comment referred to horse racing, not a sexual allusion. Little pitchers not only have big ears, but big mouths, too—and limited understanding.

Mother was able to come to terms with the changes in society much better, though she remained unaware that some of her feelings about racial inequality remained firm, if muted. It was surely a terrible tension to be an all-embracing Christian and read about "all of

God's children," yet hold on firmly to the notion that it wasn't really "all God's children," just the lily-white ones. We sanctimoniously allowed Negroes in the balcony of our uptown church, the auspicious Wesley Monumental United Methodist Church, "South," a postwar term of begrudgement. Those Negroes came only for weddings and funerals of their white employers, but mother told me that in the old days, the balcony was quite full—full of slaves who accompanied their masters to worship services. She spoke in a tone of unselfconscious pride.

I quite clearly remember our minister, the Right Reverend Albert F. Trulock, preaching sermons in which he claimed that God intended for the races to remain separate. After all, the blue bird would not mate with the red bird: Segregation was all a part of God's plan. I don't suppose that anyone ever pointed out to him that some of our kin in the animal kingdom see absolutely no problem mating with others of a different color. That would have been too much for him to take in. He also echoed the supremacist argument that God had created a separate continent for people of a different skin: Africa for the black, Asia for the yellow, the Americas for the brown, and Europe for the white. Though it seemed to me that if we are all descended from Adam and Eve, as we were supposed to believe, that notion is foolish at the very least. My older brothers left the church.

I became increasingly aware and uncomfortable about the "white only" signs on restroom doors, and I absolutely hated the same "white only" signs above the water fountains. I agonized about being a black mother with a thirsty child who was not allowed to take a sip of water. I even played a private game of seeing how long it was between the appearance of a white face, wondering if a black mother had time to lift her thirsty toddler for a surreptitious sip, quick and unseen. I identified so thoroughly with the indignity of it all, knowing that if I were told that my child was not good enough (or white enough) to have a drink of water, there would have been no peaceful resolution. All hell would have broken loose. I flatter myself, of course, as I was a wimp then and am now. I'm just a lousy armchair rebel.

It was not until years later that I learned that there were plentiful shops on West Broad Street, which catered exclusively to black clientele. They didn't even need to go uptown and probably didn't even want to. I wonder if they had signs proclaiming "no whites allowed." Probably not. The black community had their own restaurants, newspapers, motels, and everything else a society requires. That was to me, even many years later, a relief. One of the reasons I never knew is that we didn't drive on the west side of town, which would now be termed a black "ghetto," a fact which makes me gasp. The cruel irony is that Jews owned most of the shops on the west side and freely left every night and went to their homes in the best parts of town, leaving the "ghettos" to others. What a crazy, mixed-up situation; the whole world is a madhouse.

My girlfriends and I rode the bus uptown to Savannah every Saturday to eat our hamburger at the restaurant in Levy's department store and to see a movie. On the way, we passed by the "black" movie theater on East Broad Street. I was amazed by the billboards and marquees. They never showed the same films that I saw, but instead theirs had alluring titles and intriguing billboards of sexy dark-skinned men and women in lively, bright costumes. I wanted those movies to come to theaters where I could see them, too. But they never did. In fact a couple of years ago, while watching a documentary on Savannah, I found out that there was quite a class separation among the local blacks. Those on the eastside and those on the westside didn't mix, even to the point of never even setting foot in each other's movie houses. So I was not the only one left out.

Brown vs. the Board of Education had little direct effect on our lives, as in the South segregation remained intact. The homogeneity of our elementary school was maintained, except for the brief intrusion of one Romany girl (whom we referred to as a "Gypsy"), Mercedes Quato, who would dance for us in the most exotic and intriguing way, weaving her arms and hands in a sinuous pattern, while her shoes tapped out the rhythm.

There were also some orphan boys from Bethesda, the oldest orphanage in the US, located on the beautiful and famous Moon River just outside Savannah. The boys had a peripatetic education throughout the city, staying in one school only until someone was kicked out. Then the whole fleet moved on. Those boys got really cheated in life, and it made me sad. (I didn't know at that time that my great-grandfather had been a "Bethesda boy" himself in the mid-nineteenth century.) One of the boys whom I had especially liked was mercilessly derided because he had never learned to read. His name was James. Before very long, the Bethesda clan left Charles Ellis School and moved, again because one of them had caused a problem and the others were guilty by association. I never saw James again, at least not for more than ten years. We ran into each other by chance in Wright Square one day, and he proudly told me that he had married and that his wife was teaching him to read. I was immensely moved.

The high population of Jews almost disqualified them from *total* social discrimination, although I say that from the standpoint of a Gentile. They might have felt differently. After all, most were rich, and money goes a long way to buying acceptance, a universal "gold" standard.

Neither my middle school nor my high school was integrated, and we remained in our pristine, bland, colorless environment. The old "separate but equal" policy was not true, of course. The black schools lacked our facilities, and, I learned later, the textbooks they used were the ones discarded by the white schools. My mother had a Georgia history textbook, in which "race" was listed as part of the identification stamped in the front, along with, "name," "school," "grade." But I was generally unaware of these things. What *Brown vs. the Board of Education* accomplished in the South was not the desegregation of schools, as I went through middle school and graduated from high school in 1960 without a single black classmate. What it did accomplish, though, was to erode the smug, protected shell of our lives. We wrestled with the contrast of our newly formed opinions against the firmly entrenched heritage of our parents. And for some, if not most, of us, our rational grasp replaced the older assumptions of the superiority of the white race.

No blacks attended Wesleyan, though integration by this time was being enforced. It's just that, even though we boasted of several Asian alumnae, among whom was Madame Chang Kai Shek, no less, no one but a WASP (White Anglo-Saxon Protestant) would have entered the sacrosanct halls of a small, mediocre women's college, with pseudo-religious pretension and silly social restrictions. There were certain parlors into which we could not even step without wearing floor-length formal gowns and high heels. I still hear the admonishment that "Wesleyannes are ladies at all times," to which some students added, "and in all positions." Our handbook cautioned us: "Women are always seated when smoking."

I couldn't exactly have verbalized "racism" as a descriptive word from my upbringing, even though it was obviously there, overtly in society, and muted at home. As the generations changed, so did our feelings. Ranny, first of all, became a wild liberal, violating all the taboos of the times. He was an embarrassment to many of the family. Next came Windell who was greatly influenced by his older brother and put his philosophy into action, becoming a federally employed civil rights worker. The rest of us followed along, some lagging behind.

I remain very proud of my two older brothers, who were both idealistic and courageous. I shared their idealism but lacked their courage, I'm ashamed to say. My efforts were mostly verbal, most often ineffectual. My boyfriend and I went to bars on the black side of town and attended services at a black church, but all we accomplished was to make everyone else feel awkward and ill at ease. With us as interlopers, nobody enjoyed either his whiskey or his worship. We were so concerned with ourselves and our pathetic attempts at being enlightened that we didn't notice.

TRIPPING OVER THE CUSP OF ADOLESCENCE

When I was fourteen I got a job as a "page" at the Savannah Public Library. There were twenty or so high schoolers who worked in the afternoons, for the magnificent sum of seventy-four cents an hour. Four afternoons a week I worked for Frances Rees, who had once been the sweetheart of my mother's first cousin, Frank Robertson, a Methodist minister. Miss Rees was a very kind, compassionate and supportive person, and the job was gentle enough. She ordered children's books, and I double checked our holdings against the latest catalogs, and, after she decided which ones to order, I totaled up our orders on an ancient adding machine.

One night a week, Thursdays, I worked the main circulation desk. Nina Ravenscroft was the librarian assigned to work that same night, and, although she was always nice to me, I never felt comfortable around her. I had seen her be very abrupt with co-workers and even with patrons. I stepped to. She talked to me a lot about her unfortunate marriage. She had come from a wealthy, sophisticated family, but had married a ne'er-do-well who became an alcoholic. She told me that her mother had warned her that, if she married him, she would be reduced to begging. Not exactly begging, nonetheless she was compelled to find a job to support the family. When I gave her a ride home after the library closed at nine o'clock, she'd invariably ask me to drive by the neighborhood bar to see if her husband's car was parked outside. She was a very bitter woman, doubtless with great cause. She had the most beautiful wedding ring I've ever seen, a large diamond with two equally large rubies on either side.

We teenagers enjoyed our jobs and our eccentric employers, most of whom were old maids. The first one all of us met was the business director Miss Pottinger, who could not have been more aptly named. She was truly a walking epithet of herself. "Miss P," as we students called her behind her copious backside, was in charge of supplies, and she was so frugal that she issued each page two pencils when we signed up to work, and to get another one, we were required to show her the nub of the original, to prove that it was too short to use. And God forbid if we lost one. On the other hand, the library was always solvent, and there was no waste under the tight fist of Miss Pottinger. I can see her now, waddling down the marble library floor with her thighs asking permission of each other and working in tandem to propel her forward.

There was the bird-like little French lady, who had a thin beak-like nose and literally flitted from place to place, energetic and chipper. Although an American citizen, she insisted on being called "Madame Mauduit." She was a widow and the first French person I'd ever known. I liked her. The imposing head librarian was Miss Geraldine LeMay, whose tall, erect figure and salt-and-pepper hair commanded a certain respect and maybe even a little fear. She rarely spoke, at least not to us peons, and we bragged among ourselves if Miss LeMay singled us out with a greeting or, rarest and best of all, a kind remark.

Shelving books was a bore. We teenagers usually found other things to do in the stacks, like taking long breaks with someone on guard. We didn't dare do any hanky-panky. When the bookshelf was crammed full, our favorite trick was to send an eager, recently signed-on page to Miss Pottinger to ask for the "shelf stretcher" so that we might squeeze one or two more books onto the shelf. Much to the delight of us "oldies," new recruits always fell for the ruse and eagerly went to Miss P's office. Miss Pottinger, curiously enough, never complained. I guess that, as long as she had a full counting of pencils, she could relax about other things.

I met Donald Crafts, my first serious boyfriend, at the library. He drove the truck around to the various branches delivering and collecting books. Miss Rees' office was in the annex which was separated from the main library by a driveway, and Donald would always toot the horn as he passed under my window. When the boss wasn't there, I'd wave; when she was, I sat still, but she smiled. He was my transportation to and from work, giving rides to me and Sharon Clark, a friend and fellow page. Donald was excitingly intelligent, really brilliant, but not particularly supportive. We went together five years, the last of which I even had an engagement ring, too old, I felt, to wear his oversized high school ring, which I had sized down with candle wax. We never made wedding plans, as we both knew that it would have been an ill-fated union. I knew that always, and he began to realize it, too. He was a very good friend, though, and I was sad when he went to graduate school at The Fletcher School of International Affairs and disappeared from my life. He had wanted to get married and have me support us while he studied. I had other ideas. He, enlightened about most things, explained that "a wife was a mere shadow of her husband and that his accomplishments would be enough success for both." Long before feminism, I knew that I didn't fit into that mold. At Christmas I returned his ring, and he was engaged again in the spring. I was brokenhearted, not because I had been jilted, but because I had lost my best friend.

When I was in college I worked part time as a secretary for an insurance company and for Savannah Electric and Power Company, both in uptown Savannah. I enjoyed the people I worked with but didn't especially like the work. After I learned a new job, I became impatient with the monotony and lack of challenge. The most important thing that I gained from those experiences was that I had made the right decision to go to college. Though grateful for my employment, I was always ready to head back to academia in the fall.

For about three summers somewhere in the mix I worked for the Tetley Tea Company as a secretary for the tea taster, Alan Davies. That was a wonderful experience. I handled the billing, not an uncomplicated task, as I had to convert dollars into foreign currency, (I learned about such things as rupees), checking the exchange rate which varied from day to day. I'd fill in the bills of lading and take them down to the Customs House. The tea factory was actually way out on the other side of town, near the docks. Tea leaves arrived by ship in wooden boxes about the size of a medium doghouse. The shipments came from exotic places like Indonesia, India, and China. Then Mr. Davies would taste a sample of the individual boxes of tea to determine how they were to be blended together. It's interesting to know that every little Tetley tea bag contains leaves from different growers, different shipments, and, actually, from various countries. The reason that they all taste the same is due to the efforts of a tea taster, specially trained through a seven-year apprenticeship. I was highly impressed. Besides that, he was a very nice man, and the tea factory was a pleasant place to work.

The first summer I worked only in the afternoon. My desk was in the corner of a large room, with Mr. Davies' across and to the right. The rest of the room was fitted out with a long table and a miniature kitchen, decorated with a stove, brass teapots, and two large brass cuspidors. The surroundings, though not typical for an office, were pleasant, and the brass teapots and other supplies gleamed in the brightness of the fluorescent lights.

The second summer I worked all day. On my first day back on the job, Mr. Davies asked if I wanted to taste the tea with him. Of course I did. He explained how it worked. Both the teapots had to be cleaned, I think with baking soda; anyway, no detergent was used so that there would be no soapy residue. The matron, a glorified kitchen maid, brought out about thirty little white ceramic pots, a little larger than the teacups in the Chinese restaurants. Each one had a saucer. She then took the teapots and boiled the water for one minute (I think) to steam away the exact amount of oxygen in the H_2O. Into each of the thirty cups was placed a tablespoon from each box of tea. The air-free water was carefully and neatly poured into the little ceramic cups. She then placed a saucer on the top of each little pot. The tea steeped for exactly three minutes. Just at the precise moment, heeding the buzz of a timer, she uncovered the perfectly steeped tea and placed a small portion of the leaves into individual saucers.

Everything was set. Mr. Davies, with me in tow, took an ordinary tablespoon and started down the rows of the little ceramic pots on the counter. He pointed out how important the color of the tea leaves was, noting that some were red and some black, still some in between. Though it was obvious to him, I confess that they all looked the same to me. He spooned a sample from the first pot, with a great big slurp. He explained that the harder the tea hit the palate, the more flavor it gave off. It was my turn. I tried to slurp, but I simply couldn't. My Southern upbringing had not allowed me to sip audibly, and the ghost of my grandmother emerged over my right shoulder.

Mr. Davies then explained that his keen sense of taste would be dulled if he swallowed any tea, and he turned in the direction of one of the cuspidors. He spurted a neat steady stream from halfway across the room, hitting his target perfectly. I had thought that the cuspidors were merely a decoration, and I was abashed. Using a cuspidor is a true art, not to be undertaken by the hesitant, and I failed miserably. Whereas he could direct his aim from several yards away, I had to stand directly over the big brass container. No matter how hard I tried, I couldn't do any better than let the warm tea dribble down my chin. The effect was not pretty, as I couldn't produce much more than a baby's drool. It was embarrassing, and I appreciated even more his long years perfecting his trade. I made a decision, right then and there, that, since I was in no danger of spoiling my untrained palate, I would go ahead and swallow all thirty samples of tea, and I did, virtually waterboarding myself. After that experience, it took me years to like hot tea, which I now adore.

Mr. Davies then noted down how much of which box needed to be blended, so that each little tea bag would taste exactly the same. Except that he, himself, would never use a teabag, because of the paper taste. He said that Lipton tea, which had just come out with a new "flow-through" teabag, was undrinkable because of the unpleasant paper taste.

I had peon jobs when I was a student at Wesleyan. My junior year I worked in the library, which this time was not a happy experience. (Ironically enough, we were fired if caught actually reading a book!) I worked at the circulation desk, and part of my job, in addition to checking out books, was to alphabetize cards. Since I'd worked in a library for about five years and had alphabetized thousands of little 3x5 cards, I'd worked out a quick and precise system. After finishing my first group of cards, I took them to the librarian. Without even looking up from her work, much less glancing at the cards, she told me to go back and alphabetize them again. I was highly insulted. I quickly unlearned to be efficient. I somehow made it through the first year, for the fine rate for student workers of fifty cents an hour.

The next year, I became the student secretary for the new English professor, that man with the funny last name, Krickel. That is a story for a later chapter.

Sallie Krickel

The Cold War Invades the Sunny South

When I was in elementary school in the 1950s, the Cold War sent a paralyzing chill across the country. The atmosphere was tense. World War II had ended, but the USSR and the "communist menace" threatened the new peace, and we all lived under the cloud of potential, if not certain, nuclear attack. We were both vigilant and uneasy. Savannah was not only a port city but also the site of a strategic air command base, Hunter Field. Located nearby in Hinesville was Fort Stewart, an important army base. We were told that, in the case of nuclear attack, our town would be a major target, second only to New York City. We children believed this as gospel. It was a strange dichotomy, the feeling of pride in the importance of our town (we pupils bragged somberly), and knowledge that, because of it, we would be summarily blasted from the face of the earth. Maybe it was just easier to assert our self-importance than to express our collective sense of doom.

Personally, I had seen the newsreels of Hiroshima and Nagasaki. The pictures of nuclear aftermath in *Life* magazine were seared in my mind and imagination. I remember wondering how quickly the mushroom cloud would spread, how quickly death would ensue after the settling of the nuclear mass. I transposed those images in *Life* to the lazy Southern town I lived in. I did not know the term "surreal" when I was a child, but, in retrospect, that is the best description of the atmosphere we lived in.

Americans were urged to build underground shelters and stock them. Since Savannah was only six inches above sea level, that was impossible. We would have found ourselves mired down in mud or marsh. The grim reality: We were goners. Resigned to the inevitable, I took up my father's habit of eating my dessert first, hoping the bomb would arrive before the stewed squash. I made other such concessions, like trying to be nice to everyone, hoping that because of my great virtue, the mushroom cloud would billow me straight up from cloud to cloud until I reached heaven. It turns out that my resolve to eat my dessert first was more successful than the attempts to be angelic.

We elementary students were issued dog tags, just like the soldiers. We were young and naive, though, and delighted in trading our dog tags with our sweethearts. If holocaust had occurred, identification of our charred little bodies would have been difficult. The best that anyone could have determined was that, judging from the metal dog tags, these were the remains of "John Smith" or "John Smith's third grade girlfriend." Maybe that was close enough. I wondered who would even survive to collect us or to read our identification.

Several times we had bomb drills. With sirens wailing, we would be lined up to take the long two-mile trek to the train tracks on the edge of town. In case of attack we children would be loaded up in boxcars and taken to safety. Those were sober, even desperate, times for me. I knew that I wouldn't survive the claustrophobia of being crammed in a boxcar with hundreds of other children. Besides that, I would rather have been blown to smithereens with my own family than exist in protective isolation with hundreds of sniveling, whining schoolmates. I lived only a couple of blocks from school, in the other direction, and I always had the urge to run home when the drill began and hide out. I had not seen at that time all the documentaries and other films of Jews being rounded up and transported to concentration camps in the same boxcars, but something in me found the whole process not only frightening, but repugnant.

Windell, who was in middle school at the time, recalls seeing films about the destruction of atomic bombs as they were being tested in Arizona. All the facsimiles of nearby buildings crumbled, much like the towers at the World Trade Center were to do in the next century. The images were gripping and terrifying.

The political events which caused such extreme measures settled down. I was not even sure exactly what it was all about. Life resumed normalcy. My early teen years were pretty much like teen years everywhere. There was the excitement of dances, proms, where I always had pastel Benson and Hedges cigarettes to match my prom gowns, boyfriends, exploring adulthood, taking risks, trying to find my own niche.

There was the excitement of a new, youthful, idealistic president, John Kennedy. There was hope and vitality, stability, too. But only a few months after the inauguration came the abortive invasion of Cuba's Bay of Pigs, our country's attempt to counteract the "red menace" just ninety miles from our shore. Tensions reached extraordinary proportions; the Cold War was heating up. The invasion of Cuba failed, and Kennedy backed down.

But Cuba, in the firm grasp of Fidel Castro, didn't forget quite as easily as our country did. Fearing another attack from America, Castro appealed to Khrushchev, his avuncular communist ally, for protection against the US. Our radar began to show some suspicious activity. The Russians had dispatched ships loaded with nuclear missiles, headed for the small island just ninety miles from the tip of Florida. My fiancé at the time was a student at Emory, and he became alarmed when trains started rumbling through campus, heading south. The flatbed rail cars were covered with huge tarps, poorly disguising missiles and other weapons of war. Not only that, the rhythmical monotony of trains passing on the tracks was relentless. All day and all night the steel of the wheels sparked against the steel of the tracks, keeping pace with gnawing fear. Nearly all the people were terrified; the rest were hysterical.

Reports came in from Savannah that guns were being stowed along the beach on their way to Cuba. Tension mounted. There were aerial views on television of the Russian ships approaching the Caribbean on a steady, deadly course. Kennedy used the official hot line to Russia, the red push-button phone. Once again there was a standoff between Kennedy and Khrushchev. I'm not sure how the events transpired, but the Soviets recalled their missiles, and the US removed ours from both Florida and Turkey, the former pointing toward Cuba and the latter toward Russia, itself. All I know for sure is that World War III was avoided, thank God. But danger was always lurking as an undercurrent.

New terms entered our vocabulary: the Berlin Wall, the Brandenburg Gate, Checkpoint Charlie. In the early sixties, the Soviet Union erected a wall, first a barbed wire barrier, later a tall concrete structure, which isolated West Berlin, not only from East Berlin, but from East Germany as well. Hundreds of miles of the wall were constructed almost overnight, and it became the great symbol of the Cold War and communism. The supposed reason, according to the communists, was to protect the East from the residual fascist influence of the West. Our "side" saw the situation in a much different light. We needed to liberate the East Germans from the tyranny of communism. Whatever, the Brandenburg Gate was boarded up, impassable. No respecter of humanity, the wall cut through streets, sometimes even apartments, and prohibited communication between the Easterners and the Westerners. Friends and even families were separated. People were unable to get to their jobs. During the course of the next years, the democratic West thrived, while the East went through a steady decline. It was little wonder that many Easterners sought to breach the wall and proclaim their freedom. All Germans wanted unification.

John Kennedy stood in front of the Brandenburg Gate in 1963 and boldly declared, in a strong show of solidarity with all Berliners: "Ich bin ein Berliner." His intentions were nobler than his German. Instead of exclaiming "I am a Berliner," he, with great enthusiasm, cried out "I am a jelly donut." (Just as we would say, "I am a Danish pastry," rather than "I am Danish.") But the world loved this young, handsome idealist, and his message was passionately clear, though his actual political support was scant. (He privately proclaimed: "Better a wall than a war.") Ronald Reagan was president when the wall, this great symbol of communism and the Cold War, crumbled. He stood at the same famous Brandenburg Gate, shook his fist, and shouted: "Mr. Gorbachev, tear down this wall." That was in 1987, and in a few years after that, the wall did fall, though "fall" is not a very descriptive word. It didn't "crumble," either; it was hacked down, chunk by chunk, piece by piece, with fervor, the ferocity of the oppressed bursting into freedom.

Ranny's East German friends turned up on his doorstep in Munster in the middle of the night, delirious that Germany was reunited. Euphoria reigned. The hundreds of miles of wall were demolished in a few weeks' time. His friends brought with them fragments of the destroyed symbol of the Cold War, and Ranny gave me a couple of pieces, which I have framed on the sunroom wall.

About a year after the wall fell, Edward, the girls and I visited the recently reunited Berlin, with Ranny as our chauffeur. The autobahn from Munster to Berlin was punctuated with the rusted-out Trabbis, the cheap East German cars which were so worthless that they didn't even warrant being repaired. They lay on the roadside, like skulls and skeletons of buffalo in the old American West, blanching randomly in the hot sun, and of the remains of covered wagons, burned out and decaying like hopeless dreams.

We stayed with some friends of Ranny's in the former Eastern Sector, which was emerging from the constraints of communism. Though Father Christmas was bicycling through the Brandenburg Gate, an amusing but promising scene, and though capitalist kiosks sprang up overnight like mushrooms and were dotted around the square, the atmosphere was still hesitant, if not repressive. Ranny and Edward stayed with the older parents, but the girls and I stayed in the home of the young couple, Michael and Gaby, and their daughter, Bianca. Never have we had such gracious hosts. Michael, particularly, was warm and sensitive, eager to please his American guests. We Krickel girls were much taken with this kind, caring and handsome young man.

I was aware that when we were out sightseeing, Michael and Gaby were still guarded, reluctant to ask questions. I don't think they were shy; I think that they were still living under a suppressive cloud. They couldn't bring themselves to ask questions of the officials in the Bundestag, but retired to the midst of the crowd so as not to call attention to themselves. It was obvious and eerie. The Alexanderplatz was bare and lonely, the traffic sparse in the 1990s. We had seen more skeletons of Trabbis on the road to Berlin than we saw actual traffic circulating around the city.

Much of what we saw involved the wall. Michael, our warm, compassionate guide, pointed out all the checkpoints from the Eastern side, as well as all the brutal ways that were to keep people from escaping. Here was a place where dogs were trained to attack anyone who tried to cross from East to West; there were the towers armed with sharpshooters and searchlights. He pointed out mine fields, and explained the anti-vehicle trenches. He showed us crosses at the riverside, commemorating the first shot victim, as well as the last victims who were killed as they tried to swim to freedom. There were entrances where tunnels had been, subway systems which had been bricked up, then breached. At one point, Liz bent down to gather a few remaining rock fragments of the wall, and she put them in her pocket. Michael pointed out that she was in the death strip, "no man's land," and that not too many months ago, she would have been shot. According to her, those rocks suddenly got awfully heavy. We visited the site of Pink Floyd's concert, "The Wall," which was played as a cry for freedom. Liz had a picture made on the still barren landscape. Michael even took us to the spot where he used to stand and wave to his sister on holidays. She in the West and he in the East had no other communication.

Michael knew all about the various positions of the wall, of course, because he had served in the Red Guard; he was one of the soldiers who had been part of the suppression of would-be escapees. Everyone was conscripted to military duty and he had no choice. He was somber in admitting that. Michael, our lovely host, had just months before been our enemy. He might have been the very one who would have shot Liz as she wandered into "no man's land" and stooped down to collect some souvenirs.

My son, Ed, and I went back to Berlin in 2009, nearly two decades later. The skeletons of Trabbis had been carted off and buried. Everything looked prosperous. I enjoyed seeing the usual tourist sights and finding geo-caches with him. By now the big city had become thoroughly "Westernized." Tourist shops jostled to attract tourists, in much the same way pedestrians pushed past each other in the crowd. Near the site of the preserved section of the wall was an outdoor snow slide, like the water slides at our theme parks. We ate "street food" near where the Alexanderplatz had stood desolate when we had visited before. We even got a shot of a virtual geo-cache on the top of Checkpoint Charlie, still standing, though no longer armed with soldiers and rifles. It was choking with masses of people. The desolate space in front of the wall, where Liz had picked up the rocks more than a decade earlier, was thoroughly commercialized. In fact, the barriers between the sections of the city had been totally obliterated. We didn't even know when we passed from West to East. In 1990 we were the only visitors and effortlessly snapped photos. Now it was difficult get a break in the huge throng of people to take a picture of us at the same spot.

On our earlier visit, Edward, Liz, and Michael had visited the famous Pergamon Museum and seen the Ishtar Gates. They had merely strolled in the museum one afternoon. Mary was sick that day and stayed at the apartment. I had stayed home that afternoon to be with her. I had been very disappointed. So I was excited about my long-delayed visit to the museum, as Ed and I made our way to the Pergamon. There was no strolling in now; the lines were prohibitively long, thanks to tourism and prosperity. The Ishtar Gates remained unseen, and I have to be satisfied with photos, but that's all right, given the great scheme of things.

Shhh…..

Living in our big, rambling old house in Danielsville was a dream that I would never as a child have allowed myself to dream. It would have been too fantastic, and I've never been one to sit around and want something that I knew I couldn't have. After my crowded childhood, moving into this huge house was exhilarating. Everyone had a refuge, a special and private space which was his or hers alone. Booger Hill was my haven.

As far back as I can remember, our childhood houses in Savannah were bulging at their seams with the three generations who lived together. We were stuffed here and there in houses far too small to accommodate people of such diverse ages and needs. There was a single bathroom for nine people! These living arrangements seemed natural to us children, as that was the way they had always been, and most children's sense of "normal" is whatever they are familiar with.

As I grew older, I became self-conscious of our rather shabby house, whose walls always needed painting, especially the dining room in our house on 46th Street where the green paint peeled off again nearly as soon as it dried. Our furniture was always of good quality, which spoke to earlier, more prosperous days. And, of course, we had nice silver, fine china and crystal.

Sallie Krickel

The air itself was oppressive in Savannah, both the intense heat in the summer and the old oil heater blistering the hall in the winter. The air stultified, like we were suspended in time, the way the weather gets heavy and still in the wake of an impending storm. Nothing was clear and direct, merely muted allusions to the dark and unpleasant, hints, mutterings, suggestions, even obfuscations. The hushed air became even heavier and harder to breathe, and hiding things did not make them disappear. They still existed and became subject to imagination, anxiety and phobias, from the most trivial things to the highly significant

Secrets bulged from whatever spaces were not occupied by breathing bodies. They crowded up our already crowded lives. We were never told anything outright, either insignificant or important. We were not told when we were moving or why or where. We would just be packed off to Asheville to stay a month in the summers and arrive home to entirely different surroundings. The furniture always made the move, too, though the toys rarely did. Our urgent questions remained unasked, though we were disturbed by glimpses of adult secrets, heavy, heavy secrets.

We couldn't discuss our father's tuberculosis, as we considered it a disease that "proper people" didn't have. I never knew that our father was a drinker, but that does help fill in the puzzle of my parents' strained relationship, the echoes of the slamming door as my father abruptly left the house and my mother's long bouts of hysterical crying after she had locked herself in the bathroom, trying to drown her anguished sounds, as well as her unhappiness, in the running water. We were not told of our father's embezzlement, though Ranny found out when he opened the Savannah *Morning News* and discovered that strategic articles had been excised, making the page look like a gap-tooth seven-year-old child. I don't know how he found out what the "redacted" parts said. We didn't know why the police came and arrested our father (because Uncle Windell had withdrawn his bond) and why our father never went with us after that to visit our uncle and why he never visited us again as long as our father was living. When Uncle Windell took Sissy, his mother, for drives, he waited for her in the car. That was strange in itself, as our formal manners dictated that he escort her to and from the front door.

Even our father's death was a mystery. There appeared to be something scandalous involved, but what I never knew. Mother and Windell did go to south Georgia, to see if there was any sort of workers' compensation or insurance, but they came back disappointed. They were told that it would be better for them not to investigate further, and they didn't. That quelled further discussion. Just one day, poof, our father disappeared from our lives. We pretended that he had never existed. Reality was blurred by sadness and desperation.

It was fashionable in the 1950s for crosses to be placed at the sight of a fatal accident. Even now, from time to time, commemorative crosses or flowers are placed at the site of an accident, but the difference is that the state sponsored the memorials in the fifties and paid for them. More than an acknowledgement of the dead, the crosses were an admonition to the living. Knowing only that my father had been killed somewhere in "south Georgia," I brooded every time I saw a white cross on the side of the road, wondering if this had been the spot. The possibilities were endless. I never asked. Questions, like answers, were not part of the family dynamic.

Parents need to and should protect their children. Knowing what to say and what to hold back is difficult. It's a fine line to tread. I'm not sure, even to this day, that I have the answer. I do have the confidence that during my childhood, everyone tried the best that he and she could have, given his or her own personal upbringing and experience, the collective disappointment and despair. Part of the reason for the adults' reticence was the puritan nature of my mother and, especially, my grandmother Sissy. Mother told me one time, in the context of how the world had lost a sense of propriety, that, although Sissy had lived with her and my father all their married life and although mother had borne five children, they had never once broached the subject of pregnancy—or whatever term they would have used. Pregnancy was far too coarse a word! Sissy, the mother of four herself, would catch on, of course, but nothing was ever spoken. This was the same grandmother who could not bring herself to refer to a chicken "thigh" but called it "the second joint."

Our Aunt Sarah died of "cancer," always referred to generically. I learned as an adult that it was breast cancer, but we surely did not ever call it that. If we had, that would have meant acknowledging that she actually had breasts. And she was not even married. The fact that Sissy suffered from glaucoma was kept secret, even from her. Mother just told her that the daily drops would make her eyes feel better. It may even be that Sissy, herself, knew the truth, but truth was secondary to pretense.

Our parents were never able to argue openly, but argue nonetheless they did, especially in the year between Sissy's death and my father's. Night after night they glared across the dinner table, despising each other wordlessly, but desperately, hurtling insults which were louder than shouts. I never knew what provoked these scenes, probably just the difficulty of two people living together, but it was numbing as a child to see them hate each other so profoundly. They had never been able to fight out loud, of course, with the audience of both the older generation and the younger generation always present, but the air seethed. Mother exacted revenge on my father by requiring all of us to gather together at the end of the day with bowed heads, holding hands and giving a "sentence prayer." My father did a lot of squirming.

I think that if one mixed dour puritanical genes from Robertsons and pretentious genes from the Ingrams in a test tube, and dropped in a good shake of rowdiness and whiskey from the Bradford genes the explosion would shake the whole earth—or cause a house to groan at least. Nobody had a real chance.

We children lived with constant allusions to the moral failings of our father. When I roomed with Amie Dreese at Wesleyan, Mother told me that Amie's mother, Amelia, would tell me dreadful things about my father, but that they were not true. I had no idea what she was talking about, conflicted by curiosity on the one hand and guilty reluctance on the other. Amelia had worked for my father as a secretary at the shipyard during the war, but whatever the reference was to I never learned. Amelia was nothing but lovely and generous to me.

Mother alluded to the same thing when Irma Frech and I went to ballroom dance classes together, but neither of Irma's parents ever gave even a sideways glance over my way, positive or negative. I did not take it as a personal affront; they pretty much ignored all us children. My Aunt Billie, however, didn't try to conceal her contempt for my father, grumbling about him under her breath, without saying anything specific, but constantly bemoaning the circumstances of her "poor sister."

Even the good was kept secret. Madeline never got around to telling me the "good secrets" about my father, her older brother. Though I've pretty much by now pieced out the bad, the good have, regrettably, died with her.

Some obfuscations were trivial, like encouraging us to hope every year that our spayed dog would finally have puppies. There was no explanation about the "burglar" who broke into our house and smashed our piggy bank to bits, taking all the money we children had saved, without stealing other more valuable objects. When my mother's diamond engagement ring suspiciously disappeared, there was no reaction except bitterness on my mother's part.

Some secrets were damaging. We children were regarded as a "bunch," not as individuals who might have needs and concerns of our own. Things happened which never should have happened, but children were rarely heeded or, at least, they were not considered important. They merely needed "straightening up" from time to time, like the furniture. We were no more than another species, one rung higher than our pets.

The only problem is that secrets, guilty secrets, didn't go away because no one talked about them. Like the law of physical matter, they were not destroyed, they merely took on another form. It would have saved a lot of grief and anguish, certainly a great deal of insecurity in the long run, if we had dealt in our childhood with the serious subjects of abuse and breach of trust. But they were as unacceptable as my father's tuberculosis. They just didn't happen in *respectable* families. But they did.

Kindergarten Graduation

I graduated from high school in 1960, *summa* (Mother insisted that I was an overachiever) and started college at Armstrong, disappointed that I had not applied to a "real" college. I had studied extremely hard in high school, but I was so busy studying and working that I didn't know such things like how and when to apply to college. I always felt that the boys had more guidance and that it was not so important that a girl have a formal education. Armstrong was my only option.

Much to my surprise, it was spectacular! With delight and astonishment, I met Homer and the great Greek tragedians, and the Muses led me on and on for the rest of my life. The faculty were consciously approachable, and many of my teachers were true "friends." I thrived—for a while.

But teen age is an insidious time. Adolescent years are troubling for most, and mine were no exception. The transition into adulthood brought about the past and too many ghosts raised their ugly and sinister heads. It was too much to deal with. I was nearly paralyzed with troubling thoughts and memories—and hopelessness. That was the worst part: the hopelessness. My world became a deep, dark unhappy place.

At one episode in their journey through the *Inferno* Vergil cautioned Dante to avert his eyes and to hurry on, as the scene they passed would bring him too great a distress. I will take Vergil's advice and will pass silently through the next year or two, as it would serve no purpose to stay in such a gloomy, unhappy, and uninspiring place as my adolescence.

Suffice it to say that I finally spied my grandmother's corset swirling in the distance, and I latched on. I found a draught of my mother's courage and resolve and drank from it thirstily. Even so, Purgatory was a heavily laden journey.

By starts and pieces I graduated from Armstrong (*summa*), with my mother still pointing out how much of an overachiever I was. I set about applying to a "four-year" college, very tentatively and with a modicum of self-confidence. I was accepted at Wesleyan, the same women's college in Macon that Aunt Billie had attended. I packed my suitcases, and they bulged, not so much with clothes as with the unresolved disappointments of the past and the fears of the future. I set my jaw, gritted my teeth, and left home. That was the fall of 1964.

Part II

"Agricolam virumque cano...."[1]
(Of a Farm and a Man I sing)

---

1 * I apologize for the shameful corruption of Vergil's opening lines of the *Aeneid*: "Arma virumque cano..." (Of arms and a man I sing...)

Prologue

THE BERLIN WALL had just fallen when Edward, the girls and I visited Ranny in 1991. (Ed, who had recently graduated from college, was working his first job and had no vacation time accrued.) We traveled through East Germany, communist until recently, to East Berlin, which was, I thought, amazingly quickly awakening to capitalism. We climbed to the top of a building to get a good view of the Alexanderplatz, and the desolate scene contrasted with the holiday bustle of Paris, where we had recently been. Although Western materialism was on the cusp of the horizon, it had not yet arrived full force.

As there were not yet many accommodations for tourists, the girls and I stayed with a fellow stamp collector friend of Ranny's, Michael, and his wife and little daughter, while Edward and Ranny lodged nearby with Michael's parents. At dinner one night Michael's father asked us, with Ranny as interpreter, what our life was like in America. We explained that we lived in a little village of about three hundred people. A cosmopolitan man himself, he blurted out: "What in the world do you do all day in a place like that?" He asked out of genuine interest, and, although we took no offense, we felt the need to defend ourselves. We hastily assured him that we were both professors, I at a nearby college and Edward at the state university.

His question haunted me, though, and I began to brood on "what in the world we actually did all day." I concluded that we spent our days in the same way that he spent his: providing food and shelter for our family, nurturing our children, earning a livelihood, grappling with the disappointments of life, enjoying the good moments, and muddling through the bad as best we could. We all, the world over, do the same things, for the same reasons. The only difference is in the details.

So my married life was essentially like all others: dealing with the troubles of life, sometimes admirably, sometimes falling short, caring for our loved ones, searching to give our lives purpose and meaning. Given these universal certainties, the details are what make us unique, and I, in my clumsy way, will try to flesh them out.

The Goat and the Archer, the Horse and the Rat

Edward and I were as different as night and day. In the first place, he was a Capricorn and I, a Sagittarius, two utterly incompatible signs. According to our horoscopes, we are "two entirely different individuals" who are "not likely to remain with each other." To make matters even worse, I was born in the year of the Horse, and he in the year of the Rat, according to our place mats at the Chinese restaurant. The Chinese zodiac predicts "unhappiness and strong animosities" between the horse and the rat, and "personality clashes and bitter rivalries in marriage and business relations." All the forces of the universe plotted against us.

Even our own little microcosm prognosticated doom. When I called my mother to tell her that we were getting married, she was so hysterical that she couldn't talk. She had her reasons. Edward was divorced, nearly twenty years older than I, and, she suspected that he was, god forbid, Jewish to boot. The only time she had ever met him, at Parents' Day at Wesleyan, she had referred to him as that "strange little man."

We caused quite a kerfuffle at the university. If we went through with our marriage, I would lose my job. There was a strong nepotism rule which prohibited married couples from both teaching. It was ridiculous, of course, because I was a lowly teaching assistant in French, and Edward was merely a newly hired assistant professor in English. My Chair, Dr. Hassel, urged us just to live together, so I could keep my job. French teachers were hard to come by. I explained that wasn't exactly the route we wanted to take. Such things just were not done fifty years ago. Even though it was the liberated sixties, the sexual revolution had not yet made it South, not in an overt way. Good girls didn't do such things, or at least admit to it. My mother sent me to talk with Dr. Peterson, our longtime family doctor, who discouraged me, hinting in veiled terms, that incompatibility loomed ahead, alluding to, but never actually mentioning the word "sex." Such a big to-do, especially about two utterly unimportant people as we.

Edward and I

Despite the poor odds, we tied the knot, in the chapel of my childhood church, Wesley Monumental, in Savannah. I wore a cream colored silk suit that Mother bought at the exclusive shop that our Uncle Felix owned. We invited only family, and there was a modest crowd of fifty or so. My brother Windell gave me away. The organ notes were punctuated by the chattering of my little nieces and the shushing of their mother inside the chapel and the pounding of rain outside. But, alas, we formally and legally were joined in matrimony, even if by the erroneous names, "Mr. and Mrs. Kringle."

Before long, things began to look up. We moved into our little honeymoon cottage on the lake, inside the city limits of Danielsville. It was a lovely place, the home of the town doctor who had recently died, and we had a whole upstairs for Edward's books. On the work front, Dr. West, head of the Humanities Division, arranged for me to keep my job throughout that year, pointing out that I had signed my contract as a single woman and that it was binding. It didn't take many months for Mother to come round, too. She soon liked Edward far better than she had ever liked me. She eventually started calling him "Edward" instead of "Dr. Krickel."

What people didn't know and couldn't have understood is that we couldn't *not* be together. Even given the vast differences in our personalities, there was one inescapable fact: We were crazy about each other. We didn't make a decision to be together; it was quite beyond our control. As Rumi wrote, true lovers don't finally meet somewhere, they're in each other all along. In Plato's *Dialogues* Aristophanes, undeniably under the influence of strong drink and undeniably in jest, spoke of true lovers as soul mates, who find in each other their own missing half. Upon the discovery, they coalesce. *In vino veritas.*

But differences we did have, and they were fundamental ones. I was the practical one, while Edward was laid back and easy going. I cooked and cleaned. I made lunches every morning. I got the children off to school. I washed and ironed and laid out clothes. I sewed clothes and curtains. I did the mending. I even "turned" his shirt collars and cuffs when they became frayed, an old-fashioned technique, obsolete even then, not to mention now. I tried to darn his socks, using my grandmother's black darning egg. I helped with the homework. I kept the children in line. I was the room mother, the den leader, the Sunday school superintendent. I worked exhaustingly, never stopping to realize all that I did. Meanwhile, Edward sat and read. He smiled and cheered me on.

He did the nice little things, like bringing me coffee in bed every morning for nearly twenty-seven years and starting up my car to cool off in summer or heat up in winter. He read to the children faithfully every night before bed. And when Ed and Liz rebelled during their teen years and refused to eat breakfast, he humored them. He buzzed up a frothy milkshake, instead, into which he put milk, a raw egg, yogurt, fresh fruit, wheat germ, and vanilla, so that they were eating a far more nutritious meal than they did otherwise. And, most importantly, they were allowed both to rebel and to save face.

He urged me not to be too inflexible. He pointed out that the more rigid I was, the more rigid the children were bound to counteract. It was best not to lay down hard rules, but to have discussions, so that they would come up with the right conclusion on their own. That worked most of the time, or some of the time at least, and it's true that I needed some reining in. He was absolutely against corporal punishment, claiming that it taught the wrong principle, namely that the biggest and the strongest won out and could beat up the others.

Part of our difference had simply to do with our personalities. I was as driven as he was relaxed. But another part of the difference had to do with our upbringing. Edward's mother, Daisy, was the softest, kindest woman I've ever known. She exuded warmth and acceptance, and scooped up every baby she ever saw, runny nose or not, and had them gurgling and smiling and playing a secret little game that they both had known all their lives. The babies could be pups or kittens, as well, who all felt a magnetic attraction to her open arms and willing heart. She coddled us all. Her whole approach to life was kind and playful. Edward said that she was that way when he was a child and that their house was always full of the neighborhood children. I doubt very seriously if Edward was spanked a single time. I don't think his mother ever thought of it. I'm sure that she wasn't capable of lifting her hand against a child.

My parents' theory of childrearing was, what can I say, far more fundamental, more traditional. There was no sparing of the rod in our house, especially for the boys, and our strict parents and maternal grandmother administered punishment swiftly, without a flicker of remorse. While Sissy was angrily tearing up a comic book left on the floor, Edward's mother was patiently cleaning around the stacks of books that her boys had left at their bedsides.

Edward as a young boy

As a child Edward was a "picky eater," a concept which was unknown (and incomprehensible) in our house. In fact, his mother dashed out of the house early in the mornings and placed a hen egg in the bird's nest outside his window. That was the only way he'd eat his breakfast egg. We, on the other hand, ate whatever was set before us, not daring to criticize. It was not unusual for us to be sent to bed without supper. We didn't ride a pony inside the garage on a rainy day, but were consigned to walk around the house in the dark where the snakes and even alligators lurked. (There were really snakes and alligators in the extended yard when we lived on White Bluff Road.) Our grandmother kept a bar of soap handy and moist, ready to wash my brothers' mouths out with soap. I never underwent that indignity, either because I was not impertinent enough or because I was a girl, or both. My dirty mouth developed later when I was a student at a Christian women's college. I'm sure my mouth could use a good bit of washing out now. At least Mary thinks so.

My brothers and I all survived unscathed, and frankly, the tales of such childhood abuses have given us limitless fodder for stories as adults. Our existence would have been much duller, and we'd hardly have anything to talk about. But, I am glad that I married Edward— he brought a gentler civilization into my life. So, to say that Edward's and my approach to life was different was a salient understatement. I claimed that we had a marriage by dialectic: the thesis, the antithesis, and finally, the synthesis. We always initially disagreed about almost everything, but would, after much discussion, sometimes lively if not exactly heated, come to an agreed-upon solution. We enjoyed engaging in such set-tos, and I told the children that they were lucky to have the benefit of two such divergent points of view. They maintained that we just liked to argue.

Sometimes we'd get into a mode of "verbal disagreements." At such times I pointed out that we'd slipped into a habit of fighting and that we really should stop. Edward replied that I didn't know what real fighting was, hinting at by-gone times, and that we'd never had a real fight in our lives. I assured him that I was trying as hard as I could! It's true we never reached the point of insults, we never played mean or dirty, and we never lost respect for each other. In fact, we were known sometimes to burst into laughter at the absurdity of our arguments, like the way to stack the dishes on the lower rack of the dishwasher.

I learned early on that, if I wanted to stretch out my indignation and suffer my grudges, I had to be careful not to touch him. A mere brush against his arm had a metaphysical effect. My anger melted away, and soon I forgot what I was so upset about. Even this annoyed me, as sometimes I wanted to nurse my wounds and sulk a little longer. I just couldn't. Our touch was magic. We held hands nearly all the time, most often surreptitiously. It became a playful game.

We agreed on the important things and shared the same basic values. Then, too, we not only loved each other, we were, even to the last, *in* love with each other. He always told me that he could just look at me and the memories of all the wonderful times came flooding back, and I found both his voice and touch soothing and magical.

Living inside this man of incomparable intellectual brilliance was an alter ego who was totally inept in the real world. My first taste of this was when we took a trip to Florida several days before our wedding so that I could meet his parents. He took no money, no checkbook, no credit card. His idea of taking a trip was to get in the car and start up the engine. Our trip took a long time as we had to avoid all toll roads, living on the little bit of cash that my meager student budget allowed.

I came to terms with the fact that the practical parts of our life were my domain. That was all right with me. I was naturally bossy. Edward gave me his steady strength and devotion. He was the anchor, firmly fixed, no matter how the winds and sea tossed me, his little dingy, floating on the surface. I use the term "dingy" with full intent.

When we went camping, it was I who hooked up the camper, took it to the service station, cleaned it inside and out, and stocked it with food. It was I who had to figure out how to use the fence stretcher to build the goat pen. It was I who had to subtract the rectangle area of the pool from the triangle area of the lawn to estimate the amount of grass seed we needed. Strangely enough, Edward had a degree in Ag Engineering, and I'm not known for math skills. I became the navigator on trips, and I am a directional idiot, though Edward served as an astronomer in World War II. Between the two of us our family ought to heave a huge, collective sigh of relief that we are not currently living in Ethiopia.

The problem was not altogether that he was unwilling. In fact sometimes he was a little too eager. We came home from vacation once to find the tire flat on our little VW bug. Edward insisted on fixing it himself. He dutifully removed the bad tire and installed the temporary donut. Halfway down the driveway, the donut rolled off. Undeterred, he tackled the job again. With the temporary tire attached to his satisfaction, he drove off down Highway 29, headed to the station one mile away. Much to his horror and with potential disaster, the entire wheel flew off.

Our old house needed some shoring up for the winter. Edward measured the thirty-six windows which slid up and down and ordered storm windows. The six windows in Ed's room rolled out and couldn't be fitted. The costly new windows were delivered. Even though they were custom made, they still needed a little trimming along the sides for an exact fit. Edward got the tin snips and started cutting along the premeasured grooves. I was busy inside. Before too long he, exasperated, came and shrugged defeatedly, saying that he couldn't do the job. I asked what the problem was. He explained that, as he walked alongside each window and leaned over to trim the edge, he would get to a certain point, lose his balance, and crash foot first through the pane. I, always the pragmatist, suggested that he crawl alongside, rather that walk. That would give him some stability. His eyes brightened, and he went outside and finished up. And, it was truly a remarkable job, installing thirty-six storm windows, holding them up with one hand, while hammering with the other, all the time balanced on a tall step ladder. I don't see how he did it. It was certainly his moment of glory.

Not infrequently Edward was frustrated when he couldn't perform some of the most basic tasks. After he had tried to repair a pipe, tinker with the car, or start up the reluctant pump, unsuccessfully of course, he'd get discouraged at his ineptitude. I always assured him that, if I had cared about the plumbing, I would have married a plumber! It's easy enough to hire out the plumbing, impossible to buy a gentle, soothing voice in the night or a source of encyclopedic knowledge in the day time.

Like many men, Edward was not much help around the house, either. His main chore was to take out the garbage, a straightforward enough task. It, however, took him several days, as he worked in stages, first removing the full bag from the pantry, tying it up, replacing it with a clean bag. Next he put the full bag on the kitchen floor. At some time or other he moved it to the back porch, then to the bottom of the steps, and finally into the big garbage can outside. I found it maddening. In complete exasperation, I gritted my teeth and muttered: "Edward, you're a wonderful husband as long as I don't want you to do anything." He grinned and admitted with a slight tone of irony: "You're right. I don't do things." He pointed out that if we were both like him, nothing would ever be accomplished, but that, if we were both like me, life would be a dizzying hell. After some years, I came to the conclusion that it was just as hard for him to finish a task as it was for me not to. Talk about differences.

Edward always wanted to be around us. Even in the busiest, most frantic of children times, he wanted to be smack in the middle of the brouhaha. He stood in the middle of the kitchen floor as I prepared dinner, just another appliance for me to maneuver around. When Mother visited and we sat in the study to chat, she'd point out that Edward was reading and we shouldn't disturb him. That was the very point. He wanted to be "disturbed" as long as he could be with me. He had plenty of other rooms to sit in.

He accompanied me to the grocery store, to nearly everywhere, even wanting to take a daily walk with my girlfriends and me. He always said that it was better to be together. I didn't always agree. I needed some alone time now and again, but that was a precious commodity as I moved from the classroom to the house without missing a beat. I did not want to sit in the middle of the noise and motion. I craved, instead, to have some uninterrupted time for myself. I doubt that there is any mother in the world who does not know exactly what I am talking about.

One time, when Liz was in middle school, she called me at Emmanuel to ask if I would take her and her friends to the mall, to worship at the pubescent girl shrine. They wanted to celebrate the end of spring exams. None of the other parents were available, and I agreed, but reluctantly. After all, it was the end of the semester for me, too, and I was wiped out. Giving in to her pleas, I said that I would come home, take a ten-minute soak in the tub, draining away, I hoped, the stress of late spring exams and revitalizing myself for a trip to Athens. I got home, eased my weary body down into the warm soothing water, and closed my eyes.

In came Mary with some exceedingly important confidence, and she perched on top of the toilet seat at one end of the tub. In a minute or two, Liz sat down at the vanity at the other end and began primping for her afternoon pilgrimage to the mall. Before long, Edward, always eager to be with us, decided that was just the right moment to trim his beard at the sink. My ten minutes were soon up. As promised, I struggled to get out of the tub, but I couldn't. The room was too crowded. There was nowhere to step. So much for solitude, not to mention privacy.

The "alone" moments that I could steal away were rare. When I felt pushed over the limit, about twice a year, I would announce that I was running away from home. I'd tell them where I was going, (I was not totally irresponsible), and what time I'd be home. I often went to visit friends, sometimes to the movies. As a solace to my self-pity, actually I think it was more self-preservation than pity, I'd buy myself a box of popcorn, which I did not have to share with anyone, a large Coke *and* a candy bar. With the satisfaction only a well-fed glutton could feel, I'd return home to my brood, my inner self quiet and tucked in, recharged for a couple of months.

Actually, it was not unusual for Edward and me to escape together. When we needed some "alone" time, we'd drive to the Golden Pantry and buy snacks, then drive to the courthouse in the heart of town, eating our forbidden (at home) fruit. We watched the traffic go by, and sometimes never said a word. The purpose was to be together. When Edward took Ed to lifesaving classes at the Athens Y, sometimes, whenever I could get away, I'd drive to Athens, find him reading a book, and we'd go to Bell's supermarket for snacks and sit together in the parking lot, again not necessarily saying a thing. One special time, as I was leaving campus in Franklin Springs to fetch one of the children to music lessons, I spied his little VW bug coming down King Avenue. He rolled down the window and kissed me. He rolled the window back up, never stopping and never uttering a word, and we went on to our respective duties.

I need to make it very clear that taking care of animals was not a chore to Edward, and, happily, that included us two-legged ones. In addition to coffee in bed, he brought me breakfast in bed every single morning for our last fifteen years together. He read to and chattered with the children, supporting them, too, in their chess ventures, 4-H competitions, and art lessons. He tirelessly drove them to violin, piano and guitar lessons in Franklin Springs and to lifeguard classes in Athens. He shared my suffering attendance at youth basketball games. He accepted me, with all my shortcomings. He did all these things naturally, and with ease.

He shared in the care of the babies, whether kids, pups, or our own children. Every single night after Mary was born, he got up when she cried, changed her, and put her in bed for me to nurse. Sometimes I never even woke up. He cared for his mother, in the most intimate way, unblinkingly, after her stroke. The animal world was something he understood, somewhere he belonged. We were lucky to be part of his menagerie.

When Edward died, a friend of ours wrote an article for the *Athens Banner Herald*. Among other things, she pointed out that every time she saw him, every time, she'd think: "How lovely, there he is." Several years later, she decided to divorce her husband, who was also an academic. She complained bitterly that he did absolutely nothing to help her out. With the gutters falling off, the roof leaking, the weeds choking the patio, her husband, oblivious, would come home after classes, pick up a book and retreat to his corner to read.

I pointed out that Edward was exactly the same way, yet she loved Edward dearly. We talked for a while and realized that the difference was that Edward valued me, always sided with me and thought that whatever I did or said was wonderful. He made me feel good about myself. He listened to all the unimportant happenings of my day, while making them important. We'd steal a moment sometimes, with me stretched out on the sofa, my feet resting in his lap, while he listened to me and massaged both my weary soles and my weary soul. That much support and devotion go a long, long, way and far outweigh stepping around a big bag of garbage on my kitchen floor—or a rain puddle or two dripping through the ceiling. At least for me.

Edward lived his life on a little higher plane than most of us. It's not that he couldn't be bothered by mundane things in a smug way: He did not feel that he was too good to do menial tasks. Not that at all. There was never, ever anything arrogant about him. He just never got the hang of living in the same world that most of us inhabit. I learned a lot from his world, a benign and gracious place, thoughtful, honest, free from the pettiness and envy which sour our faces and diminish our souls. After years, now decades, of feeling grateful to him for all he did, I realize that I helped him too. I helped him find his way, though ever bemused and befuddled, through my more imperfect, practical world, the one where, like it or not, he had to live.

There is no denying that our differences were vast and that we voiced them frequently, but we survived despite them, maybe even because of them. We found in each other our missing halves. The Capricorn and the Sagittarius, the horse and the rat, lay down together in peace and in unpredicted but profound harmony.

BOOKS

Edward doted on me and on the children, but he loved books, too, at least as much, if not more. He had loved them ever since he was a little boy. He held them in a gentle, reverent way, a combination of awe and tenderness. When I first saw him, walking to the podium in Shakespeare class with an armful of books, he seemed to be hugging them, rather than just carrying them. Even his book jackets were in pristine condition. If, perhaps, a book had no jacket when he bought it, he painstakingly made one out of waxed paper, cut precisely, with the flaps tucked neatly inside the front and back covers.

He didn't devour books, but, as a friend said, he nibbled at them, reading a few pages here and a few there. He wrote inside the front cover the date he bought each book. On the first page he wrote the date he started reading it; inside, the date he resumed reading. Finally, he wrote on the back cover the date he finished it. In the margins he made interesting notations, sometimes commenting on the passage itself, but oftentimes scolding the author.

Occasionally he even wrote insults, like "ass," in his clear, neat handwriting. He took pains to explain to the children that he meant that in the British sense, which was not at all vulgar like it would have been in American English. I found that amusing, but back then I soaked up every word he uttered. Mary was later to become an

English major, and she always delighted in using his books, with all the notes, kind of a more polished and insightful Cliffs Notes. This very year she found a file card, used as a bookmark, on which he had written a list of suggested essays for "Winesburg, Ohio." He had dated the list "3/3/58" but the topics were still timely. Liz, Ed, and I too, have also enjoyed picking up one of his books full of notes, an ongoing conversation with him. In his big schoolmaster's desk in the corner of our bedroom, in the upper right-hand drawer, he kept a list of every book he read. Many a night, after turning the last page, jotting down the date on the back cover, he would pad over to his desk, open the file drawer, and add the latest title to his vast list.

He was a slow reader. He studied style, language, development as much as he followed the plot. And he never, ever forgot anything he read. I tried to read more slowly, too, following his example, hoping that I could comprehend better and longer, but that just didn't work. Forty years later he was able to remember better the details of a book that I had read only a week before. Oftentimes, and this is absolutely true, he would recall the precise page where a certain passage was. A compendium of knowledge, he was truly a genius, a very modest one.

Edward and his books

When we got married all his books were in boxes, and I made it a priority to have them on shelves. It took a while, but we finally got them up. Several years I taught summer school for the sole purpose of having a section of bookshelves built. We ended up having ceiling-to-floor bookshelves in the playroom, and the upstairs hall, in addition to a whole cedar-lined room upstairs, which had books encasing the windows, as well as on the long walls. I guess that we shelved our walls the way that some people wall-papered theirs. There was certainly no need or expense for a professional decorator. I loved the mismatched arrangement, tall and short books side by side, all the colors jumbled up.

Edward retired about the same time that Ed finished college and left home, so we converted his bedroom, an upstairs sun room, into another library, with shelves built on three walls. There were, of course, random, individual bookcases throughout the house, nice ones in the study, and makeshift ones in other places. Both our "bed-side tables" were shortened barrister bookcases with glass doors, lamps and a radio standing precariously on top.

People used to ask me if Edward kept a catalog of his books, but there was no more need for that than to make a list of the names of his children. He arranged his books "Krickel-style," by subject, century, and genre, and he knew where every book was. Even when he was desperately ill, just a couple of days before he died, I remember his asking Liz to run upstairs to the back study and get him a specific book, telling her that it was on the back wall, three shelves from the bottom, about the third or fourth volume from the right. He was incredible. She read to him the passage he requested.

And what is amazing is that he had read most of the more than eleven thousand books in his collection and remembered what was in them. When we used to go to professional meetings, he was hounded by former students and colleagues who would come up and ask him a question. They had saved it over the year, knowing that he, and only he, would know the reference or the title, or whatever. Tom Landess said that Edward's friends "came to feel a kind of personal pride in him, as if somehow [they] were major shareholders in his omniscience" and that "while reference books sometimes contained errors, Ed Krickel was totally devoid of them." When Emmanuel needed their library assessed, he sat down and wrote sheerly from memory the authors and titles, publishers and dates, of books that a college library would need for their basic literature collection, primary and secondary sources.

What is equally amazing is that he was totally unassuming, seemingly unaware of his vast intelligence. He was ever polite and encouraging, incapable of making people uncomfortable. He began most sentences "Perhaps it might be…" or "If I remember correctly…" or "Is it possible that…." Rather than having a sense of superiority, he seemed almost embarrassed, even apologetic, to know so much. His knowledge was so encyclopedic that he could talk with ease with nearly anyone about nearly anything.

It was not in his nature to boast. The only time I knew him to do so, though this happened long before I met him, was recounted by his good friend Tom. Apparently, there was a guest speaker, an expert on Irish literature, at Converse College where he and Tom taught. The man was insufferable, egotistical and arrogant. After this stuffy academic had finished his talk, Edward's colleagues begged him to quiz the man on Irish literature. Edward replied that he couldn't do that. It would be rude, and besides, in his usual self-deprecating way, he, himself, didn't really know that much about Irish literature, anyway. They knew that he did and put their friendship on the line. Finally, they goaded him into a sparring match.

At dinner that night Edward asked the guest speaker about this particular Irish book and that particular Irish author, which the man admitted he had not read. Before long, the visitor, embarrassed and uneasy, started saying that, yes, indeed, he had read whatever Edward asked about, even though it was obvious that he hadn't. So then this usually gracious man, later to be my husband, started making up fictitious titles and phantom poets, and yes, the visiting scholar had read those, too! Edward's colleagues, aware of the bogus literature, stifled their laughter—for the time being. Had they been able they would have "cheered [him] through the market place."

Talking about literature was as easy (and as fundamental) for him as breathing is for the rest of us. It was an essential part of who he was. In a time when most professors had very narrow specialties, Edward was a universalist. Although his field, technically, was modern British and American literature, he was equally conversant with literature and literary history of all ages and cultures. He was already familiar with every Nobel Prize winner, when everyone else, after the announcement, scrambled to find out who he was and what he had written.

As our friend Patti noted, "He wrote and studied and talked literature for the pure love of it." When he and his buddies, Ernest, Carl, and John, got together, their conversation electrified a room. It was thrilling to sit and listen. They played literary games sometimes, like quoting the first lines of novels and trying to stump each other. Some months after Edward died, maybe some years, I don't remember, I picked up *Dinner at the Homesick Restaurant* and read: "While Pearl Tull was dying, something funny crossed her mind." That, I remembered, was one of the first lines he used in the "title guess" game, and for a few moments I was again part of those wonderful literary sparks and relived those afternoons of warmth, excitement, and total awe.

The four of them, Ernest, Carl, John, and Edward, were legendary in the English Department, and they ate lunch together every Tuesday. When Edward became too ill to leave the house, Carl and John came every afternoon for weeks, making the trek from Athens to Danielsville, and they talked literature. (Ernest was in Mississippi, dealing with his own cancer demons.) Even in his diminished state, Edward contributed to the conversation, if, by then, in a weakened whisper.

Edward "felt" poetry the way some people have an ear for music. On hearing a poem for the first time, he would most likely know who the poet was just by the style. I remember studying really hard for a Spanish exam for which we were to identify lines of poetry. I was at a loss about how to distinguish between Santa Teresa and St. John of the Cross, two seventeenth-century Spanish poets, both religious mystics who used identical themes, allusions, and rhyme schemes. I was struggling terribly. Delighted by one particular passage, I clumsily translated it into English. Edward, unaware of my inner frustration, immediately said, "Isn't St. John of the Cross magnificent." I was deflated. How could he know everything, even when he did not even read the language? I was grateful, too, that he was so kind, for things like that could well have undone me. He never, ever made me feel inadequate or dumb, however inadequate and dumb I was. Belittlement was neither in his vocabulary nor in his heart

For my prelims in French I (quite truthfully) studied for six months. I was responsible for knowing morphology and phonology (changing of words, their sounds and meanings), as well as everything of importance that was ever written in French, from the *Oath of Strasbourg* and the *Song of Roland* to twentieth-century literature. I worked exhaustively, and, for the first and only time of my life, I actually felt knowledgeable. The morning of the exam, the very morning, after six months of studying eight hours a day, I prepared to face the grand inquisition. Edward mentioned, in an off-hand way, a contemporary French poet I had never heard of. I was exasperated, and he felt terrible. I was reassured by the fact that, frankly, I doubt if any of the professors in the Romance Language Department had ever heard of this obscure modern poet either. I put the matter out of my cluttered-up mind.

After that desperate Saturday night when he drew his last tortured and labored breath, there were the necessaries to be taken care of. It was easy to see the hospital bed being carried away, to have the oxygen machine returned to Care Medical. The hospice nurse flushed the leftover medication down the toilet. I wanted no more signs of illness, no reminders of suffering.

The Lady of Booger Hill

I was touched to discover at the back of his closet the green suit that I had tailored for him years before, preserved carefully in a zippered plastic bag. Poor dear Edward had even worn it one Easter morning. Over the months after the funeral, Ed took his father's new shoes, the shoes which I had encouraged him to buy just two weeks before he died, in a desperate attempt to keep him walking and to ward off the inevitable as long as possible. He was too weak to go into the store, but, by damn, he was to have new shoes. The clerk came to the car and fitted him. Liz claimed a couple of jackets, Mary some pajama bottoms, and for years I slept in the cozy warmth of his undershirts, soft and comfortable, which still held his scent.

What was unbearably difficult, a task I put off for a long, long time, was the undoing of his bedside table, the tucking away of the last notes he made, the reshelving of the last books he read, the obliterating of the last things he thought, the tidying up of the last music CDs he'd listened to.

As for his books, it took me twelve years to figure out what to do. The children took the ones they wanted, probably a couple of hundred. I gave some to friends. I stored the bulk of them in two climate-controlled warehouses. I consulted his colleagues. I knew that the resolution of the books was in my hands, and that it was a final gesture of love and respect for me to see that they were taken care of. I sold his entire Henry James collection, more than one hundred books by James' as well as criticism, to a very nice professor in Belgium, Gert Buelens, the president of the Henry James society. He and I corresponded, and we became on such informal terms that he would email me that he had held such and such a book in his hand with reverence, as it was a book he had always heard of, but never seen. His university had a library attached to every department, not a general library. He placed "Edward's collection," as he called it, just outside his office door, so that he could visit it every day. Although marginalia generally devalues a book, Gert took delight in reading Edward's notes, and he loved the books as much as Edward had. That was an immense satisfaction. Harold Wilson bought much of the World War II collection as a donation to King College, and I made a donation of the rest on my own. I wasn't in the business to make a profit as it was more important to find people who would appreciate the books. Several years ago, the library at the University of Georgia contacted me, and I donated all the rest of the collection to them. Even after giving many away and selling some, there were more than 10,000 volumes.

I was taken aback at how sad it made me to have the books carted away. Like so many other things, it had to be done, and I am a do-er. No one person had room for the entire collection, and we all have the ones we wanted most. Now hundreds of people will have access to them. Those things were logical; those things were true, I know. I kept reminding myself. But it was such a personal loss, as if the last vestiges of Edward, himself, were slipping through my fingers, his words muted, with echoes fading in my heart.

THE LONG SKINNY MAN WHO ONCE LIVED IN EDEN
(WITH APOLOGIES....)

My life with Edward was not only a life of discovery, but one of sheer astonishment and delight. One day, in the first blush of marriage, we turned into the little lane which ran down to Dr. Bond's house, our honeymoon cottage. A huge snake stretched the entire width of the road. Edward rolled to a stop and tooted the horn. The snake, soaking up the sunshine, remained oblivious. Edward tooted again, but the snake stayed put. Finally, he got out of our dirty little white Volkswagen and gently nudged the snake with his foot, until he, the huge snake, lazily crawled to safety.

Edward didn't even get flustered when a little green snake sunbathed alongside of us in our front yard. I screamed out "snake!" but Edward

188

was more astonished by my reaction than the appearance of the innocent little creature. All of this amazed me, yet I felt increasing confidence in this man who could have a gentle approach to all of life's creatures, without once reproaching me for being so fearful and silly. It was his nature to accept, rather than criticize, even me, or maybe especially me.

I had grown up in an apartment in the city, with concrete sidewalks instead of grassy fields to walk on, and people, not creatures as neighbors, though a few of our neighbors might have qualified as more a part of the wider "animal kingdom." I fell asleep to the roar of traffic and the unsettling intrusion of headlights, rather than the drone of crickets and tree frogs. We avoided cars, not brambles and red bugs.

I shared the citified notion that "the only good snake is a dead snake." My heritage, both the religious and the popular lore, emphasized a hatred of serpents. Who was it, after all, in the Garden of Eden who caused the wrath of God, the downfall of man, and, ultimately, the curse of all generations? We learned all that in Sunday school and it was pretty heavy stuff, stuff which really captures a child's imagination. I learned later that it was the python, too, who presided at Delphi, even after Apollo slew him. Therefore, we were made to understand that snakes are sinister and cold-blooded. We were led to believe that they are slimy to the touch, despite the fact that they are dry and scaly, not slimy at all.

We encountered an occasional snake during our childhood picnics in the woods. Our reaction was exaggerated hysteria, though I'm sure the slithering snakes were more frightened of us than we of them. There was a lot of commotion, and they were lucky to escape the wrath of the blustering machismo of my Uncle Windell. Our only other real contact with snakes was at the house on White Bluff Road, where our fear and loathing of the creatures were reinforced. According to Ranny, the house had stood empty for several years before we moved. Well, it had not exactly been empty, as several nests of snakes had taken up residence, some inside, some outside, and some in the well house. We encountered them all too frequently. Usually, our dogs barked a warning and we dashed out to see the excitement, maintaining a safe distance, as my parents or grandmother expeditiously dispatched the creature with a few whacks of the hoe. As squeamish as Sissy was, she had grown up in the country and lived her early married life there. She knew how to handle such situations, and she did so with unexpected and undignified vehemence.

I remember that several of the fearsome snakes puffed up their necks when cornered. They looked like the Indian cobra who splays his hood as he sways from the basket, hypnotized by the tune of the charmer's flute. We were told in exaggeratingly excited tones that these were "spreading adders" who mixed their venom with their breath, and spit their attackers with poison. The primary target was the eyes, and blindness was instant. We were terrified. It turns out that all this was apocryphal. The truth is that these particular snakes are nonvenomous and nonaggressive. But you could never have convinced us back then. We felt the imminence of danger, if not death.

The fear of snakes, carefully cultivated by our parents, was used as a means of punishment. Ranny's penance for a misdeed was to have to walk outside around the house at night. The number of times was determined by the transgression. He would be nearly paralyzed with fear, especially at the dark side of the house, the one closest to the field where we found the baby alligator. But it was either obey or tangle with our father, so he walked. The only provocation that I can recall for this particular sentence was his saying "I swear" at the dinner table. He was a teenager. By modern standards, this is absolutely innocuous, but we were held to pretty high standards. The punishment was sometimes mental pain rather than physical abuse, and I don't know if it was particularly effective, but it is memorable. Until his dying day, Ranny suffered greatly from irrational fears, especially of snakes.

For several years after we moved into our house on Booger Hill Road, we shared our attic with varmints. They didn't stay in the attic, but spent the nights scurrying up and down inside the plaster walls. In the still of the night they sounded like a thunderous herd of buffalo. I'm a very light sleeper, and I was restless and annoyed. Of even greater indignity was their intrusion into my private time. At night when I was soaking away the stress of the day in the downstairs bathtub, I had to listen to their racing little feet scratching on the plaster walls above my head. In my fertile, yet ignorant mind, I was convinced that they might scratch straight though and subject me to unsavory and sinister acts, though I didn't admit such a foolish thing to anyone. Edward said that they were squirrels and were actually worse than mice, as they tended to do more damage. Squirrels were capable of gnawing through electric wires and causing a fire. Not a soothing prospect for an imaginative, paranoid young wife.

The situation was thoroughly brought under control by an unexpected source, a big blue racer who took up residence under the eaves. We never actually saw the snake in the attic, just the shed skins, but we saw him outside occasionally, and I eventually began to adopt a certain proprietary feeling toward him. There was never a problem with rodents again. Edward explained that the mere presence of a snake was enough to deter other pests. Not overly excited to have to share the house with a huge snake, I preferred it to the mice and squirrels; at least snakes were quiet and didn't keep me up all night. Edward didn't mind having snakes around, but I confess that I checked the doors to the eaves from time to time, just to be certain that the wooden latches were firmly in place. I would not have been happy co-mingling. I pretty much stayed clear of the whole area.

Later, on Booger Hill Road we came home one evening to see a snake stretched out at the doorsill outside the playroom. He had taken refuge from the rain and was barely visible, blending in with the doormat. Edward approached the snake and again gently nudged until it crawled under the house. We were repairing the porch floors and there was a gap still of about three feet. With a snake in the attic and one under the house, the city girl in me had to come to terms with them. I was never comfortable, but I endured. I didn't complain, at least not out loud.

My attitude was transformed when I watched a show on public television, called *The Joy of Snakes*, featuring Okeefenokee Joe. After seeing that, I gained respect for the serpent species, and my irrational fear diminished, though I don't admit to any real affection. Over the years, I became able to mow the lawn brushing shoulders with a green snake lazing in the hedge of spirea alongside the driveway. I confess that I found other areas to mow that day, going quietly along with my business and leaving him to his, waiting for some hapless bird or field mouse to come his way. I mowed under an oak tree while a long, skinny black snake clung to a big fat branch right above my head. I gave the oak tree a wide berth, but I stayed rational. I didn't even panic when I lifted a stone and a whole "clutch" of baby snakes was wriggling underneath. Though I wasn't exactly fearful, I didn't stay around to introduce myself to their mother.

I even got to the point of being able to "handle" a snake. I don't mean to imply that I was into "snake handling" in the way that some religious sects are. In fact, at Emmanuel I once saw a film in which a Holiness minister performed "snake handling" as a testament of his faith in God. My experience was certainly neither religious nor voluntary.

The Lady of Booger Hill

One of my students, Susan, a beautiful girl with long dark hair and deep brown eyes, gave a report in World Lit class about Anthony and Cleopatra. As a prop, she borrowed the biology department's boa to represent Cleopatra's famous asp. This beautiful, innocent girl had a thing for snakes, which I doubt that she, in her innocence and naiveté, fully comprehended. She stood in front of the class and talked with the snake looped lazily around her neck. After a while he stretched out and slowly began to move. Susan was wearing an unfitted plaid jumper with buttons at the shoulders over a cotton shirt. As the snake crawled between her jumper and her blouse, I asked if she needed any help. She replied that "no," she had everything under control.

Not long afterward, the expression on her face changed. The boa was exploring. When I asked a second time if she needed help, she quickly replied, "yes!" We went into my small classroom next door, closed and locked the door. I unbuttoned her jumper at the shoulders, and it dropped to the floor. She explained to me that it was important to lift the snake, not pull him, as pulling on a snake makes him mad. I eased the boa from around her neck and laid it gently on the worn green carpet. I had no intention of making the six-foot boa angry! Dressed again and undaunted, Susan lifted the snake, draped him again over her shoulders, and walked down the two flights of stairs to the biology lab.

I, again, apologize for this lame allegory, for, of course, this section is not really about snakes, or at least only tangentially. It's about stepping out of the darkness and numbness of ignorance. After all, it's ignorance which feeds irrational fear. It's about growing up, gaining self-confidence, and expanding my narrow little world. It's about acceptance and respect for things different from myself. I was fortunate, indeed, to have met and married the man that I did. He taught me so much, without teaching, with merely being who he was. It's just easier to talk about snakes than it is to discuss private, intimate, abstract matters like love, acceptance and trust.

This brings me to wonder what actually happened to the serpent in Eden. We are told that God cursed him and consigned him to crawl on his belly in the dust. But there is a rational disconnect. Wasn't he already a belly-crawler when he encountered Eve? Didn't he already live in the dust? After all, God, the creator of everything, created the serpent, too. God placed him, or at least Satan in the snake's form, in Eden. After the "fall," did God hurl him out with Adam and Eve, or leave him there? In all the scenes I've seen of Adam and Eve leaving Eden, I don't ever remember seeing the serpent going with them. I wonder.

And, what happened to Eden, anyway? It's clearly not to be confused with heaven. Does it still exist somewhere in the Muslim Middle East? Are we planning to bomb it? Or did God in his anger and disappointment smite Eden? Did pieces fly throughout the universe like fragments of a meteor? If so, maybe a little part of it landed on the Booger Hill Road. Maybe I, too, along with God's other creatures, even the slithering ones, lived in the near perfect state of trust and love, if only for a while.

OUR HOUSE ON BOOGER HILL

Edward and I first met our house on Booger Hill Road in June of 1969, about one month before the first moon walk. It was love at first sight. The sprawling white house was a genteel representation of what was good about the South at the beginning of the last century. It was charming, yet unpretentious, lovely without being exactly grand, dignified, but totally without airs. I say intentionally that we "met" our house, as it was more an entity of its own, engaging and friendly, than it was something to be bought and sold. We regarded ourselves not as owners, but more as friends who shared thirty years of our lives with the Lady of Booger Hill.

In mid-June, 1969, we still lived in Dr. Bond's house. I was heavy with my first pregnancy when our beloved Labrador retriever "Danny Boy" disappeared. We had taken him for his usual afternoon swim at the South Fork of the Broad River. He had a mad passion for the water and leapt excitedly out of the car as soon as we opened the door, furiously wagging his tail which looked like it was propelling him, speed-boat fashion, down the dusty red clay road. We heard the splash, but when we reached the river's edge, there was no Danny Boy. We called and called. Edward searched the woods nearby, oblivious to the knee-deep brambles, but we couldn't find him. For three days we continued our search. Edward scoured the woods up and down the bank, calling as he walked. Together we knocked on doors of every house in the area. People acknowledged that they had seen the unexpected and strange sight of a black dog making his way tirelessly back and forth, up and down, swimming the South Fork. We heard reports of him from one end of the county to the other. We missed him terribly. On the third night, we were awakened by the familiar thud on the screen door at the back porch. Danny Boy had made his way home!

In our search for Danny Boy, we had driven up a long, winding driveway, a beautiful driveway, lined on one side by spirea bushes and on the other by crepe myrtles. What a surprise when we discovered this beautiful house at the end of the drive. It was not imposing, like an antebellum columned mansion, as its columns were modest, set on a waist-high brick foundation. But the house, itself, was instantly warm and inviting, with its large open porches wrapped around the front and side. The ceilings of the porches were painted light blue to ward off evil spirits, so the local legend held it. Joining the two porches was a concrete patio bordered by a huge box of pale petunias, the old fashioned, perennial variety. The gardenia bushes encircling the porch were beginning to bud, and bees and butterflies hovered around the long hedge of abelias.

The little windows upstairs were a collection of diamond-shaped panes, and the roof sloped gracefully in many directions, with gables studded around. We walked up to the front door and knocked. No one was home, or at least no one came to the door. I realized later that it was impossible to hear a knock on the front door from the far away back kitchen. I couldn't help but take a peek into the house, through the beveled glass window in the front door. The living room was enormous, and behind it was a hall which, I learned later, was the size of single-wide trailer.

We marveled at the wonderful home nestled on the crest of a little hill. Though it was right off two highways, literally, no one could see it because of the dense pines and oaks. It was a private haven, a step into a world of quiet peacefulness, set apart from the frenzy of the busy world and the din of ever increasing traffic. It was astonishing. We had driven by it hundreds of times on Highway 29 on our way to and from Athens and had never known it was there.

With Danny Boy safely home and Ed safely delivered, we settled into our little honeymoon cottage, Dr. Bond's house, converting the dining room into a nursery for the baby. It was a pleasant, if busy life, juggling Edward's teaching schedule, my graduate classes, and the care of an extraordinarily active little boy who wasn't as keen on sleeping as we were. We bumped along happily for a couple of years.

One June day just two years later, we were startled to see a "for sale" sign on the side of Highway 29, just down the bluff from where the house was hidden. On a whim, knowing that we couldn't afford such a thing, I called the local realtor, and we made an appointment. I was so overwhelmed when I went inside that I was speechless. We walked through the house, from one wonder to another. All the rooms were large, and the kitchen, with three pantries no less, was big enough to have a sizeable table in the middle of the floor. There were even walk-in closets, a rare feature for a house built in 1920s. The ceilings were tall, with intricate moldings at the top of the walls and again at the baseboards. There was even a picture molding about twelve inches down, so that we did not have to mar the thick, old-fashioned plaster walls by driving nails into them. The heart-of-pine floors, with their wide boards, were a warm, rich brown color and were so sturdy that there was nary a creak anywhere. There were fireplaces and mantels in every room. The doors, even the interior ones, were solid oak with brass knobs and keyholes. It was beautiful and, what's more, it felt comfortable and good.

Though we were as poor as proverbial church mice, we managed to buy it. The owner, Jack Sorrells, who was an administrator in the College of Education at the university, gave us a second mortgage. I think that he, too, recognized the instant bond we felt with this grand, old house, and he knew that we would love it and take care of it. Jack's father had built the house for his second wife, Jack's step-mother, as a wedding present, and theirs was the only other family to have lived in it. So it was saved from the abuse of many turnover owners or renters. Mr. Rufus had recently died at age ninety-five, and the family decided to sell. During the following years, I became friends with Jack's sister, Louise McLott, who had grown up in our house and was as lovely as it was. She and I were in the same bridge club and spent many a pleasant evening playing cards, sometimes at my house, sometimes at hers. The entire Sorrells extended family visited us often during the years, or, rather, visited the house. That was the effect it had on everybody. Everybody loved it, related or not.

Jack explained that back when his father built it, there were very few homes which were planned by an architect. Ours had been, which explained some of the nicest features, like every room having access from two directions, allowing for the constant circulation of air. Even the dining room, in the middle of the house, had a large bay window. Spacious bathrooms were constructed, even though the two-seater outhouse was used for another twenty years or so. Electricity did not come to the area until the 1950s but our house had had its own generator, and there were electric outlets in all the rooms, except, surprisingly enough, the dining room. Our bedroom upstairs was so large that, when I first saw it, two double beds sitting side by side were dwarfed in the spaciousness of the room. Connected to the hearth was a Franklin stove, the old kind which was coal fed and which had a flat top for boiling water or making tea. There was a sister stove in what was to become Elizabeth's room across the hall.

Moving day arrived. We had lots of help. My brother John came over to help Edward move the hundreds of boxes of books. Friends lent a hand and a truck or two. It was a joyous occasion, much hustle and bustle, and I prepared a huge picnic lunch for everyone, ham, potato salad, fresh tomatoes, pickles and bread. The entire Montgomery family arrived, with all five children in tow, and "set up" my kitchen.

We had been cautioned that moving was particularly confusing to a two-year-old, and we were prepared to make the transition as smooth as possible for little Ed. No need at all. He loved the commotion and the attention. He thrived in the house, dashing through all the big rooms and down the hall. He was in a children's wonderland.

Unfortunately, we had not taken as much time to reassure Danny Boy. He was wild with all this excitement, but confused and insecure. We tried to keep him inside, but with the doors constantly being opened and closed, and even propped open at times, he got out. The frantic dog saw Edward driving down the driveway in a pickup truck to get another load of things from the old house, and he panicked. He must have felt that he was being abandoned. He followed Edward's truck onto the highway, running hard to catch up.

He was hit by a car and died instantly. We stopped the moving long enough to dig his grave and lay his body down. It was particularly ironic that Danny Boy was killed the day we moved, as it was because of him that we discovered our house in the first place. We were all distraught. I cried and cried that night after everyone left. Though surely his heart was emptier than mine, Edward consoled me for hours. He was strong in that way.

Unlike most young girls, I never had expectations, so that I never had to live through disappointments. So, moving into our wonderful house couldn't be called a dream come true; it was as if I had stepped into an enchanted world. The house was so fresh and inviting, with its long sheer curtains billowing in the breeze from the tall windows. Over the years, I painted and papered, had bookshelves built. I refinished the long banister and all the oak mantels on the hearths. I'm sure that I touched every inch of the big old house, and I did so with tender care. In turn, it nurtured me, too, and gave me a refuge from the madness and uncertainty of the outside world. We were a good fit.

It was the breeze that I loved the most, the freshness of the air. The curtains danced almost all the time. The house "flowed well" and held the crispness of spring long into the summer. In the shade of the immense oak trees, with an attic fan and ceiling fans, and after a late evening skinny dip, we stayed cool all summer long. There was no need for air conditioning. The open windows invited the delicate scent from the gardenias in the front and the huge wisteria tree trained outside the back porch, the Confederate jasmine winding around the fence near the well house, as well as the music of the crickets and tree frogs. It occasionally brought in the not-so-sweet aroma from a passing skunk, whereupon we'd jump out of bed and run to the hall to turn off the attic fan which sucked in the outside air.

We had lots of parties, grand and small. My mother and brothers, with their families, gathered there many a Thanksgiving. My nephew and his family, along with my mother and brother Ranny, and yet another friend, fled hurricane Floyd to the safety of our house. My dear friend Martha and her family took refuge with us after the tornados hit Athens in 1973. We had reunions. We had birthday parties, a retirement party, swimming parties, a wedding reception, and even an all-night graduation party, after which I stepped over sleeping bodies, boys and girls, the next morning on the way to give final exams at Emmanuel.

We had a formal little girl tea party, with a punch bowl and lots of homemade goodies. Liz and Mary dressed in their red velvet jumpers that I had made, and Liz insisted on wearing the cream-colored fur jacket that she had received from Santa. There was a good turnout, but all of her guests arrived in jeans and tennis shoes. The little girls spent the entire afternoon dashing excitedly throughout the house, doubtless sugar charged by the sweet punch and cookies. So much for my efforts. After that, we stuck to summer parties in the pool for the children.

People always commented how wonderful and relaxing it was to come to our house in the country, apparently unaware of how we toiled, cooked, cleaned, and prepared ahead of time. But the truth is that we loved it, every minute, even the cleaning up. I liked to stay up late, far after the guests had left and the family had gone to bed, clearing things up, washing up the dishes, tucking everything away, and reliving the evening, always happy about our friends and the life that I shared with my family in our wonderful old house.

The local rumor was that the house was haunted. Edward always replied that, if so, it was a very friendly ghost. The rumor was based on the fact that Mr. Rufus had died there. But, heck, everybody dies, I thought, and what a pleasant place to leave from. Liz's friends, whenever they spent the night, always had to go home about eleven o'clock. It was absolutely predictable. Annoyed, nonetheless I loaded them up in the car and delivered them home. Years later, Liz confessed to me that she would begin to tell them about the ghost who lived in our house, who appeared about midnight and roamed methodically throughout the house, checking to see if there were any strangers around. She would weave a terrifying, if inventive, tale, building up the suspense until her girlfriends, seized with fright, would flee, highly traumatized, to our room and, after a quick call to their parents, to the back seat of my car. I wondered why they all left, all at approximately at the same time of night, why they left without apologies, and also why there were few repeat visitors.

There are the downsides of living in an old house in a rural area. The winters were challenging, quite an understatement, even after we installed storm windows and had insulation blown into the attic. I laughed that I wore as many clothes to bed as I did to work. We all dressed in layers, even in the daytime, and my heavy long-sleeved green bathrobe even had a hood! We had lap robes draped around all the chairs in the sitting room. We couldn't afford to heat the whole house, so we darted from room to room across the frigid hall. It turned out that the wonderful breeze which kept us cool in summer kept us cooler in winter.

The upstairs had no heat at all, so Edward would dash up about an hour before bedtime to turn on the electric blankets. The window panes were known to freeze on the inside. It got so cold one time that the upstairs toilet bowl literally froze. Most of the time, we coped without too much grumbling. We perfected the snuggle, even occasionally a group snuggle, predating the group hug. And there is nothing quite so warming as a good cuddle-up on a cold, cold night.

There was no such thing as cable TV out our way. There was not even any natural gas. All lines stopped at the South Fork River, which, mind you, is barely larger than a creek. It amazed me that we could lay cable across the Atlantic and Pacific and could even put a man on the moon, but the south branch of the Broad remained impenetrable.

The first winter our pipes froze, and we had no water. We insulated, of course, after that. But we never managed to keep the pump from freezing, even after we put a light bulb in the well house. Ice storms were the worst. Since our pump was electric, if we were out of power, we were also out of water. We were the last house on the "trunk line" and, therefore, the last to have utilities restored. Once we were without electricity and water for seven cold, long days. We had some heat from space heaters in the kitchen and bathroom, but not enough to warm a cup of coffee. Despite all this, life's challenges became mere inconveniences because we all weathered them together, Edward, the children, and I—and the old house that we shared all our seasons with.

The thought of the cold, cold winters paled when we woke up to the delights of spring. First, little pastel crocuses literally popped up from the ground. Then buttercups appeared, some yellow, some variegated and fragrant. The spirea burst into bloom, its tiny white flowers emerging before its leaves, creating a winding snow bank up the driveway. Pristine white dogwoods, azaleas, bright yellow forsythia and even a lilac tree, rare this far south, wove a multi-hued tapestry in the yard and the woods. Patches of thrift dotted the yard. Miniature Confederate violets carpeted the field in lavender. Then a whole mass of daylilies emerged, some bright orange and some yellow and fragrant, which mingled with the scent of gardenias. The pine trees at the end of the field donned a lacy cloak of delicate wisteria blossoms, dripping from their uppermost branches and fluttering in the light breeze. We opened our doors to the freshness and beauty of our little world. How inconceivably lucky we were. Even if I had been a dreamer, I could never have thought up all of this. Never.

My friendly house and I spent thirty years together, mostly splendid years, certainly satisfying and fulfilling. I found myself alone, although not really alone in many senses. Edward had died in the same room as Mr. Rufus, and I always felt his presence, though I wouldn't exactly characterize it as a ghost. It was more like a guardian spirit.

My energy was dwindling in inverse proportion to my age. I found it difficult to drive at night on the highway. The upkeep of the large house, the sweeping of the porches, the mowing of several acres of yard, the care of the pool lost its purpose. There was no one to work for, no longer anyone to please. I sighed at reality. When the time came, I said good-bye, with surprising acceptance and without regret. It was time. I rolled up the original architect's drawings in the original cardboard tube and placed it on the mantel in the dining room.

I had taken very good care of the dear old house, loved it exceedingly. In return, it swaddled me in a warm blanket of acceptance and security. It gave me years of memories. Under its aegis I grew from being a timorous young woman who was afraid of her own shadow, and everyone else's, to being a confident, mature woman, unafraid of shadows or snakes or storms or most other things. I was a lifetime removed from the girl who had strung alarm bells across her bedroom door before going to bed. Rather, I now slept comfortably in the middle of the woods with all the doors unlocked.

NANNY

Edward's mother, Daisy, was an immense presence in our lives in Danielsville. She was the prototype of an ideal grandmother, the kind we read about in fairy tales. She was loving, kind and exceedingly squeezable. Daisy reminded me of my own Grandmother Bradford, with her naturally curly snow white hair and her inviting plumpness. Her hands were as soft as a newborn kitten. When my children were born, I asked each grandparent what he or she wanted to be called. That way, they would always be pleased with the sound of their names, and we could avoid such names as "Granky." She chose "Nanny," which is what Ed and Liz called her, but Mary always referred to her as "Nana," in a private, conspiratorial sort of way.

Nanny was born Daisy Evans Wilson in Nimrod, Perry County, Arkansas. Her earliest days were precarious. She told us that she was born two-and-a-half months early and weighed

Nanny's parents: James and Mary Sue Wilson

three pounds—or she was born three months early and weighed two-and-a-half pounds. I can't remember which. Whichever, it was miraculous that she survived at all, as rural Arkansas in 1902 afforded few hospitals and no neonatal units. I doubt even that the term "neonatal" was in the lexicon. Her heart, she maintained, was on the right side of her body, instead of the left, a result of her premature birth.

She told us that her grandfather said that she looked just like a baby rat, a remark which wounded her to her dying day, but by which I'm sure he meant no harm. Her parents put the newly born baby in a shoe box and placed her behind the wood stove, so the story goes. Since she was born in July, not all the details ring true, as it must have been hot as blue blazes in Arkansas in the first place, but she repeated this story as gospel truth. The doctor, Dr. Evans, who delivered her, instructed her parents to give her a dropper of whiskey mixed with honey every day to stimulate her heart. Ed said that Nanny told him it was called the "little-nip." Somehow she survived, whether through the warmth of the July stove or though the glow of the whiskey or the tenacity of her own brave little spirit. Her grateful parents gave her the middle name "Evans" in honor of the doctor who saved her life.

Her challenges and troubles were far from over. Her older sister, Nell, was assertive, and Daisy lived in her shadow. She was closer to Lola, her younger sister, and virtually idealized her one brother, Tom. But her littlest sister, Marjorie, was the darling of the five. Marjorie was a beautiful little girl who, unfortunately, contracted some kind of childhood disease. She developed a high fever and lay delirious for days, on the verge of dying. One day she took a dramatic turn for the better and "woke up." She chattered and laughed. Everyone was elated, and no one seemed to know or at least to recall the story of the swan's song. Although the older children were cautioned that Marjorie must rest and not get overly excited, Nell got her to laughing so hard that, according to the story, the little child suddenly fell over dead. Legend says that the swan's song, like the melody of little Marjorie's laughter, is only heard just before death. Daisy said that her mother never recovered from little Marjorie's death and subsequently died of a broken heart, and that she, Daisy, always held Nell responsible for both the death of her little sister and the melancholic state of her mother.

Daisy's father, James Wilson, was elected to the Arkansas legislature. In his pictures, he resembles highly his grandson, my husband, Edward, with the same square shoulders and distinctive shape and tilt of the head. Their deep-set eyes and shock of wavy hair are nearly identical. But tragedy struck once more when he came down with tuberculosis. Back then, TB was practically always a death sentence, which it was, indeed, for him. He was committed to the sanitarium where he lived his last years, quarantined even from his family. As tuberculosis is highly contagious and, in an effort to protect the family, everything he had was burned. Daisy witnessed this with great sadness, especially when the writing box and quills, which she particularly associated with her father, were consumed by the hungry flames. Daisy was fifteen when he died, and her main contact with her father throughout her life had been through letters.

Her mother, Mary Sue McElwee Wilson, was left to care for the children. Like many modest women of the age, she refused to go to a specialist when unpleasant symptoms emerged. Her own father got so far as to get her into the wagon for a doctor's appointment. They made the trip from Pine Bluff to Little Rock, but she would not get out of the wagon, much less into the doctor's office. They returned home, and it soon became evident that she was dying from uterine cancer. I can't even allow myself to imagine what pain she endured, and I don't mean only the physical pain, which must have been considerable. She knew that as soon as she died, her remaining four young children would be orphans, if not technically, at least essentially, because their father remained in the sanitarium.

Daisy's grandfather, Sue's father, took them in. The children called him "Billy-Pa," though his real name was Thomas Fletcher McElwee. He was a Civil War veteran who never recovered after the war. He had walked home from a Yankee prison camp battered and broken. When he finally reached Pine Bluff, he sewed coins in the hem of his trousers so that he would never be that broke (and broken) again.

According to family legend, seven (!) horses were shot out under him, yet he survived. Not many of the soldiers were fortunate enough to ride, but those who were boasted about having their horses massacred when they were in the heat of battle. Actually, the same legend was perpetuated among many of the other rebel veterans, though the number of unfortunate steeds varies from tale to tale, from one to six or even more.

After the war, more accurately after the defeat, Billy-Pa suffered from what we would now call "post-traumatic stress disorder," but back then people said that their "spirits were just broken." He wrote articles for a newspaper and received a pittance for that, and he had a small inheritance and a good many acres of land, but, otherwise, he had no means of support. I asked Daisy how they managed, and she said that in her adulthood she had wondered the same thing, but they lived well enough and never lacked for anything.

I don't know exactly when he died, but he lived to see all the grandchildren, or, as he referred to them, "Sue's scruffy-haired young-uns," reach adulthood. Daisy told such wonderful stories of growing up, and I am keenly aware of how much more I know of her childhood than I do of my own grandmothers'.

The four children were a handful to look after, and Billy-Pa took an attitude of gruff permissiveness. She and her sisters would sit on their grandfather's lap and braid his long beard, decorating it with colorful ribbons. One day, he forgot that he had been to the "Wilson girls' beauty parlor," and he went to town with all the ribbons still tied in his hair, much to the amusement of the Pine Bluff residents.

She told me about going down to the creek when it was forbidden and sneaking round and round the house, skirting the woods at the edge of the house until they saw her grandfather's head droop to his chest as he took his afternoon nap on the front porch. They would then make a mad dash to the back door and dry their clothes out.

One time, they couldn't hide their mischief. It happened before their mother died, when Daisy was a young girl. She had a new green dress, and she thought it quite beautiful. She was told that, no matter what she did, she was not to soil the dress. But she and her sisters soon found their way back to the creek, and the cool running water was too much of an enticement. Daisy took off her new dress and very carefully draped it on a limb before she joined her sisters in the fun. After a while they were horrified as they looked up and caught sight of a goat eating the very same new green dress. No hiding their behavior now, no sneaking into the back door. She never once mentioned getting punished. She was cheerful to the core.

There's no way to account for Daisy's pleasant disposition. She surely lived through more unhappiness in her life than most of us do. Not only was her childhood fraught with tragedies, she even lost one of her own children, Jimmy, who was named after her much beloved father, to pneumonia when he was less than one year old. She didn't "endure" the way the women in my family did, but she was not a Pollyanna, either; she just handled things differently. I'm not sure I can explain it. But I can appreciate it. Her warmth and good nature were irrepressible. Edward said that theirs was the favorite house in the neighborhood, and I can well believe that it was. She loved everyone and nearly everything. The one exception she made was with child abusers, who, she, using uncharacteristic language, said "should burn in hell."

Daisy warmed to everything that was vulnerable and needed protection. She'd enter a room and every child there would flock to her. I think it was in part that she always remained a child herself, open and trusting, loving and affectionate. Daisy had been a full-time homemaker, except for the few years when Edward and his brother, Jack, were in college. Her only "paid" position was as the head of the toy department of a large store in Nashville, the name of which I've forgotten. What a wonderful job for her, making children happy all year long.

Nanny and the children

So it's not surprising that her grandchildren were the focal point of her life, first Jack's three, then ours. (It's unfortunate that August, Edward's son by a previous marriage, never really got to know her.) When she lived in Florida and we visited, she and Ed, a toddler, spent hours and hours in their little camper, taking imaginary trips and pretending their snacks were finely prepared gourmet meals. They were both thrilled with their bold, fantastic adventures. After she and Papa, my father-in-law Edward Sr., moved to Danielsville in 1977, she spent glorious hours with the children. One girl spent every Friday night with her and the other every Saturday night. As I snuggled them after they returned from their Nanny's house, the lovely scent of her perfume, Opium by Yves St. Laurent, still lingered in their hair. The visits to her house were pure enchantment. She served the girls breakfast on a tray each morning, decorated with a freshly picked flower. They cooked together, played countless games, mostly imaginative and creative. She and Mary had their dolls, a world of make believe which was more real than the actual one. Long after the doctor told us not to give Mary her pacifier any longer, for health reasons, Nanny kept one hidden at her house. I was not pleased, less than sympathetic, which, in retrospect, I regret.

Daisy and Liz made numerous "road trips," throughout the red clay back roads of Madison County, some of which had potholes and others which had never been paved. Their adventures were conspiratorial, and they knew where abandoned houses were and where every creek meandered through every pasture. After Papa died, Ed kept his Nanny's checkbook for her. Though he was only in the third grade, he could add and subtract, and he felt very important and very much needed. He was just as kind and compassionate when, during the time she lived with us, he helped out with her care, even her personal care, without the least hesitation.

Daisy had lived her life completely under her husband's "umbrella." It was not that she was meek, as that word would not describe her at all, but hers had been a very old-fashioned marriage. Papa had taken care of all their business and all other practical matters, including grocery shopping. She had absolutely no clue about insurance, taxes, or other fundamentals of life. But she was kind of spunky, too, in her limited way. She held her own in the verbal give and take of the marriage. Like all people who have lived more than fifty years together, they had their petty squabbles and little dramas which, though trivial, sometimes reached epic importance and which at the same time brought them comfort, like a ragged threadbare bathrobe, familiar and comfortable, yet not much help keeping out the cold. Every single morning at breakfast, as Daisy let her coffee cool, Papa would remark: "Daisy, your coffee's getting cold," to which she would reply: "Yes, I know. I like it that way." It was a scratchy old record played day after day for more than five decades.

Papa died two months to the day after they moved from Melbourne Village to Danielsville. It was a beautiful October morning, and he was outside changing the oil in his giant Cadillac. He had suffered with heart disease for years, and his recently installed pacemaker suddenly stopped working. He died instantly and fell to the ground. The years had not been kind to Papa, and he had become nearly stone deaf, with his heart so weak that he struggled unlocking his steering wheel mechanism. It was frustrating to him and pitiful to us. At 79, having suffered the ravages of childhood diabetes, he had little quality to his life. And the future promised nothing better, only worse.

After the initial shock of his death, when Daisy's blood pressure reached stroke level, she adjusted very well. She went on with her life, telling us occasionally that she had awakened during the night to find Papa standing at the foot of her bed. She didn't get upset about these "dreams," and reported them rather matter of factly. But I'm sure she missed him far more than she admitted.

Daisy didn't sit around mourning her life away. She and Naomi Adams, a lady from the Sanford Community whose son had recently died, worked through their common grief by establishing a local "Clothes Closet." They accepted used clothing, which they resold from a small shop on the square across from the courthouse. Mostly they charged twenty-five or thirty cents for an item, except for maybe an overcoat. But nothing was priced more than two dollars. Even at such a reduced price, they raised an amazing amount of money, with which they bought Christmas toys for the indigent children in Madison County. Santa didn't have to make the long journey from the North Pole to see our local children, because his stand-in, complete with white hair and plump and rosy cheeks, ran the North Pole, South, down on the square.

With a sudden burst of independence, Daisy announced that she was going to get a driver's license! We were stunned, as she was seventy-five years old and had never, ever driven. With a mixture of excitement and considerable trepidation, we went to the State Patrol office and got a driver's manual. She studied it like some people study the Bible, and she could quote the whole thing, chapter and verse, just like a Holiness preacher. If I stopped at the stop sign, she pronounced that "one must come to a complete stop," not a rolling one.

She passed the written part of the exam with no problem. But it took a while longer to get the actual mechanics of driving, itself. Whenever I had a little time, she and I would head out to the cemetery. She liked to practice there, because there was no traffic or hills, but a lot of sharp turns to master. Besides, she explained, she liked driving back and forth in front of Papa's grave, as she felt more secure and sure of his blessing. It briefly crossed my mind that she was also being certain to show him her newly found freedom.

His big Cadillac was too much of a challenge, and we decided that she might do better in a smaller car. So she and I headed to dealerships. I'm sure the salesmen could spot us as suckers the minute we drove up. She decided that she wanted the blue, two-toned Cutlass Supreme, the one with only two doors, so the children would be safe in the back seat. We were right in settling on a smaller car, and her improvement was dramatic. The man in charge of the driver's test came to Madison County on the third Wednesday (I think) of the month. We'd heard that it was better to take the test locally, and she signed up. She didn't quite make it on the first try, but she passed the test the next time he was around. She clutched her license with more pride and excitement than any sixteen-year-old. It was two days before her seventy-sixth birthday. Several years later I discovered that we had bought a sports car with a souped-up eight-cylinder engine. All we had cared about was the color, and it was really pretty.

On her own, she restricted her driving to town, going to church, the pharmacy, the doctor, and the little local grocery store. She drove to our house, too, which was one mile south of town on a busy highway. Always after she left, Edward and I stayed on the porch until we were sure that she had managed to turn left onto Highway 29. Occasionally we heard the screeching of brakes of another car, one time of a semi, or the blaring of a horn, but she managed never to have an accident. Thank God.

Daisy loved and accepted all creatures, animal and human, perhaps even in that order. Though never a really good player, a fact which wouldn't have bothered her a bit, she felt comfortable playing cards with the bridge ladies and going to big parties.

She was equally comfortable with the Hart family, all of whom were mentally challenged. I think there were other children, as well, who lived on their own, but Mr. and "Ole Miz" Hart lived in the center of town, one block from the courthouse, with two daughters and their son Cecil. Notable was the daughter Lucille who clutched a doll and brushed its hair over and over, all day long, the whole time swaying back and forth and muttering incomprehensibly.

Cecil was smart enough to "work outside the home," that is whenever he was not scouring the town dump. It was a family preoccupation that Cecil get married, and he said that he had had a vision from God that He was going to bring him a wife and that he,

Cecil, would find her in the front porch swing. He quite content-edly bided his time.

When one of the Hart daughters got married, she bought most of her trousseau at Daisy's Clothes Closet, as well as the outfits for the whole wedding party. The other daughter, Lucille, even though she looked lovely dressed up in a lavender satin dress, crisp and look-ing like new, was too shy to appear at the actual wedding, a "garden" ceremony. She watched the whole affair through a little peephole in the fence with her brother Cecil.

The Harts' yard was not dirt, not grass, but littered knee deep with rusted-out metal parts and other "objets d'art" salvaged from the local dump. In addition to "stuff," there were lots of cats, too, and some chickens, despite the fact that the Hart family lived in the heart (no pun) of downtown Danielsville.

Poor Ole Miz Hart one time ventured into the world of quasi-respectability and hosted a Tupperware party. She sent out thirty in-vitations and did some cooking. Sadly, not one single invitee showed up, except for Daisy and little Liz. Daisy was sensitive, loyal and supportive of everyone, and she knew that the party was not going to be a huge success. She did tell Liz that she mustn't eat anything, and that, whatever happened, she was not to sit on the front porch swing.

One of my favorite stories about Daisy involved my first visit af-ter Edward and I were married. Though I had met his parents brief-ly, I didn't know them well, and they didn't know me any better. All they knew is that I was some college girl who had taken up with their middle-aged son and had married him forthwith. Both of my in-laws greeted me warmly, even Edward's usually gruff father, with whom I felt an immediate bond. He did confiscate my copy of *Portnoy's Complaint* which I had taken along to read, and he read it himself, telling Edward that it was not appropriate for such a young thing as I. The first morning of our visit, Edward brought me coffee in bed, which he did the whole twenty-seven years of our marriage. Rather than in a mug, he had poured the coffee in Daisy's fine china, successfully balancing the dainty cup on its equally dainty saucer. Never being truly adept at anything, I was horrified as I spilled nearly the whole cup on my mother-in-law's "company sheets." Dear Daisy appeared and reassured me. She was so warm and kind and actually seemed delighted to be changing the linens, implying that a cup of coffee was the very thing that her sheets needed.

Lovely as she was, Daisy could be highly excitable. There was the time that Mary's fever spiked when she was visiting her grandmother. Daisy sent someone to "Bill's 'N D'ville" to see if Edward and I were eating supper there. The entire town was in a frenzy. Finally, the judge thought to come to our house, and there Edward and I sat, reading, oblivious to the state of emergency. Everyone in town had been notified – except us!

There was the time that young Liz was visiting Daisy and disappeared. The neighborhood alert was sounded and even Mr. Perry, the elementary school principal, joined the search. One of the low points of my life was giving the sheriff a description of my little seven-year-old daughter. There was a happy ending, fortunately, and we found Liz safe and sound, calmly eating cookies with Elcoe Huff, the retired bank president down the street. They were innocently passing away the afternoon, oblivious to all the excitement going on outside.

Daisy's love and her presence certainly added a wonderful dimension to our lives. Sometimes it was difficult for me to understand her, and Edward pointed out that "she thought with her heart and not with her mind." He encouraged me to read the story, "The Darling," whose protagonist could well have been his mother with another name. I am, sorry to admit, a pragmatist, and I beat myself up for being so. But, goodness knows, my husband and my mother-in-law needed someone to handle everyday life for them. I do know that I learned a lot from Daisy about love and acceptance. And, I do know, emphatically, that I loved her and that I am forever grateful for what she gave our children.

The last few years of her life were cruel, as she suffered stroke after stroke, never rebounding from the last when she would have another. That's not the way any of us wanted her life to turn out. She, who had early on suffered the premature deaths of her parents, her little sister, and even her own child, who had brought so much love to so many, and who had survived the death of her husband of more than fifty years, certainly deserved better than that.

The Pool

When Mary was a barely a year old, she fell ill with a serious, life-threatening illness. Suddenly her little body rebelled. Night after night, her fever spiked, sometimes reaching 105 degrees. I remember one awful night, in February, in the cold, cold old house, when her temperature got so high that it registered higher than the thermometer. She seized, rigid as a board. I jerked my nightgown over my head, filled the bathtub with lukewarm water, and climbed in with her in my arms. The tepid water soon became chilled in the frigid bathroom. After a while I announced to Edward, who was looking on helplessly, that I thought her fever was down. He replied, in his droll manner, that he imagined my temperature was pretty low, too.

Since her high temperature returned to normal after the sudden nighttime spikes, the doctors were unimpressed. They said that she looked fine to them. But they weren't with her in the middle of the night when her fever soared and we had to change her sheets soaked with sweat. After about a week, her legs gave way, and she crumpled when she tried to pull herself up to the side of her crib. Then her wrist became red and painful and swelled double size. The doctors panicked, and we were told to rush her to the Scottish Rite Hospital, now part of the Atlanta Children's Hospital network. Our first night there, when her temperature spiked, I walked to the nurses' station to tell them. I was rather casual about it, as this had become part of our routine. When they took her temperature, they went into emergency mode. Apparently, though I don't know why, no one had taken me seriously. Why any parent would exaggerate a child's illness is beyond me, then and now.

We spent a couple of weeks at the hospital. Mary underwent daily x-rays and tests, from the fairly benign procedure of the daily drawing of blood, to the excruciatingly painful spinal tap. Edward and I were not allowed in the procedure room. It was parent proof. It was not, however, sound proof, and we listened, helpless, in the hall to the terrible screams of our little baby as the large needle was inserted into her spine and fluid was drawn out. For the first week and a half, I was there day and night, sleepless and frantic. My mother drove from Savannah to Danielsville to care for Ed and Liz. After Mary was diagnosed we stayed another week to get her medication stabilized. At that point, I drove to Franklin Springs every day, and her grandmother Daisy stayed with Mary while I was gone.

The diagnosis was Still's disease. Although it was a serious condition, we were almost giddy with relief. The doctors had ruled out lung cancer and leukemia and other such illnesses. Not all of the children were so fortunate. One little boy, three years old, had unexplained lung cancer. His prognosis was poor. One little girl, about seven, lay on a stretcher in a body cast, unable to move. She was Latina and spoke no English. I ached to think of her transported from her little village to a hospital in the States, separated from her family, unable to understand anything that was said to her, not knowing what was happening in the first place. I tried to chat with her in my stiff, textbook Spanish, but either my accent was so poor or she was too intimidated and confused, because she never replied, just stared at me with her large, haunting black eyes.

The doctor explained that Still's disease attacks joints, but more importantly, it attacks vital organs, too. It was imperative that we keep a strict regimen, giving her four baby aspirin every four hours, on the dot. The active ingredient in aspirin is salicylate, an anti-inflammatory, and that was the best treatment, despite aspirin's negative effect on the body. It was crucial to keep the salicylate level at a therapeutic scale, so that her joints and heart would not become perilously inflamed. The dosage was based on weight, and being little more than a year old, she didn't have much leeway. If she vomited and her weight dropped even a pound, her salicylate level would spike and she'd become comatose. Four or five times, we had to rush to the emergency room where they would revive her.

After a few visits to the physical therapist, we learned to exercise her arms and legs at home. One particularly obnoxious pediatric rheumatologist told us to be sure to exercise her, not to "bring me back a crippled-up baby." Bring *her* back. The very idea. Oftentimes it seems to me that scientists become so accustomed to dealing with tests and numbers that they forget there's a human body involved— and a human soul.

We were diligent caregivers. I remember thinking that I was happy that we were Mary's parents. Her chronic pain made her very fussy, which was hard on everyone. But we had minds and could separate the fact of her crying from our feelings of frustration. Even I became uncharacteristically patient. We worked hard for several years, never missing either her medication or her therapy. Our combined efforts, Edward's and mine, and especially Mary's, were successful, as Mary has grown up with strong legs, a healthy heart, and a sense of courage and determination which were born from adversity. She is amazing. We all had a difficult couple of years. Liz had life-saving bladder reconstructive surgery while Mary was very ill, and I was called to the emergency room from her bedside because Ed had been admitted with his fifth broken arm!

Mary's illness and need for physical therapy were, then, the primary reason we put in our swimming pool. It was a bit of an excuse, honestly, as much as it was a reason. I grew up in Savannah, near the ocean, where abundant rivers and creeks wended their way through the marshes. I missed living near water. So we had a big pool installed, for Mary's therapy and for the pleasure of everybody.

Our pool was one of the first ones in the county, and we loved having people share it. I used to explain that it was like having a birthday cake and eating it all alone if we had a pool with no one to have fun with. We were delighted to have lots of company, and there were unexpected perks, because, when people came, they insisted on bringing us something, and we were inundated with fresh vegetables during the summers. We all enjoyed swimming. One summer Ed and Eric Temple, his best buddy, swam a hundred laps a day, day after day. Ed earned his lifeguard certification and taught swimming lessons from time to time. Liz, too, enjoyed the pool, though she had genuinely grieved when the trees outside her window had to be cut down so that we could have it installed. Mary blossomed. In fact, she could swim before she could walk up and down the porch steps. That was a real, if unfortunate, advantage, because we didn't have to worry about her escaping to the pool unattended. Some Sunday afternoons the whole church, the tiny Danielsville Methodist, would come over after lunch.

Though all children and even their parents were welcomed to swim, Edward and I took over the pool at 10:00 every night, and nobody else was invited. After dark, in private, on our own property, after all, we didn't bother with swimsuits, but, instead, took our night clothes outside and put them on after toweling off. When we went back in the house, Edward made me a gin and tonic, which he traded for a kiss. He claimed that he preferred his gin secondhand. We turned on our attic fan. Even though we had no air conditioning, we stayed cool all night, our temperature lowered by the cool water and the fan pulling in the freshness of the night air. Our summers were glorious.

However happy the memories, there were serpents in Eden, literally. Before swimming in the morning (and especially at night when Edward and I were particularly vulnerable) we had to check the skimmers, discovering the occasional snake, mouse, frog, even baby rabbit whose misfortune it was to cross our yard and stumble into the clear, inviting water, only to be poisoned by the chlorine. We wanted no company at all, human or otherwise, alive or dead. We did have to share the water with a thirsty bat or two, those despicable winged rodents. Once I came across a cluster of fire ants, who clutched each other into a ring and were placidly floating on the surface. I know, specifically, that they were fire ants, as I tried to scoop them up with my hand to throw them onto the lawn. The stings burned for several days.

The serpents were not always the live ones. Other calamities slithered about. One rainy fall afternoon, the girls and I arrived home about 3:00 and we were startled to see Edward's clothes strewn haphazardly on the side porch. He greeted us at the door of the porte-cochère with a sheepish expression on his face and said "Something happened to me today, and I guess it's funny." He proceeded to explain that, in the drizzling rain, he put on all his rain gear, hat, trench coat, boots, and went out to winterize the pool. He gathered up the skimmers and stored them; he unscrewed the ladders and put them in the pool house. He then tackled the diving board. He removed one large bolt and put it on top of the board; he then unbolted the other side, whereupon the first bolt rolled into the pool. No problem. He got the net and set about scooping up the sunken bolt, which turned out to be rather obstinate. Instead of being gathered up in the net, it rolled along the bottom.

After a while, to catch a second breath, he sat down on the diving board to rest. But the diving board was no longer attached, so both he and it tumbled into the pool! Poor Edward, we envisioned the image of him mounted on the diving board and plunging into the pool, just like he was riding a bull at the rodeo.

Much to my embarrassment, I topped his story. One very hot summer afternoon, we were working in the yard. I was riding the lawn mower and Edward was weed-eating at the foot of the driveway. Lost in deep thought, I was mesmerized by the drone of the engine. Suddenly I was jerked into reality. I was probably driving a little too fast in the first place, but before I knew what was happening, I had leapt over a large planter at the edge of the pool. I was headed straight in. No mere riding the diving board for me; this was a scene worthy of Dr. Strangelove, wild eyes bulging, careening madly through the universe on a bomb, as the big Snapper mower and I roared down the steps and made a big splash right into the pool. It turned over on me on the second or third step, but, luckily, did not pin me down. It sputtered, then drowned. I sputtered and bobbed to the surface.

In shock, I shouted madly for Edward. I followed the sound of the weed-eater and headed down the driveway. He met me halfway and wanted to know what had happened. It was not easy to admit that I had ridden the lawn mower into the pool, but I had to. Edward didn't get mad, that was not his style, and he calmly asked: "Shallow end or deep?" I thought that was a rather dumb question, though I was hardly in a position to cast aspersions. We hurried back to the pool. We both got in and were actually able to lift up the huge lawn mower onto the concrete skirt, thanks in large part to the buoyancy of the water. Never mocking, though often amused, Edward pointed out that if it had gone in at the deep end, we would have had to call the wrecker! Thank God for small favors.

Deservedly, I was the subject of many jokes. For about six months, whenever I entered a room, people cut their eyes my way and started to smile. Even the family doctor, not known for a robust sense of humor, teased me the next time I saw him. Meema, my very own mother, broke out laughing so hard on the phone that she had to hang up.

No one seemed to care that I was injured! I had big black bruises on my leg and upper thigh, as well as on my chest, but everybody was so amused that they didn't even notice. Everyone, except the mammogram tech whom I saw several weeks later at a routine examination. She inquired probingly about my many bruises. Weary of the teasing, I said that I didn't really want to talk about it. She soberly drew a couple of chairs next to the machine, directed me to one and sat in the other, and asked in a low, confidential tone, how I had gotten the bruises. She thought I was abused. I laughed and reassured her; then I told her the humiliating story of the lawn mower. She must have believed me, as ludicrous as it was, because she pushed the chairs back and proceeded with the X-ray. I healed, not only my body, but my pride, too; though the subject, even after all these years, rears its ugly head at nearly every family gathering.

After Edward died, I took over the maintenance of the pool. It turned out not to be so difficult if I kept the chemicals balanced. I was relieved. Poor Edward had suffered greatly from all the tasks of daily living. I took control with little problem. When it was time for repairs, I went to the local boat company and bought a special epoxy compound to paint the steps with. It was tricky to apply, as I had to wait until the dew dried up but before the heat set in. Though not professional, it was a pretty good job. I congratulated myself and even enjoyed a day or two of smug satisfaction.

The pool needed a new liner, too. Boosted by my recent success with the steps, I decided to save $500 from the cost of the installation by draining the pool myself. Letting the water out of the shallow end was no problem; I merely backwashed most of it and then popped in a sump pump which ran for several hours a day. So far, so good. But, then it came time to empty the deep end, which was nearly ten-feet deep.

The water in the pool was not nice and fresh. Since I knew that I would have to replace the liner in the spring, I had not winterized in the fall, and the water was like a murky, slimy swamp. Unlike the shallow end, which had been no problem, the deep end had so much decayed debris in it that the sump pump would have clogged up. I was able to run a little of the water off, but there was a good bit left, several feet at least. My confidence was waning. I considered that, just maybe, I was in "over my head," figuratively, at least. But, the deep end had to be drained too, so I gritted my teeth and faced my enemy with resolve.

I tried lying on my stomach and leaning over the side of the pool, lowering a bucket eight feet down, drawing up the malodorous muck, and emptying it time and time again. Down, fill, up, struggle to the yard, empty, a little bucket full at a time: That would have taken forever. The plan was disgusting, inefficient, and time consuming. Someone advised me that there was no alternative but to walk down the slope and to bring up the putrid water one bucket at a time. That didn't sound like a good idea either, because the slope would become slippery as I dripped the slimy water on the way up. But not knowing anything else to do and too proud, frugal, and stubborn to have to admit defeat to the pool man, I hesitantly headed down the slope, bucket in hand.

I've never had a great sense of balance, even in the best of times, and, sure enough after only two or three trips, I found the slope slippery as ice, filthy, dirty ice. I slid down into what can only be compared to the fifth circle of Dante's *Inferno*, where the souls are damned to live in putrid muck, some raging on top, while others remain submerged. This was one of the most demoralizing moments—or, unfortunately, hours—of my life! The sides were too high for me to scale, the ladder was stored for the season, the sliding board was out of reach. Horrified, I tried to make my way back up the slope, but I was so wet and nasty that I could not get my footing and I'd just slide back down. I tried crawling on all fours. I slid back down. I tried fanny-ing up on my backside and pushing with my feet. I slid back down. Then I just sat down in all the filth and sobbed.

It was some time later that Mary came home. Following the sounds of my cries, she discovered me, and somehow we managed to pull me out. I'm not exactly a light load. Feeling like a sewer rat, I struggled to the shower and scrubbed...and scrubbed...and scrubbed. Ed called me that night and told me that he would come the next weekend and for me not even to go out to the pool again. Bless him, he came and set the matter right in a couple of hours. Several weeks later, he confessed that there had been the bloated body of some kind of animal among the debris. He thought it might have been a big swollen rat, so apparently there had been two of us. I had saved my $500 from the pool man's bill, but it cost me a high price of pride, humiliation and disgust.

I kept the pool up for several more years, right by myself. I rarely ventured out, telling myself that it was unsafe to swim alone, though, in truth, I had lost interest. It was no longer inviting, and I swam only when someone visited. We had installed air conditioning when Edward was sick to facilitate his breathing, and I could cool off in the confines of my house.

Like most other things on the Booger Hill Road, the pool had lost its allure. I looked back on all the good times, with babies and children splashing around in the cool, refreshing water. I remembered with nostalgia the late-night skinny dips. But my glance shifted more and more past the pool and over the red tip hedge to the highway which climbed the nearby hill on its way to Athens.

Down Through the Chimney Come Santa Claws...

True to the magic of Christmas, when Ed was a little boy, he declared that he had heard the reindeer land on the flat roof of the back porch, just outside his windows. He heard the hooves of all nine reindeer, and they were as real to him as the sunrise every morning. Since we had no less than six fireplaces, the only choice for Santa and others was which one to use. We loved the appearance of ole Saint Nick, but when people live in an old house in the country, he is not the only one who comes down the chimney.

During the spring of 1973 I wrote my doctoral dissertation. I sat at the dining room table and spread out my papers on my makeshift desk. The only companions I enjoyed were the space heater, which cozied up the room by keeping the chill out of the air, and our black Lab Dynamite, who dozed all day on the floor near my feet. I plodded on with the dissertation, a totally unnecessary edition of medieval *fabliaux*. Day after day, week after week, month after month, I drudged through my material. I had to keep on going because I had a dual deadline, both a graduation date in mid-August and the impending birth of my second child at the same time. In fact, Liz was born just two days after the commencement exercises, a double happiness of having a precious new baby and fancy degree. The imminent birth of my daughter provided a good excuse to miss the folderol of graduation. I've never liked such tedious, predictable affairs, with the names of hundreds of students called out, frequently mispronounced, and the same platitudinous speeches, full of encouragement and admonition at the same time.

What a bore. Besides, all of my (modest) achievements have been for personal satisfaction, not public approbation.

Nineteen seventy-three was also the spring of tornados. The first one occurred in March, hitting Athens pretty hard. Even though Danielsville, fifteen miles away, was spared any actual touchdowns, we watched as one twister swirled madly over our house. For weeks, we uncovered debris which had blown from Athens. Fragments of linoleum landed in our little orchard, pieces of this and that, largely unidentifiable, were sprinkled about the yard. Edward even discovered a sterling silver teaspoon monogrammed with "P" half buried in the side yard. At first, I fantasized that the spoon might be part of a Civil War trove buried hastily as the Yankees approached. My hopes were dashed when Edward pointed out that the spoon was manufactured, not handcrafted, undeniably postwar.

The second tornado hit in May. It was even more destructive. But not even natural disasters interrupted my studies for long. After we assessed the damage, I went back to my work. A day or two later, I heard a scratching sound coming from the living room. It was slight at first, then more frantic. I concluded that a bird had blown down the chimney and was trapped. I felt sorry for the bird, and, I confess, sorry for us, too, as he would die and the smell of his rotting corpse would linger for several weeks. But I plowed away at my studies. The noise persisted, but the timbre of the scratching changed into more of a metallic rasp. The bird had actually gotten down from the chimney itself into the space heater.

Suddenly an enormous shadow, and I do mean enormous, loomed across the living room. It was a large wild duck. In the wild, a duck might not seem so big, but, believe me, its three-foot wing span was enormous, even against the background of our unusually large living room. Dynamite went berserk. I leapt to my feet. The frantic duck flew into the study, down the long hall, then back to the front of the house. Dynamite went into his duck-chasing mode, barking furiously and cavorting with glee as he chased the poor, terrified creature. During one trip through the hall, Dynamite even managed to grab a few feathers. The confused, frantic duck retaliated by pooping on the floor. What a sight!

I managed to close the huge duck off in the two front rooms, and then I propped the front door open, hoping that it would find its way out. Back to the books for me, "deadline" reverberating through my weary brain. Dynamite resumed his place on the floor, curling his body up at my feet. During the course of the afternoon, the duck made occasional fluttering sounds. I'd let Dynamite back into the closed-off front rooms. He'd dash about for a while, then come back into the dining room with me. The fluttering in the front room was unsettling, but the fluttering in my own belly was a constant reminder of the imminent childbirth, so I kept on task: "Neither rain, nor sleet, nor snow" the saying goes, and I added "nor tornado, nor wild duck, nor birth of a baby."

After a couple of hours, the house noises stopped. I concluded that the poor creature had finally left. I worked on, unaware of the passage of time. As morning turned into afternoon and afternoon, itself, was waning, Edward and Ed came home. I told them what had happened and showed them the small pile of feathers and the droppings, which I had kept as evidence, fearing they would never believe such a bizarre tale. I assured them that the duck had made no sounds for hours and that it must have escaped through the front door. Checking things out on their own, they opened the study door, with Dynamite in tow. Suddenly, all hell broke loose. The duck, still there, had been hiding. It had perched up atop some tall barrister bookcases, behind a row of books. It panicked at the intrusion and took flight. Ed, then four years old, squealed with delight, while Dynamite jumped madly onto all the furniture, sending the sofa cushions flying. Edward flailed his arms, shouted, and managed to flush the duck out the front door. Everyone was thrilled, Ed and Dynamite with the whole adventure, Edward that the duck was safe and sound. Everybody except me. I shrugged my shoulders, tucked my work in for the night, and dragged myself to the kitchen to start supper. We saw "our" duck fly by many times after that; apparently it had a nest on a nearby pond. It kept to its high flight pattern, though, and never again took a tornado-induced detour down our chimney.

But other critters did drop in from time to time. One summer night as Edward and I slept we felt a sensation, really just a slight hint of movement, pass over our feet. We both woke up, but nothing seemed awry. The same thing happened the next night, but we were more alert this time. We spotted a flying squirrel. Ever gentle and respectful, Edward ushered it out. There were no more for many years.

One night, however, when Edward lay very ill, Mary discovered another flying squirrel in her bedroom. Ed had come home to be with us during this painful time, thank goodness. He assured me that he and Mary would take care of the situation and guided me out of her room. I'm not sure exactly what they did, but it involved excited noises, a broom and the curtains. They were confident that they had resolved the squirrel problem.

A few nights after Edward died, I again felt the same whisper of something moving over my feet, again not really touching them. It was unmistakable. I knew that a flying squirrel was back. In the middle of the next night I was awakened by our schnauzer, Kati, with her toenails clickity-clicking on the hardwood floors, running from room to room. In our study-turned-bedroom where I was still sleeping, she held sentry in front of a bookcase so low to the floor that she couldn't get under it. She literally "dogged" the hapless creature who dashed madly away, down the hall toward the kitchen. Kati took the challenge and threw herself into the chase. Shortly after, she calmly returned to my room and settled down on her dog mat near the bed. The following morning I found the squirrel's lifeless body in the butler's pantry between the kitchen and the dining room. Kati had snapped its neck, clean and quick.

I was relieved that the squirrel intruder was disposed of so efficiently. Problem put to rest--except the next night Kati clicked her paws around again, running about all night long. This time her stalking lacked focus and she dashed from room to room. Neither of us could settle down. The next morning I called Merritt Segars, our friend and knight in shining armor, though he hardly looked the part. He was a ruddy-faced country farmer, a salt-of-the-earth man, who took on heroic proportions when we ladies were in distress. Merritt investigated and discovered that the mother squirrel had come down the chimney in Mary's room. When Ed and Mary thought they had scared her off, she had merely burrowed down in a nest of dirty laundry. There were at least three babies, which explained Kati's seemingly random chase, a busy night trying to herd all three. Merritt wryly observed that Mary's room was such a mess that, if he were a wild creature, he would have made a nest there, too. Mary was a teenager and, like her brother and sister before her, actually prided herself on her unkempt bedroom. Edward used to say that teen age was temporary insanity, and this was a case in point. We were grateful to Merritt, and he was grateful to us. His pet snake was hungry.

A bat found its way inside one night. Where it came from, how it got in, I don't know. As I remember, Edward put a glass jar over it and eased it into the jar with a piece of cardboard, then released it outside. Bats are totally nocturnal and very docile during the day, so there was no problem in collecting it—or at least no problem for *Edward* to collect it. Awake or asleep, bats are not my favorite creatures. When we were in the pool at night, a bat or two would occasionally swoop down to take a drink. I didn't like that at all, though Edward assured me that bats have such good radar they would never bump into us. They were just thirsty. I didn't like sharing the pool with anyone when the two of us swam together at night, *au naturel*, not children, not friends, not dogs, and certainly not bats!

I doubt that there is a single house in the country without an occasional mouse, despite the ubiquitous yard cats. Even in the local breakfast and "meat 'n three" eatery on the square, Edward and I were having a ham biscuit one morning when we spied a mouse nervously running back and forth along the wall. A respecter of all creatures, Edward calmly went to the door, pushed it open, and let the mouse out, just as if he had opened the door for a well-bred lady. I doubt that any of the other customers even saw him. Although we had our share of mice over the years, Edward always managed to take care of them. Gentle as he was, he finally resorted to setting out traps.

After Edward died, Merritt "mouse proofed" our house. Despite our best efforts, however, a mouse invaded. I didn't want to kill him, conjuring up the images of Neil's tale of my grandmother's mouse-slaughtering scene. I didn't have the stomach for such things. I bought a trap that would catch it alive. Placing a generous smear of peanut butter inside, I set it up under the kitchen sink. The instructions explained that the mouse would enter, tripping the trap door, and would be contained inside without being injured. Surely enough, the trap worked and the mouse was captured alive, though agitated. He was well nourished, thanks to the generous serving of peanut butter, as healthy for rodents as for children. Foolishly, I had not anticipated step two: what to do next.

I reasoned that letting him go in the yard would be self-defeating, as he would soon sneak back in. I was reluctant to put him into the car. So I walked about a half of a mile down the Booger Hill Road. I was aware of what a ridiculous sight I was, trudging along in shorts and bright yellow latex gloves, holding a mouse cage as far away from my body as my arm could stretch. My rather paranoid mind started playing tricks, though my brain knew better. I fantasized that the mouse was plotting his revenge. I envisioned his hurling himself on me with his sharp claws and teeth as soon as I released him. The further I walked, the more real this vicious attack became and the larger the mouse grew. I mustered up my courage and set the cage down, with the door facing the woods. I released the latch and prepared to run for my life. The poor mouse was stupefied with fear, even more so than I, and I actually had to pick the back end of the cage up and slide him out. I grabbed the empty cage, but didn't stick around to see if he recovered from his trauma, as I was too occupied in recovering from my own.

As I walked the half-mile back home that morning, the thoughts of returning to the city began germinating in the dark recesses of my mind. Challenges of mice and bats and wild ducks, all of which we had conquered with such gusto before, had lost their luster and appeal. I slowed my gait and wearily realized that, without Edward, I had once again become faint of heart.

AN EVENING AT THE J & J

The J & J Center was the Mecca for rednecks. It featured such artists as Conway Twitty and Ivory Jack. It hosted line dancing to the strains of Billy Ray Cyrus. In addition to honky-tonk music and a large bar, it sported a room full of slot machines and a couple of electric bulls. It was also the venue for rastling matches, a favorite yokel obsession. Rastling should not be confused with the (finer?) art of authentic wrestling. It is far more theatrical, more animated, and assuredly more vocal. It lacks even a tiny iota of finesse.

In his elementary school days, Ed was a huge rastlin' fan. God knows how his interest was piqued, probably through the other kids, but his young days revolved around Ricky Flair, Rick "the hammer" Valentine, Dusty Rhodes, Wahoo McDaniels, and the imposing Andre the Giant. These rastlers became household names and real personalities, in much the same way that his grandmother Daisy had regarded the performers at the Grand Ole Opry. Living in Nashville, she and her friends gossiped about the Opry people as if they were family and even rode en masse to "spectate" at their funerals. It was reputed that Papa Krickel had one time dated Minnie Pearl, whose signature was the price tag always dangling from her fancy straw hats.

Although I knew that most of the rastlin' matches, which came on television every Saturday morning, were faked and the outcomes rigged, I could not help but cringe at their raw brutality. The rastlers grunted, groaned, and yelled as they threw themselves onto the mat or catapulted from the ropes around the ring. They sputtered in the throes of a choke hold; they grimaced in pain from arm locks and leg locks. God only knows what long-term effects resulted from the stress on their bones and joints, not to mention the repeated blows to their heads. I have the unhappy notion that they obliterated the *sapiens* part of their genus, whatever was there in the first place.

Their costumes were equally absurd, from the skimpy tight shorts to muscle tee shirts, wide capes, and even, occasionally, masks. Mr. Wrestling #1 wore a solid white mask, while Mr. Wrestling #2 wore a white mask with a black stripe. Part of their schtick was their opponents' attempts to unmask them. I don't remember that they ever did. The current champion, the champion "du jour," sported a wide black belt and an enormous buckle, with a copious layer of his belly-fat drooping over it. Most amazing of all was Johnny Weaver whose special move was called "the sleeper." In a reverse choke hold, he cut off the windpipe of his opponent, leaving him gasping for breath. After a few seconds, his victim passed out. Johnny then slapped him into consciousness, and the match carried on. Ed was enthralled.

Like the rest of our family, Ed was not the most agile of people. He had broken his arms four times by the time he finished grade school and had had so many other injuries that we started alternating emergency rooms. When he was about eight, I, the scout den mother, had taken the troop to the elementary school playground. There was a huge sixteen-foot antique slide there, which had several waves on the way down and waist-high bars on either side of the top. I was talking with one of the fathers about my liability as a scout leader, when out of the corner of my eye I saw Ed plummeting through the air. He landed, thud, at my side, a flip worthy of even the best rastler on the circuit. He had attempted a somersault on the bars at the top of the slide that went miserably awry. I was horrified as he lay motionless and speechless on the ground. We called the ambulance and the EMTs loaded him up on a board. I directed the driver to Athens General, as we had visited St. Mary's only a few weeks earlier.

Ed was very fortunate. First of all, he had missed the concrete support slab by only inches, hitting the soft, forgiving ground. In addition, he landed on his entire side, not at an angle or on one specific bone. Nothing was crushed, nothing was even broken this time, and he ended up with only massive bruises. His whole left side was black from his ankle to his shoulder. In considerable discomfort, he was totally immobilized for nearly a week. Back home, we set up the sleeper sofa in the playroom, and he lay there hour after hour watching TV. Usually a highly active child, he was bored lying on his side all day and night. We kept him company as best we could. Saturday morning after this latest accident, he was particularly bleak. He begged me to watch the rastling match with him. I stretched out on the sofa bed, too, prepared to make it through the taunts, grunts, groans, shouts, leaps, and choke holds.

I was unimpressed with the massive, sweating, and I supposed smelly, hulks posturing around the ring. I yawned and shifted my position. My thoughts turned elsewhere. My boredom was suddenly interrupted when, for real, on live television, with Ed and me stretched out on the sofa watching, Rick "the hammer" Valentine broke Wahoo McDaniels' leg. I was aghast. That was too, too much. From then on out Ed was on his own when rastlin' matches were on. I imagine Ed's injuries healed more quickly than Wahoo's, though Wahoo did resume his career some months later.

Ed was as active mentally as he was physically, very intelligent, with a quick, keen sense of humor. Those are wonderful qualities, no doubt about it, but they didn't always stand him in good stead in the classroom. It didn't help, either, that we encouraged all our children to voice their opinions. While that was fine at home with just a couple of highly opinioned "experts" to contend with, it didn't work so well in the classroom.

Third grade, the year of the slide dive, was particularly trying. His teacher was Louise Jordan, a highly unattractive, unimaginative spinster, the daughter of a Pentecostal preacher. If her mind had been as expansive as her waistline, she would have been a more tolerant teacher and, in my opinion, a better person. The only thing that she was really noted for is playing the "Holiness piano," trilling up and down the keyboard with a grand flourish. I do give her credit for that. She was spectacular. Miss Jordan and Ed had, at best, an uneasy relationship. Ed has recently confided in me that she paddled him every single day. He wasn't really complaining, just reporting, as I'm sure he knows that he provoked every lick. A crisis arose in the spring. I can't remember exactly what happened, but the teacher-student situation took on enormously contentious proportions. I do remember telling Ed that I thought he had a good point and was sympathetic to his case, but that Miss Jordan was the teacher and he simply had to do what she said. As the reward, if he could "keep his nose clean" for the rest of the year, we would let him do something special that summer, something of his very own choosing. Without missing a beat he said that he wanted to go to a rastling match. I told him that his father would take him.

Ed behaved. I fretted. I knew that I had to make good on my bargain, but I couldn't envision my dignified husband in the midst of such crudity. I fretted some more. The only conclusion, I decided, was that I go along, too. Putting the matter off as long as I could, I finally called the J & J Center and made reservations. We arrived at the parking lot jammed with dusty, unwashed, battered-up cars and pickups proudly fitted out with gun racks. Making our way guardedly to the ticket window, I gave them our names and announced that I had made reservations. They guffawed, took my money, and gave me the tickets. (Apparently one didn't usually make reservations at the J & J.) We elbowed our way into the huge auditorium trying to blend in with the regulars.

I could never, ever have imagined such a throng of humanity! Where in the world had they all come from? A good many, I suppose, had migrated from Georgia's largest flea market, also called the J & J, a mile or two down the road. Halfway between the Center and the flea market is an eatery which boasts "the best food in Athens," interesting enough in itself, as it's not really in Athens at all. Off-putting, too, is the port-a-potty business next door, which has twenty-five or thirty bright red potty booths in the yard, ready to be rented, which is not exactly a come-on for lunch. One of my favorite touches in the neighborhood is what I refer to as the "recumbent Jesus." There was, quite literally, a statue of Jesus resting on his back on top of a mailbox, stretched out the entire length, with his feet nearly touching the mailbox door. He had on a beautiful bright blue gown, which could be seen from some distance away. When I drove closer, I saw that his blue gown matched his eyes perfectly. A lovely fair-skinned, blue-eyed Arab.

Back to the J & J, I felt intensely ill at ease. Edward, unflappable as always, directed us to our seats with the same ease he would have used at a chamber music concert. I surveyed the crowd. A policeman was positioned at each corner of the ring. All four faced the seats, not the wrestling mat, and constantly scanned the audience, like the secret service men do when the president is speaking. From the bar people returned, jostling each other and spilling beer from their oversized paper cups. The whole place felt sticky, sticky with beer and sticky, too, with human sweat, both accumulated over time. I observed that we were the only ones there with a full set of front teeth. Many of the women, dolled up in bright red lipstick and dark black mascara, wore tight cotton halter tops. Little round bubbles of breasts peeped out. This was the 1970s, before breast enhancement and spandex had caught on big. These ladies were really noticeable, standing out even in such a rough crowd.

Finally, with a great deal of whoop-la, our rastlers made their entrance. They were preceded by a couple of dour-looking cops and followed by their worshipping minions. The crowd cheered one and booed the other. Passionately. On the "programme" that night were Tommy "Wildfire" Rich and Tony Atlas, a black body builder. They were both on the Atlanta Circuit.

They threw off their robes and capes, and the struggle began. The live match was anti-climactic, if not downright boring. It lacked the exaggerated sound effects of a television production, no thumps and thuds of bodies hitting the mats. The grunts and groans were muted without microphones and were lost in the expanse of the large auditorium. The rastlers were just hulks hurling themselves and each other around the ring, then strutting about like peacocks. I was much more interested in the spectators, who were far more animated that the rastlers, jumping up and down, shouting things like "kill him" and "gouge his eyes out." Except for them, it would have been yet another long evening.

I was relieved to get in our little white Volkswagen, which had turned pink from the dust of the red Georgia clay and whose back window was too small to hold a gun rack. As we headed home, I consoled myself that I had braved a real live rastlin' match, with honor and virtue intact, and, what's more, that at least nobody broke anyone else's leg. A couple of years later, Edward and Ed went back to another match, this time seeing the famed Andre the Giant. I didn't feel the urge for a return trip; it would have been too much of a good thing.

THE CURSE ON MISS BERTHA'S HOUSE

Our house was situated on the corner of Highway 29 and the Booger Hill Road, up at the top of the hill. Our only close neighbors lived in a house at the bottom of our driveway which faced the Booger Hill Road. In fact, it more than "faced" the road, it was so close that the front door was a matter of yards from the traffic.

When we first moved in, Miss Bertha Sorrells still lived there, with her son Will Jr. Miss Bertha's husband, Will Sorrells Sr., had started building the house in about 1919, just before Mr. Rufus Sorrells had our house built. Unfortunately Mr. Will died before the house was finished, and several tragedies, both personal and financial, befell the family. The house was never finished, and the locals concluded that both the family and the house were cursed. This so-called "curse" loomed heavy and lasted long.

Though the downstairs had some nice features, like the tongue-and-groove walls and gorgeous heart-of-pine floors, the upstairs was merely studded in, with no walls at all. Times had gotten progressively worse for Miss Bertha, after the simultaneous death of her husband and the bankrupting invasion of the boll weevil. By the time we moved in, the large house was in shambles. The original tall wooden columns lay decaying in the back barn, and in their place stood two stacks of rectangular concrete blocks, ugly and incongruent with the two-story clapboard façade. The front porch, itself, was barely visible, except for a small portion in the middle, from which the monstrous concrete columns had been constructed to hold up the roof.

The sides and back of the house were inaccessible. Weeds, unchecked privet bushes, and volunteer brush of various sorts grew harum-scarum up to the very foundation, and wild vines snaked up the clapboard sides of the house, a weathered gray structure which had never enjoyed the stroke of a paintbrush. One could literally not see the side or the back doors, so dense was the foliage smothering three sides of the house. It blended in with the rest of the woods.

Miss Bertha herself was straight out of a Faulkner novel. Every morning, wearing a tattered housedress, she faithfully swept with her worn-out broom whatever was left of the front porch. She conducted herself with great dignity, indifferent to the shabbiness, always wearing two large diamond solitaires in her ear lobes. She was a nice lady, and we chatted from time to time. More than once, I apologized for our Lab, who investigated her yard every day after supper, but she claimed that she loved dogs and was happy for him to visit. She was very gracious.

Miss Bertha died and Will Jr., unable to care for himself, went to live in a "facility." When I went into the house, I was appalled and sad to see the conditions in which they had been living. They used just a few rooms, a small one, eight by twelve, in the back of the house. The ashes from the fireplace spilled onto the floor, nearly reaching the middle of the tiny room. I guess that they, Miss Bertha and Will, merely walked around them. Along the wall was a single cot where Will slept.

The only other occupied room was in the back, on the west side, and that was Miss Bertha's bedroom. It was large enough to accommodate a wooden cook stove, whose metal vent exited through a window. So this enormous house, whose upstairs hall could easily have housed a bowling alley, was reduced to two barely livable rooms, two rooms and an immaculately swept front porch.

Miss Bertha's family sold the big house, the curse included. It lived on, as the subsequent owners suffered divorces, miscarriages, business failures, bankruptcies, and even a suicide. I enjoyed the neighbors while they were there, though no one stayed for more than a couple of years. Alf, a professor in history at UGA, who recovered the house from the strangling weeds and vines and constructed the cement block columns, and his wife Carol, the most self-centered woman I've ever met, who locked her toddlers out of the house so that she could take a nap. Pat, an unstable nurse, and her husband, Charles, a genial hospital administrator. Sharon, who was always on the verge of making millions, though spiraling madly into bankruptcy, and her vain, not-so-bright second husband, Marty. Richard, a brilliant biochemist and his wife Sandy, patient, accepting, yet strong when tested, a veritable Penelope on the Booger Hill Road, staying the course at home while her extraordinary Odysseus travelled the globe. Rick, a lawyer, and Karen, who had stared down a would-be robber, wrestled goats to the ground, spun and wove wool from her very own goats, all while house breaking two Great Danes and a Vietnamese pot-bellied pig. And last, a young couple, who lived the high life on borrowed money and lived through the horror of the young husband's suicide.

They were the last neighbors I had. I moved to Athens within a year, though for reasons unrelated to anyone in Danielsville. After I left, Miss Bertha's house was first turned into a restaurant, the

"Georgiana." The restaurant venture failed. Next, a bunch of verifiable loonies moved in. Their plan was to house troubled teens on the second floor and to rent out the first floor for weddings and parties. Apparently it had not occurred to them that there might be a problem with what to do with the "troubled" kids when an "untroubled" wedding was taking place. Send them off? Tie them up? Bind their mouths with duct tape? The county refused to issue them a permit.

I'm not sure what the state of Miss Bertha's house is now. I have long since moved, and I have the memories of what was, not bothering about what is and what will be.

Life on the Farm

Edward aspired to be a gentleman farmer. He managed the gentleman part well, though he never quite caught on to the other.

He had always been both a lover of nature and a lover of literature. So when he entered the doctoral program at Vanderbilt after World War II, he found kindred spirits. Vanderbilt was the center of the Agrarian Movement, which had been established in the late '40s and early '50s. Basically, these teachers and writers, who referred to themselves as "The Fugitive Poets," urged a return to rural life and basic values, a Southern Renaissance. They eschewed the modern, especially industrialism, and took refuge in the past. They were passionate and talented, but, as far as I can tell, their pens were more prolific than their plows. In my opinion, though they would be horrified to hear me say it, they held some of the same positions as the Amish, though most of the Agrarians, except for Andrew Lytle, were content with philosophizing and writing rather than actually tending the soil. They fashioned words, not crops or furniture. Leaving their axes idle, they were armchair Luddites. Edward thrived in the Vanderbilt atmosphere. The influence of his professors and the friendships of fellow students made a lasting impact on his life. They reinforced his natural leanings and defined him and his philosophical path.

Having a little subsistence farm was a dream for him, and he longed to "return to nature." It was hardly a dream of mine. My childhood had not exactly been filled with the mysteries of the natural world. Other than the year we lived on White Bluff Road, which was a desperate time in our family's life, my acquaintance with nature's wonders was highly limited. I knew the names of a few trees and several flowers, but nothing much else. Pines were obvious, as were oak trees, and crepe myrtles were fun to climb. I loved wisteria vines, especially in our yard on White Bluff Road, where we children competed with lizards as we scrambled up the giant oak. There was a vine on 46th Street, too, that we used to scale, swinging out to the edge of Crescent Circle. So, although I was aware of a couple of trees, I never really knew, nor thought much about them. I had an oft-held urban notion that, although we might use the other creations of God's domain, we were inherently removed and superior.

Other than humans and our dog Lassie, I was fairly oblivious to the rest of the world. I knew palmetto bugs, a euphemism for the gigantic roaches which scurried in profusion along the sidewalks in Savannah at night. I tickled roly-poly bugs into little round balls. I caught lightning bugs. I stirred up the tiny inverted pyramids which we found by the hundreds under porches and houses, singing the chant, "Ladybug, ladybug, fly away home, your house is on fire and your children are gone." But it was all a great deception, as no ladybugs ever flew out. I doubt seriously that they were ladybug homes in the first place. It was merely something to keep us children busy— and outside. Nature's creatures existed solely for my entertainment.

I wasn't particularly fearful, as I picked up the caterpillars from the neighbor's Catawba tree, I grabbed lizards by the tail whenever I could catch them, and I played with fiddler crabs in the marsh grass along the brackish creeks, with a masochistic delight at the sting of their little pinchers. I taunted large red ants as they crawled along the wooden steps on Hall Street. Those were childhood preoccupations, and my innocence and natural acceptance of the world diminished as "…down [I] forgot as up [I] grew…." I assumed the comfortable disdain of dirty things, like bugs and earth and everything else that was not just like myself. I had a lot to learn.

I had never even heard of the Agrarians before I married Edward. But I quickly became sympathetic to the cause, or some of their tenets at any rate. After all, Edward was so taken with the movement, and anything he admired I automatically held in high esteem. I got caught up with the idea of moving back to the earth, or, in my case, more precisely moving to the earth in the first place.

I was as avid as I was ignorant. The truth is that I was madly in love, a one-woman groupie. In my mind, Edward's knowledge had no bounds, and his opinions left no need for opposition. The sole purpose of my life was to please him, and my devotion had no rational boundaries. Whatever he wanted was wisest and best, irrefutably. Everything he did and said was superior, and I wanted very much to please him. I even pondered the jeopardy that my soul was in if I was expected to love anyone, mortal or divine, more than I loved Edward. I couldn't imagine it.

When he talked about wanting a little farm, I devoted all my attention and energy to making his dream my dream and to making it come true. I dug a modest flower garden and tended to it, working every day. While I was pulling weeds, Edward read books about farming and sent in a subscription to the *Dairy Goat Journal*, which, by the way, arrived the same day as *Opera News*, all from the comfort of his armchair in the den. So intent with what I was doing, the implications never sank in.

The Lady of Booger Hill

We moved to our house on Booger Hill Road when Ed was two, so both Liz and Mary were born when we lived there. It was, in every sense, our family home. We flung ourselves headlong into the rural life. Before long, we had dogs, cats, a pony, milk goats, and chickens, even bees. Largely, we lived off the land, as people say, going to the grocery store only about every six weeks. We gathered wild blueberries, called huckleberries, and wild strawberries, little tiny strawberries which were incredibly sweet, as well as blackberries and several varieties of wild plums. I made jams and jellies with them, and even a couple of times we made wine. We grew a few crops, mostly lettuce, herbs, and tomatoes, a little salad garden, but mainly we bought our vegetables from the locals, a bushel at the time, which we then "put up." We either drove to the mountains in the fall for apples or we bought them from Mr. Laierd's truck in Royston. We, or more correctly I, canned, froze, pickled and preserved most of our food. We took to drying some things like apples and bananas. We bought half a cow, not literally of course. Even Madison County didn't have half cows limping around. We would order a cow from the abattoir, already slaughtered and dressed, and we would split all the meat with a friend, dividing it half and half. Therefore, we had beef, as well as chicken. We bought locally produced sausage and "fresh" cow's milk (before we had our own goats), which means unpasteurized, with its thick cream nearly halfway down the jar. We skimmed the lovely cream off the top and whipped it into soft clouds for our strawberries. We had a flock of chickens, and, for a time, a hive of bees. It was hard work but we thrived. Edward was pleased and proud, and I glowed.

Our own family grew. I had babies, and the dog had puppies. The hens hatched out a flock of chicks. The yard cats multiplied. Big Mama bore kids. The freezer and the extra refrigerator on the back porch were well stocked. The pantry shelves were lined with jars of colorful fruits and vegetables. At one point we walked from room to room, each with its own fragrance, slightly pungent cheese aging in the pantry, sauerkraut soaking in a pottery bowl in the kitchen, and wine quietly fermenting in the dining room.

My sewing machine whirred, as I made many of our clothes, from underwear and lingerie to dresses, play clothes, bathing suits, and even Sunday suits. I created sundresses with little butterflies and diaphanous wings, a trick that I learned from my Athens Tech "machine embroidery" class. I created a suede jacket for Ed with fringe on the cuffs and the bottom, and in a v-pattern on the back. It had real mother-of-pearl buttons on the front and on the cuff, attached with a "stapler-type" grommet setter. Edward wore a handmade silk bathrobe with a navy blue paisley print. Homemade draperies hugged the windows, curtains fluttered in the kitchen and matching placemats lay on the table, a handmade bedspread and a quilt lay on the bed. The days were hot and busy and the nights were cool and delicious. All was well with the world.

Black Berries and Green Cheese

We had lots of fun "living off the land." Edward and I, by ourselves at first, and later with the children, gathered wild fruits and berries. I remember the first summer after we were married, I gathered, solo, little teeny, tiny strawberries, about the size of very small peas, and made strawberry shortcake. The berries grew alongside the road down to Dr. Bond's house, the place we lived for the first four years of our marriage. It took me several hours to pick a mere cupful, but the result was wonderful. The tiny strawberries were naturally so sweet that they needed no sugar at all. It's strange, too, as that was the only year that the crop appeared. Perhaps weed killers were sprayed on the nearby field, or perhaps the weather conditions were never quite the same; perhaps it was the magic of honeymooners. It was a one-time glory.

The Lady of Booger Hill

We picked wild blackberries and wild plums. One time we came across an apple tree way out in the woods. We parked the VW bug on the side of the road and went to gather the ripe fruit. The tree was so full of red apples that it looked like it might collapse on itself. We figured that we would do what we could to lighten its load. Harold Wilson, who was to become Ed's godfather, was visiting us at the time, and he scaled the tree to shake the apples from the branches. We loaded up our gathered treasure and set out home. As we rounded the next curve on the isolated dirt road, we were ashamed and embarrassed. Within a matter of fifty yards there stood a house, undeniably the owners of "our" apple tree. We thought that we were in the middle of nowhere, when in fact we were virtually in someone's back yard. We felt terrible, but we didn't even stop. There were still lots of apples on the tree, we rationalized, as we slunk off toward the afternoon sun, feeling like the thieves that we actually were.

Our blackberry outings were fun. We learned to wear long sleeves and long pants and to spray ourselves with repellent, especially our ankles, wrists, and around our waistbands. We wore good, sturdy shoes. Dressed in that way, we were thorn proof and avoided being "chigger bait." I always "stirred up the bushes" ahead of time with a stick, flushing out any snakes and other creatures which might surprise me. Not Edward, though. He was probably more sympathetic to insects and even wild animals than to his stick-wielding wife. We picked buckets and buckets full. I made scores of pies and many jars of jelly, stocking the pantry and the freezer for winter. We even made blackberry wine. Plum wine and wild grape, too.

Our dogs went with us, and the children, too, as our family expanded. The Labs were unfailingly happy and exuberant. One afternoon, as Ed was toddling along a country, berry-lined road, Danny Boy ran into him full steam, and Ed was catapulted into the air as if shot by a cannon. I'm sure it was not intentional, and Ed picked himself up laughing. He was an easy-going, fun-loving little boy, rarely daunted by anything. Another hot summer afternoon when Liz was a baby, Ed pushed her up and down a red, dusty road while we picked berries, the bushes so heavily laden that they bent nearly in half at the edge of the road. Liz cried out in sudden shrieks. Her brother had upended her stroller in the ditch. We rescued her, she more indignant and dusty than actually wounded. We had to presume this was unintentional on Ed's part, though I'm not certain, because he was as mischievous as he was fun-loving. I'm surer that Danny Boy's intentions were purer than my impish little son's.

The next year we took Ed and Liz, by now just past the toddler stage, on an early summer foraging trip. The juiciest berries we found were in a thicket of dense briars. Thinking that the children were too young to brave the thorns, we plunked them down in a nearby huckleberry patch. Huckleberries are wild blueberries, very small and very sweet, and they grow low to the ground. Also, they have no thorns. The children happily bent down with their pails, and we cheerfully picked our blackberries down the road. We heard no fussing, and we figured everything was all right. We even picked longer than usual. With our buckets full, we went to collect the children, wondering if they had actually gathered any little berries in their small pails or had merely run around tromping down the bushes. Right on the edge of the patch, stretched out the entire length of it, was a long, long black snake. The children had been unaware of him (Isn't it interesting that we refer to a snake usually if not always as "him," echoes from Eden?), and he apparently had remained undisturbed by the children. He might as well have been babysitting. All safe, we headed home with a lot of blackberries and a few huckleberries, leaving the snake to gather his lunch in peace.

Wild plums were both orange and yellow. The yellow ones were sweeter to the taste, but they lacked the sharpness of the orange ones and their jelly was insipid. Occasionally we found crabapples, and crabapple jelly was one of my favorites, tastier than just plain apple jelly, with a rich, clear red hue. When we had peaches I made pies and peach/orange marmalade, which I much preferred to plain peach jam. We gathered pears, picking them from the trees before they ripened, fell from their limbs, and became bruised. I'd wrap each one in newspaper, and store them in a cool dark place, single layers, to ripen. Often I put them underneath the bed in the downstairs guest room, which was on the "cool side" of the house. The wood floors never got really hot.

We had a huge fig bush right outside our kitchen window. It bore prodigiously, doubtless due to the fact that it was right above the grease trap. Notwithstanding, the figs were the small Brown Turkey variety and were delicious. We dried some and I made preserves out of others. Edward even managed to make one batch himself. We ate them fresh and gave plenty away.

We did everything imaginable with tomatoes. I made ketchup, chili sauce, tomato juice. I froze whole tomatoes. I canned stewed tomatoes. But the best thing of all was what I grew up calling "gumbo," but which in north Georgia is referred to as "soup mix," made with fresh tomatoes, young, tender corn, sweet baby butterbeans and that unique Southern delectation, okra. Even though I'm citified now, I still make soup mix, though most often not entirely with fresh veggies. We picked muscadines, but I never acquired a taste for these wild grapes, though Edward did and so did Danny Boy, who followed Edward around faithfully and mimicked whatever he did.

With our goat milk abundant, we made lots of homemade dairy products. We churned ice cream, using vanilla and fresh fruit. We bought a Salton yogurt maker, and Ed and Mary both had winning 4-H projects making homemade yogurt. Mary included in her demonstration a recipe for yogurt and cucumber soup, and she was a state winner in the Dairy Foods Competition. I made cottage cheese, the long process without rennet. I heated the milk, added a starter of buttermilk, and let it set for fifteen hours or longer. After the curd had separated from the whey, called by Southerners "blue john," I cut the curd into pieces and strained it through my cheesecloth. I solved my puzzlement about Little Miss Muppet who sat "eating her curds and whey." As a child it sounded mysteriously exotic to me, but she was merely eating cottage cheese and blue john.

I even tried my hand at making cheese. I used colored rennet tablets to shorten the process and to make the cheese yellow. I was surprised to learn that making cheese is merely one step further from cottage cheese. This time, after I gathered the curds up in a ball in my cheesecloth, I squeezed the cloth extra hard to get all the whey out. I rolled the cheesecloth firmly around the ball of curds and then put it in the handmade cheese press that Edward's father had made me out of a large tin can. I placed it on the pantry floor and for weights I used a full can of paint and some bricks. I had to wait for several months for the individual curds to compress into a smooth lump of cheese and for the cheese, itself, to age. It turned out well.

I had always thought it bizarre to refer to the moon as looking like "green cheese." I had eyes, and the moon was *not* green. But when I gathered the curds up into a round lump before placing them into the press, I suddenly realized that "green" referred to being unripe, not to being colored! If left in its natural state, the ball of milk solid looks just like the full moon on a clear night. I learned as much living on the farm as I did from my books, or nearly.

Because we were fairly isolated and wanted to be fully independent, we spent our early lives together with not much adaptation to the outside world. When spring came, we refused to change to "Daylight Savings Time" as everybody else had done. We kept to what we laughingly referred to as "God's Time." We didn't have television to confuse us, and we left at 6:30 in the morning to make our 8:00 classes. That was all right with me, as I don't wake up until 10:00 am, no matter what time I get out of bed. The nice thing was that we left Athens every day at noon, but arrived home at 11:30. We loved it, with some of the morning left for ourselves. It was as if we played a private little trick on the whole world every day.

We all cooked. The notion of "fast food" didn't enter our minds, even at our own house. When I made pumpkin pies, I started off with a real pumpkin. Edward would halve it, and I removed the seeds and toasted them. I steamed the fresh pumpkin flesh and mashed it up. We recycled the leftover skin in the compost heap. I made my own pie crusts and baked cakes and cookies from scratch. We ordered large tins of loose tea and brewed without the convenience of a tea bag. We soaked all our dried beans overnight. We used a meat grinder. I bought a ricer to make the applesauce. I made apple butter in the Crock Pot. I had two big canning pots, an extra refrigerator and a full-sized freezer on the back porch. I conscientiously spared my children such things as Hamburger Helper, which they "discovered" at some friends' houses. They proclaimed it the best thing they'd ever eaten. So much for my labor.

Edward's main contribution was making our bread. There was no such thing as a bread machine at our house, and he was a purist. He bought cake yeast from the A & A Bakery on Lumpkin Street in Athens, convinced that it was far superior to the powdered envelopes at the grocery store. He had a half-dozen bread cookbooks and used dozens of recipes. Through the mail, he ordered rice flour, dark rye, light rye, whole wheat, high-gluten, and low-gluten. He ground oats for oat flour. He baked breads of all kinds, adding a variety of seeds. My favorite of all was Anadama bread, made with flour, a little cornmeal and molasses. Or maybe it was his oatmeal bread, which had such crunchy crusts. Or maybe it was Italian, made with a special

Pyrex cylinder so that it was perfectly round and crusty on all sides. He made rolls, though he claimed that his hand was "too heavy" to make really good rolls. He baked hot-cross buns at Easter, stollens at Christmas, scones for a special treat. He tried his hand at bagels, which have to be boiled before they are baked.

Every Saturday morning Edward would head to the kitchen, and the day-long process of bread baking began. The proofing of the yeast, the mixing of the flour, the rising, the "punching down," the rising again, the kneading, the next rising "just to be sure," and the final kneading. He placed the full bread pans on the flat hot-water heater in the corner of the kitchen. And, by later afternoon, the exquisite aroma of baked bread emanated from the oven and diffused throughout the rest of the house. It was such a delicious affair that I was hard pressed to point out that he had been so busy making bread that he'd not helped out with the weekly housework at all. As I say, Edward was always smarter than I.

Ed had never eaten "store bought" bread until he was in kindergarten. We were asked to bring ten peanut butter and jelly sandwiches to a picnic. Knowing what the little children would expect, I conceded and bought some bland pre-sliced "Wholesome Sunbeam" at Dills supermarket in Royston. Ed ate his first piece on the way home. It was the most delicious thing he had ever eaten and he demolished half a loaf by the time we arrived home from the grocery store. He referred to it after that as "that delicious Wholesome Sunbeam," and he was hooked.

Sometimes we made a "group pizza." We'd all go to the kitchen and, armed with a grater, a knife, or a frying pan, we'd have at it. Edward, of course, made the pizza dough. We'd chop, grate, peel, sauté, sprinkle, and drizzle. Our special touch was fennel seeds. The result was always an unmanageable slice of pizza which was so laden with cheeses, meats and vegetables that we'd have to eat it with a fork. We all ate supper with great gusto, and I pretended to be delighted, though, honestly, I wasn't too impressed with the conglomeration of heavy toppings, which soaked into the crust and made it soggy. I didn't subscribe to the notion that "more is better." I would have preferred a light, thin crust with a generous layer of pepperoni, a little sauce, and a sprinkle of cheese. But the end product was not as important as the process, which, as they say, was "quality time together." Inevitably all the enthusiastic little chefs quickly disappeared, sneaking noiselessly away like the morning sun burning away the fog, as soon as the last slice was eaten. I was left alone with my serious indigestion and an indescribably messy kitchen.

MEETING BIG MAMA

The first milk goat we bought was already named "Big Mama," and it doesn't take a real stretch of imagination to know why. She was a very well-endowed Nubian goat, who had a gentle nature and a very kind face. Nubians are an expensive variety of goat which produces a lot of milk, far different from the herds of scrub goats in the fields up and down the highway. She was nearly as tall as a deer and had a very distinctive head and face, with long droopy ears framing the sides of her head and a curved Roman nose. Edward had explained that we were more suited to having a goat than a cow, because cows require much more grazing land than goats, and our little farm was just shy of five acres. Cows generally produce several gallons of milk a day, and a goat gives only one gallon, which was sufficient for our family. So, Edward put up a fence (under my instructions, no less) and converted the two-seater outhouse into a goat parlor. Goats hate getting wet. We drove to a farm outside of Watkinsville and brought Big Mama home. I'm pretty sure that we were scammed and paid far too much for her, but we bought her nonetheless, and she became part of our family.

Goats are browsers, not grazers like cows. That means that they prefer green leaves and tender tree bark to grass. Big Mama decimated the unwanted privet bushes inside the pen, which was good, but she also stripped the bark from the two ancient plum trees and a couple of crabapples, which was a terrible disappointment. After all the bushes and small trees were eaten, Big Mama, and later her offspring, were thrilled when we lopped off some wisteria from the huge wisteria vine outside the back porch or some honeysuckle at the end of the field. Our goats always preferred to be hand fed, even though they had a regular good diet of Purina Dairy Goat Chow. People say that goats will eat anything, but to our experience, that is far from true. They are, in fact, extremely finicky. If we dropped succulent honeysuckle vines or a sprig of wisteria on the ground, even inside her pen, Big Mama would not even bend over to eat the leaves, but waited for us to stoop down and retrieve them for her. People also claim that goats eat tin cans, but that's really not true. They actually like only the sweet-tasting glue on the labels, never eating something so hard and indigestible as a can. Goats are much maligned.

Big Mama was a very good milk producer, and her one gallon a day was enough for our needs. Goat milk is different from cow milk in several ways. For one thing, it is much richer, much higher in cream content. In fact, when our goats "went dry" and we had to buy cow's milk from the grocery store, Ed and Liz complained that it was sour. The milk they were accustomed to was much sweeter. Goat milk is also naturally homogenized, so that the cream is mixed up with the milk, rather than rising to the top. That makes it easier for humans to digest, but it also means that we had no cream to whip. Separating machines are available, but too expensive for our small operation. We were never interested in selling our wares; they were for our consumption only. I couldn't make butter, which requires the fat milk be separated from the thin "blue john." I was able to make yogurt, cottage cheese, ice cream and even cheese.

It's also reputed that goat milk tastes bad, though goat cheese, on the contrary, has become a gourmet delight. Edward always maintained that the milk doesn't taste bad; it just tastes different from cow's milk, which most Americans drink. Actually, the majority of the world drinks goat milk, as goats are easier to maintain than cows. They not only require less space, but can live on poorer soil and can manage steep, rocky areas. Truth to tell, people drink milk from whatever source they have. Some people drink sheep milk, some even drink yak milk! (My clever daughter Mary once claimed that she was "yak-tose" intolerant.) Pig milk is supposed to be very sweet, though I wouldn't know and don't intend to find out.

Another reason that goat milk might have a strange taste is that goats, being browsers, tend to eat a greater variety of vegetation, not just grass. And whatever a mother animal eats naturally flavors her milk. Everybody knows that cow's milk can be really, really bad, undrinkable in fact, if the cow eats wild onions. But since we fed our goats commercial dairy goat chow, their diet was standard and their milk didn't vary in taste. Even so, I must admit that goat milk didn't taste like it came out of a carton from the grocery store.

Since we were determined to be self-sufficient, Edward cleverly suggested that we keep a good supply of chocolate- and strawberry-flavored Nestle's Quik on hand, and, whenever the children's friends came over, we'd simply offer them either chocolate or strawberry milk, not mentioning that it came from our goats. With a "quick" stir of flavoring, no one could tell the difference between the milk at our table and what they drank at home. Everyone was blissfully happy and ignorant.

Big Mama provided us with a bit of drama from time to time. Once when she was sick, I took her to the Comer vet, unfortunately by myself. We drove a tan, two-toned VW van, which had an aisle between the driver's and the front passenger's seats. She was apprehensive about riding in the van, so she came up to stand beside me, and we drove the eight miles from Danielsville to Comer, side by side, eyes straight ahead. When we got to the vet's, I went in to ask someone to help me get her inside. She was very strong, very stubborn, and I felt that she might not take well to a leash around her neck. I could envision myself being dragged along the highway, right there in broad daylight, my shoes making little furrows in the dusty shoulder.

While we were waiting for someone to come out, I put my arm around Big Mama's neck and stroked her gently. We had been sitting a little while when along came two men in a gray pickup truck. They glanced over our way. Their necks turned and their eyes stayed glued to me, that crazy woman in a hippie van who was hugging a goat. Their heads jerked back forward only after they drove off the road and barely escaped landing in the ditch.

Animals produce milk only for their babies, or so Mother Nature intended. When Big Mama "went dry," we set out to find a daddy goat, and in the process, discovered the source of another myth about goats: Supposedly they smell to high heaven. I remember when I lived in Savannah, there was a "goat man" who traveled around with his herd of goats, noisily ringing the bells around their necks. Later, when I taught at Emmanuel, the peripatetic group occasionally made their appearance down Highway 29. We knew when they were coming, not only from the clanging of the bells, but from the putrid, heavy musky odor which preceded them for half a mile at least. We could smell them long before we could see them.

I had experienced the goat man and the ghastly odor, yet our dignified lady goat smelled like a rose. I merely assumed that smelly goats were part of the unfounded myth and considered the possibility that maybe even the goat man's herd took on his sweaty, unwashed odor, not the other way around. The reality hit me, to my horror, when we took Big Mama to a nearby farm for her important date. When we stepped out of the VW van, we might as well have stepped out into the middle of the goat man's herd. The odor was rife. And so was her gentleman caller. It turns out that the putrid, nauseating musky odor comes from the male, particularly when he is rutting. That lubricious male goat (and I never even learned his name) dashed up to Big Mama and darted his tongue frenetically in and out like the repeated salvos of an automatic weapon or a snake exploring unfamiliar territory. Without any proper introduction, much less any foreplay, he discharged his duty in a hasty, lascivious manner. It was the most disgusting thing I've ever seen. I felt as if I had betrayed Big Mama. We had exposed our dignified lady goat to a grimy, smelly, lust-laden redneck of a buck. I have to admit that she didn't seem as offended as I was and she, as the saying goes, "stood for" the obnoxious creature, that "dirty old goat."

Five months later, Trixie was born. There is nothing, nothing cuter than a baby goat. Trixie's whole purpose in life was to amuse us! Up on top of the doghouse she jumped! Once she even balanced all four of her hooves on a single fence post. She cavorted constantly,

Ed with Big Mama and Trixie

with little or no provocation, just for the sport of it. She played with the children, just Ed and Liz at this time, racing up and down the pen. She overtook Liz at one point, and I heard Lizzie shouting out with indignation, though not pain. She was sprawled on the ground, face down, while Trixie was standing on top of her, all four hooves. The little goat was nibbling at Liz's beautiful blond (and apparently delicious) hair, doubtless attracted by the fruity shampoo which was in vogue then.

We really loved Trixie. She was irresistible. Since we wanted her to share Big Mama's copious output of milk, Edward took to milking Big Mama and then putting some of the milk in the fridge for us, as well as putting some in a bottle for Trixie. We had a special stainless steel milking bucket, which held about three gallons of milk. For safety and sterilization, it had no seams.

We bought bottles from the hardware store, and ordered goat-sized nipples. Edward, as agreed upon ahead of time, always did the actually milking of the goats. In fact, I never even learned how. I don't think that my puritan squeamishness would ever have allowed me to commit such an intimate act on a four-legged animal. I did feed the baby with the bottle, and she was precious. We became buddies.

One of the most horrible things that ever happened in my entire life concerned Trixie. Milk goat owners don't want their goats to have horns, for obvious reasons. And dehorning a goat can be costly. So, in our frugality, Edward and I decided to dehorn Trixie ourselves. If done at a young age, we were told, the procedure was fairly painless. We ordered the dehorning solution, and started to work. What a terrible mistake. For some reason, we thought that the mixture was a paste, but it turned out to be a liquid. Instead of covering only the small nub of the budding horns, it streamed down her face. She screamed in pain. We groaned in horror and dismay. The caustic solution burned her hair wherever it ran and made furrows down her face. Thank God, none of it went into her eyes! We daubed the liquid up as fast as we could, and the hair did grow back, so that we couldn't even tell that anything had ever happened. But the caustic that seared our minds burned for a long, long time. The idea that we had hurt something so playful, so gentle, and, what's more, so trusting, was awful. Edward was a mild, gentle soul and he was undone. Though not as kind and gentle as he, I was hysterical, my usual reaction to any unfortunate situation. Trixie, bless her heart, must have forgiven us, as she was soon enough running around performing her usual antics. She didn't seem to hold a grudge.

The next time Big Mama was bred (and I did not go this time), she had triplets. So there was triple the fun—and triple the trouble. Because of my teaching schedule, it fell to me to give bottles to the three new kids, Pipi, Heidi, and Bucky. As they were always eager and impatient at feeding time, I quickly learned how to hold three bottles at once, feeding them through the fence. No one was willing to be second in line. And Bucky was the worst of all. Invariably, in his gluttony, he would pull so hard that the nipple flew off and the milk spilled into the grass. So I had to go back inside, pour and warm up yet another bottle. Mind you, I was teaching at the time, so this chore was in addition to my already busy schedule. Every morning, since my class started later than Edward's, I warmed the milk and fed the babies, and every afternoon, still in my high heels and stockings, I dashed out into the backyard and fed them again.

As they grew up, our goats became increasingly hard to handle. It was a constant struggle to keep them in their pen. Goats have a keen intelligence and a strong urge for independence. They also have a sense of humor. Every time we'd repair part of the goat-damaged fence, they would find yet another way out, either over or through the wire. It was a game to them, and they were hell-bent on winning it. Some mornings I backed the Volkswagen Beetle out on my way to work, only to discover that the goats were out again, and I would herd them back into the pen, the car bolting erratically and maddeningly through the yard, the tinny beeps of the horn sounding the roundup. I'd return home in the afternoon to the same thing. At times they lumbered across the porch, thundering like a herd of wild horses. Back into the pen again. For a while at least. The game went on.

Our place was too small for the growing herd, so we sold the triplets, which was the plan from the beginning. We felt awfully guilty, as if we had sold off some of our children, and we missed them a lot. The new owner allowed us to visit. It's amazing how smart the kids were and what good memories they had, because for a long time we drove up to the fence of their very large pasture, full of many other goats, and called their names. They bounded up to the fence and allowed us to chat with them and to rub their long, Roman noses.

Sometimes I'd get my students going by telling them that we had run out of room for our kids and that they had become so much trouble and so expensive that we had sold them. I assured them that we felt it our obligation to visit them from time to time, and the kids remembered us and were always happy to see us. I could tell such things with an absolutely straight face. Right to the point that the students were undone, I'd confess. I explained that I always referred to my children as "children" because "kids" in our house were goats.

One of the good things about having Nubian goats is that they are a dairy breed and, therefore, are never sold for meat. One just wouldn't pay several hundred dollars for a young kid and then start up the barbeque pit. Such was not the case with our next-door neighbors, the Heggoys. Alf had been brought up as a missionary child in Algeria. When the family moved to Danielsville, they bought some scrub goats to clear out their land. Dubbed Honeysuckle and Wisteria, their kids were pets, just as ours were, though theirs were not, I snobbishly add, purebred. We were the only two families in the neighborhood and grew fairly close. Since Alf and Edward were colleagues and our children about the same age, we socialized back and forth. One evening the Heggoys invited us to eat dinner. Alf was to prepare couscous, an exotic dish back in the '70s, and we looked forward to the adventure of eating something new. After we arrived, Alf announced that he had prepared the couscous with wisteria, which I found a bit curious.

I had never heard of cooking wisteria and was surprised that it was indigenous to Algeria. I thought that it was pretty much contained in the southern US and Asia. But, I was willing to try. It turned out that he meant Wisteria with a capital "W"! He had barbequed his very own pet goat. We had a terrible evening, mustering our courage and good breeding (ha!) in order to be the least bit polite, picking around the stew, and eating only the couscous and vegetables. Edward was an avowed animal lover, on the side of the hunted rather than the hunter, he always maintained. I still had enough of concrete and asphalt on my citified feet to be repelled by the notion of cooking a pet.

Alf's philosophy was sensible, of course, my mind tells me so. But there is certainly a caveat: If you raise an animal to eat, you shouldn't give her a name!

CHICKENS ARE UNDENIABLY FOUL....

I've never liked feathered creatures of any kind. Even when I was a child and was taken to Forsythe Park to feed the pigeons, the urban vestiges of wildlife, I was less than enthusiastic. They were insidious with their jerking heads and evil, nervous eyes. They had the habit of frequent, constant pooping, with no regard for propriety. I was always alert to the possibility of their tangling in my hair, pecking and doing unspeakable things. They cocked their heads when they looked at me, and I could never warm up to a cockeyed creature, certainly never trust one. I fed my peanuts to the squirrels who, tamed, would look directly at me and would eat out of my hand. Besides, they had the decency to relieve themselves in the bushes, out of sight.

When I was a little girl I went to the chicken market every Saturday with my father. Through the glassed-in front of the shop, he chose three live chickens. The shop owner seized them, took them to the back, and chopped off their heads. The chickens, still twitching, were hung from a conveyor belt by their lifeless cracked orange claws. As they circled around, perhaps ten at a time, the workers plucked. It didn't take long. Soon our chickens were naked, all pink and pimply, and we picked up our parcel, wrapped in brown paper, and headed home. I was repulsed by the process and by the stench of the shop, but I admit to being delighted when, at Sunday noon, my grandmother presented us with a huge plateful of crispy, perfectly seasoned fried chicken. Somehow there was an amazing disconnect between the market and the dining room table.

The year we lived on White Bluff Road our father tried to raise quail, without success. Quail are very skittish, and we couldn't go anywhere near their pen, especially if the dog was with us, as the poor quail got hysterically het up. Then they wouldn't hatch out their eggs. The only problem was that snakes and other predators didn't know the family rules, and they didn't stay away. The wildlife population grew increasingly fat, as the neurotically nervous quail disappeared. We were soon out of the quail business.

We even had a chicken yard for a while, and I hated it. The pen, grass stripped bare by endless pecking, was fraught with dust and droppings. The rooster was mean. At one point my father bought the wrong kind of corn, and the food swelled up in their chickens' caws. They suffocated and died. Or that's the way I remember the story. At any rate, the chicken business crossed the same deadly road as the quail business, and we were left with carcasses, neither fine fried chickens nor delicately smothered quail.

For several years when we lived on 46th Street, we got baby chicks in our Easter baskets, a fad at the time. The little chicks had been dyed lovely pastel colors, pink, blue or green. We played with them a day or two, but they never survived for long. We'd wake up one morning to find their pitifully still little bodies. We never knew the cause of death, but I now realize that dyeing them, while appealing to little children, was less appealing to baby chicks. They succumbed either to the toxic dye or to the humiliation.

I confess that when I read Gabriel García Márquez's "The Very Old Man with Enormous Wings," I would have sided with the ignorant townspeople. The gist of the plot is that a molting angel with not enough feathers to support him fell from the sky onto a peasant's farm. The unwitting farmer put him in the chicken pen, to join the other feathered creatures. The bedraggled intruder, holed up in a corner of the filthy pen, immediately became a curiosity. The townspeople paid a fee to see him, like some freak show in a traveling circus. Despite the miracles which suddenly began to happen, supposedly unrelated, the villagers and the family continued to revile this dirty creature. Later, his molting finished and his feathers full again, the angel flew heavenward, leaving the ignorant and ordinary to resume their ignorant, ordinary lives. It's hard to reconcile the notion of the purity of an angel and the filth of a bird, but, after all, wings are wings and feathers are feathers. I know that I would have been among the throng of the reprehensible, even though I have a mind that knows better.

Though Alfred Hitchcock in *The Birds* knew exactly how I felt, Edward and the children didn't. When Ed was a little boy, we were somewhere on vacation, maybe Disney World, and there was a flock of swans gliding gracefully on a pond. People tried to entice these beautiful birds to the shore, but the swans ignored them with haughty disdain. Ed, very young at the time, bent down and tickled his fingers in the water, very subtlety. The whole flock swam straight up to him. There was a natural affinity. From somewhere deep inside him, my own little cygnet knew how to speak swan.

Liz, always a gentle little creature herself, still loves chickens and birds of every sort. She has raised a dove (shhh…that's against the law) and a family of finches. And some chickens, too. When the Heggoys moved away, they abandoned their flock to fend for themselves, which in the country meant trying to escape from predators. One afternoon, two of the orphaned chickens walked up our driveway and Liz tenderly took them in. She deemed them Daniel and Claudia. She loved and cared for them, even training them to eat from her hand. Claudia was strolling through the woods one day, like Little Red Riding Hood, where she unfortunately met her own version of the wolf. There was no grandmother's house to take refuge in, to Claudia's doom. Daniel was around a long time. All our animals were friends, and that was true for Daniel and the goats, even the dogs and cats. So when a neighbor's Chow came up the driveway one afternoon, Daniel sauntered over to tell him hello. But the stray didn't share our family values, and poor Daniel paid a high price, the ultimate one in fact, for his hospitality.

Liz also rescued Lindberg, so named doubly for a basketball star at her high school and a friend of her father's. He was a scruffy white rooster who had worked himself free from a chicken truck headed for the abattoir, the Auschwitz for chickens. Lindberg stayed around a long time. He actually preferred cat food to chicken feed and circled around the cat food bowl along with our two yard cats. Although cute, that turned out to be a serious problem, as chickens don't digest cat food very well. Since Lindberg spent a great deal of his day roosting on the rail of the back steps and left the signs of his poor digestion on the stairs, I complained constantly. But Liz loved him and loved the fact that he roosted right outside her bedroom every night and crowed her awake in the mornings.

At one point she sneaked a nesting of eggs into her bedroom and nestled them down in her Barbie doll clothes. She sat on them faithfully every day. But her considerable talents didn't lie in her nesting ability, and we discovered the cache by sniffing down the source of an unpleasant odor emanating from her room. She's had much better luck with raising her finches, and Edward-bird, who has far outlived a normal Finch life span, now sings her awake every morning.

Well, it came time to get chickens for our little farm. I was amazingly supportive, strange I know, given my fowl associations. I can't explain it, not even to myself, but whatever Edward wanted I suddenly wanted too, even if it defied all logic and reason. I didn't have to pretend; I honestly was convinced of the rightness of all his desires and opinions. I didn't even blink when we placed our order through a mail-order catalogue.

I did stipulate that I'd never kill and "dress" a chicken, a strange euphemism for plucking a dead bird and pulling out his entrails, but I agreed to handle anything related to the kitchen. Edward restored a long neglected, dilapidated chicken house in the backyard. He installed nests along one wall and on another wall, a largish section for roosting. This roosting area had the effect of seeing a house with the roof rafters running parallel—just the rafters, no roof. All the connected roosts were hinged at the back and sloped a bit toward the front, so that Edward could lift the roosting boards all at once to clean out the chicken droppings. Sounds like a great plan. And it was, in theory.

Most of the hens remained confused about the system, and, though some roosted on top of the boards, some roosted in the space underneath. The roosting place wasn't lifted often enough to suit me, and it was all terribly untidy. We had plenty of "guano," which only rarely got shoveled onto the compost heap—a slower process, even, than taking out our own garbage.

We started our own flock by ordering twenty-five day-old chicks, twenty-four hens and one rooster. I was told then and I've read since, that the Japanese have perfected the technique of determining the sex of day-old chicks, a very valuable talent, indeed. It is a carefully guarded secret and is very lucrative. Because of the Japanese talent, baby chick producers are able to guarantee that there will be only a single male chick in the batch. People don't want to end up with a yard full of roosters, because just one single rooster can easily handle twenty-four hens. Interesting analogies here, giving credence to all the cultures in the world which practice polygamy.

We set up a store-bought brooder in the smokehouse and went to the post office to collect our order. The postmaster was always nice, even though we were the only patrons who ordered creatures, bees and birds, through the mail. Everyone else had more sense. We returned home and deposited our chicks in the brooder. I pitched in, lifting the soft fluffy baby chicks from their mailing box into the clean and fresh brooder. They were adorable, and I think that baby chicks would be absolutely irresistible if they could be litter-box trained.

They were kept warm by a couple of lightbulbs and had feeding and drinking troughs like the ones in bird cages, except much longer, running nearly the whole length of the brooder. We were pretty successful with our little ones, and soon enough they were ready to be moved to the chicken house. Edward clipped the left wing on each chick before he put it into the chicken yard. That way, the entire flock would be thrown off balance and couldn't fly out. The problem became harder, soon enough, as their wings grew back out and we'd have to chase them down (more correctly, *he* had to chase them down) for a re-clipping.

As agreed upon, I stayed in the kitchen. We kept our chickens in their remodeled chicken house day and night for several weeks, so that they would become accustomed to roosting there. After that, we let them range free during the day, and they would "come home to roost" at night. We needed to lock them up to keep them safe from any predators who might be looking for a tasty nighttime snack or a very fresh egg for breakfast.

"Free range" chickens are an especial delicacy because the variety in their diet produces more flavorful eggs, with bright orange yolks, creamy and as bold as a bright harvest moon. But "free range" also means that they not only get their food from everything in the yard, they leave droppings everywhere, too. I never went barefoot again. They even followed the goats around and pecked at the goat droppings. Edward explained that they were after the undigested corn in the goat scat, and he was probably right, but I maintained that, if anyone really knew what chickens were like, they'd never eat poultry again.

We collected the eggs. Fresh eggs are hard to beat. Liz's first job was to gather eggs, wash them, and hawk them (maybe not the best choice of words!) to Edward's colleagues in Park Hall. After a few years of good production, our hens underwent their own special "hen-opause" laying fewer and fewer eggs. It was time to replenish the flock, and we let one of the hens hatch out some baby chicks. I vividly remember the time that Liz ever so carefully picked up one of the biddies to cuddle gently in her hands. The nearby mother hen spied her and let out bloodcurdling squawks as she went into her attack mode. Flapping her wings furiously, she headed toward Liz. I had been looking out the kitchen window, and when I saw what was happening. I grabbed my dishtowel and flew down the back steps, squawking and flapping just like the other mother hen. We each saved our babies, and I realized what a common bond all us mothers have, the same old maternal instinct, whether mammal or fowl.

The rooster was mean and aggressive. He intimidated me so much that I was afraid to go into my own yard. He sensed my fear and took especial pleasure charging me. When Liz was about three, she was standing next to Edward as he knelt down to milk Big Mama. The rooster attacked Liz, spurring a gaping wound in her back between her shoulder blades. She screamed in pain, and I dashed out. I was absolutely livid and shrieked for Edward to kill the rooster. He let me calm down, and he refused, saying that the rooster was just doing what roosters do, that it was in his basic nature. I still remain unconvinced, even to this day, as, even if the rooster were doing what was in his nature, so was I. I needed to protect my little flock as much as he had to protect his harem. I wanted him dead.

When Edward decided in the first place to get some chickens, I made it clear that I would help out in any way that I could *inside* the house, but when it came time to kill the hens after they stopped laying, he could count me out. And I meant it. I really did. My resolve was set. Well, the inevitable day came. Much as I wanted to and much as I had planned to, I couldn't desert him in his time of trial. I guess that "for richer, for poorer, for better, for worse," implied "in the kitchen and in the coop." So, out to the yard I went.

I will spare the details, but, believe me, it was a grisly affair. Edward and I worked and worked, singeing and plucking, removing undesirable parts, being certain not to pierce the bile sac, all that stuff. After hours and hours we were still working on the original birds, he on his and I on mine. Neither one of us knew what we were doing. I think that the heap of headless chickens ready to be plucked had more sense than we did. We put through an emergency call to Gladelle and Dewitt, our wonderful babysitter/surrogate grandparents, and over they came to our rescue. In less than an hour they had the whole operation taken care of, with seeming ease and certain deftness.

One time we were given a group of culls from the university, the specimens that were rejected from poultry experiments. I'm sure this all was highly illegal, but through Alf Heggoy we obtained some (I grudgingly admit) really cute little baby chicks. They were all bantams: some were game chickens, but mostly they were Japanese silkies, some solid white and some solid black. Silkies have no spines in their feathers, so they are entirely fluff. They have topknots, too, which were soft and fluffy, and even had downy feathers on their legs and feet. They look like cotton balls. They laid tiny little eggs, like the other bantams. I used to make thumbnail-sized deviled eggs, which were always the hit of a party.

We also bought a flock of Araucanas, which some people refer to as "Easter egg chickens," because they produce light green, light blue and light pinkish-tan eggs. It was fun to take friends out to the chicken house to let them gather the already-colored eggs, and we did enjoy that, even I. Little did we know that the chickens who laid blue eggs had a blue tinge to their skins, and those who laid green eggs had a slight greenish color. We were shocked when we plucked them (actually Gladelle did this for us). The prospect of making vegetable soup with a green tinge to the chicken stock was, at the least, off putting. Maybe Dr. Seuss knew what he was talking about all along.

Our lives started filling up with other things. The children became interested in recreational sports, Ed started lifeguarding, Liz was much into art, and Mary, our late surprise, was ill and needed care. We turned our attention elsewhere and gave our hens away. I remember with some poignancy when Clyde Oliver, a dining hall cook at Emmanuel, at our request came and took the rest of our flock of chickens away. He caught them deftly, placed them in the trunk of his car, and drove off on a date.

I think that even Edward began to clue in to the fact that we were better suited to the classroom than the slaughtering block. There was no doubt in my mind at all.

A Bee in my Bonnet

One morning I woke up in great excitement. I had a "bee in my bonnet," which buzzed around in my head and commanded my full attention. We already had an almost totally independent little farm. We had goats for milk, chickens for eggs, the woods for wild berries, an orchard for fruit, and neighbors' gardens for fresh vegetables. All we needed to be truly self-sustaining was honeybees. I hatched my plan, and Edward, as usual, supported me—from his armchair.

I wanted authentic honeybees in a real hive, not the kind that took up at Miss Bertha's house next door. After the Heggoys moved in, they discovered that a swarm of bees had made a hive in the dining room ceiling, flying in through a hole in the side of the house. No telling how many years they had been there, as Miss Bertha and her son Will had lived in just a couple of back rooms from who knows when. The first spring the Heggoys were shocked to see newly made honey dripping through the tongue-and-groove ceiling boards and making a puddle on the dining room table. They couldn't use the honey, of course, because it was tainted with decades of dust and dirt. It just made a gigantic mess! They hired an exterminator to take care of the problem. I had a different thing in mind for sure when I planned my hive.

We had a friend in Franklin Springs, Alton Shealy, who had bee hives himself, and he constructed me a homemade wooden hive. There was a shallow box on bottom, a brood chamber for the queen, then a bigger box on top where the workers made their honey. There was a barrier of some sort, also made of wood, between the queen's residence and the work chamber which kept the queen from coming up into the honey box. It's best not to have the queen laying her eggs in the honey.

The "honey box" was the actual workroom for the worker bees and drones, and it was called a super. It was about one-foot deep with frames hanging down from ledges on the inside, and it looked like a horizontal file cabinet with hanging files all in a row. I placed wax sheets on the frames, ready for the bees to use as a foundation when they created their honeycomb. There was a lid on top to keep the hive dry, snug, and safe from predators. It was painted white. Since the top was slightly slanted for good drainage, the whole thing looked like an outhouse for elves.

I read up on bees, even before computers and Wikipedia. I learned that worker bees buzz around all day, disappearing into one flower for a few seconds, and then flying to the next one. Sometimes they travel miles looking for just the right tree, plants or flowers. In addition to sucking up the sweet nectar, they carry pollen on their tiny little legs, fertilizing flowers and even crops. Back in the hive they digest the nectar and turn it into honey. Over and over, day after day, they "drone on." Everyone in the hive is either a "drone," a male, or a "worker," a female who can't reproduce. The queen stays in her chamber, doing nothing at all except laying eggs. According to popular lore, the "queen bee" is a spoiled, pampered lady, who lolls about while everyone else works. But I'd say that producing 1,500 eggs per day qualifies as pretty hard work.

I went about setting things up. Though there was not a water source close by, and bees, like everyone else, need water, the South Fork of the Broad River was less than half a mile away, near enough, I figured, for a new hive of healthy drones and workers. I placed my wooden hive on top of a brick foundation down in a stand of pine trees near the orchard. I bought official beekeeping garb, heavy rubber gloves, bright yellow, with long, canvas "sleeves" which were long enough to reach halfway up my arm. They were secured by elastic just below my elbow so that no little workers could get in. I bought a bonnet, a round, wide-brimmed hat. It was covered in a net, a loose one, which tied snugly at my neck, again to keep the bees out. I always wore long sleeves, of course, heavy socks, and long pants, with rubber bands around the ankles. Though I looked like a cross between a Martian and a scarecrow, I felt completely immune to a bee assault.

I bought a hive tool, a metal rod with a flat end to prize apart the frames. I also got the very important smoker, which looked like a miniature fireplace bellows. I was instructed to gather up a few bits of burnable material, in my case pine bark and pine straw, and make a little fire inside. Before handling the bees or fooling with the hive in any way, I was to blow a few puffs of smoke inside. That would make the bees docile. I confess that I always puffed the hive up pretty liberally.

I ordered my honeybees through the mail. I bought Italian brown bees, which are bred to be gentle and are recommended for amateur beekeepers. I don't know exactly what I expected to find, but I was really surprised when I arrived at the post office, though maybe not as surprised as the postmaster. I picked up the wooden and screen-wire package which was about the size of two cereal boxes. It was buzzing so loud that I felt that it was actually vibrating in my hands. I was holding 15,000 worker bees and one queen. When I peered inside they were so smushed up together that they look like a box of raisins, highly animated raisins.

The queen was in a candy cage, taped inside to the top of the box. My instructions were to remove the candy cage and unplug the small cork, which would expose the candy. The drones and workers would eat the candy and, in that way, release their queen. Simple enough, I thought. Even I can do this. But catastrophe struck! I was really, really nervous, and my shaking hand dropped the candy cage. It dissolved from sight down through the thousands of bees into the bottom of the carton. The plug was still in, the candy not exposed, so there was no way for the other bees to release the queen. A hive has to have a queen to survive and function, and mine was trapped. I was horrified. All the planning and expense were for naught.

Pulling myself together, I called the Entomology Department at UGA and asked to speak to somebody who knew about bees. I explained my predicament. The man was very nice, patient, and understanding, but he told me that the only solution was to reach down through the thousands of bees and retrieve my queen. He said that I could even do it with my bare hands! Bare hands, indeed; not in a million years. After arguing with myself a while and fussing at myself a great deal for dropping the cage in the first place, I summoned up all my courage, put on my gloves, and lowered my hand tentatively down into the swarm of 15,000 bees. The only force stronger than my ineptitude is my stubbornness. I wouldn't be defeated. Screwing up my courage, I grasped the cage, and pulled it out. The professor was right. I didn't get one single sting! Without any further disaster, I unplugged the candy and placed the queen in the hive. I then tumbled all the bees into their new home and put on the top. I walked back to my own old house, feeling both relieved and even allowing myself to feel just a little bit smug.

Over the months, I tended to my bees. From time to time, I'd put on my gloves and my bonnet, take my smoker and hive tool, and check on them. Everything went along pretty well. I harvested the honey, and my fruit jars were filled to the brim with lovely amber honey, a smidge dark from the smoke, and just a bit of honeycomb. We delighted in chewing the honey-soaked wax like it was chewing gum.

The bees and I settled in. My pamphlets and books warned me not to wear perfume or hairspray or even fruity-smelling shampoo when tending to my hive and not to work with my bees when I was sweaty. Otherwise they pretty much ignored me, and I grew more and more confident.

One hot summer day at the end of June, we all went blackberry picking. Since I was in long sleeves and long pants already, I decided that it would be easy enough to tie on my bonnet and give the bees a look-see. Big, big mistake! I shot a puff or two of smoke into the hive as usual and took off the top. My gentle Italian brown bees had transformed into a raging army of aggressive fascists, who flew up my sleeves, up my pant legs, down my shirt, and into my bonnet. I lost my cool altogether, and started running back to the house, shedding my clothes as I ran, first my bonnet, then my shirt, and finally even my pants! To hell with propriety. Nearly naked when I got into the house, I jumped into the shower, turned on the water, and shrieked from pain and humiliation. A gawky runner always, I've never moved so fast in my life.

It was not the bees' fault; I knew that. After all, if perfume is enticing, how much more so is blackberry juice! And, nothing can bring up sweat more quickly than picking berries on a hot summer day. I had been irresistible, wearing my own special fragrance of berry perspiration, maybe not appealing to human creatures, but highly desirous to a swarm of bees.

I should have known better. Later, when I had calmed down, I realized that the bees could always, at any other time, have breached my protective clothes if they had wanted to. They'd always been able get inside my bonnet, up my sleeves, down the neck of my shirt. They had just been nice and occupied with their own business—until that fateful day when I provoked them.

I continued to take care of my bees, though my heart was not in it anymore, and I was never again relaxed. Soon enough, I found a home for my hive, gave away my equipment, my tools, my gloves and my hat. Worst of all, I admitted defeat. I consoled myself that, after all, I was a city girl and a neophyte. I should never have undertaken beekeeping in the first place, without advice from anything except a book and a couple of pamphlets.

I was no dummy either. I knew that I could buy honey from a grocery store. It was merely a matter of finding the right aisle.

GINGER

Our life with Ginger was doomed from the beginning. Ginger was a Shetland pony, a gift from my Uncle Windell, not to be confused with my kind, gentle brother Windell, his namesake.

One day when Ed and Liz were little, he called us and said that he had a pony for the children. He had trained her himself and her name was Ginger, the very same name of the pony that Edward had when he was a child. He even threw in the saddle. Excited, Edward and Ed drove to Savannah and met a pretty little brown Shetland pony. The ride back to North Georgia was precarious, as

Ed and Liz with Ginger

they were ill equipped to transport a horse, even a very small one. She was secured in the back of a borrowed pickup truck, with a makeshift support on the front and sides. They arrived after an anxious trip for both them and the frightened pony. Since we had had to collect her on short notice, we'd had no time to prepare at home either, and she spent the first night in the goat pen, with no shelter.

The next afternoon was Sunday. I, knowing little of animals, was concerned for Ginger's health and safety if she were left out in the elements. That was absurd, of course, as animals are well equipped to deal with weather. I urged Edward to make her a shed right away. He, as usual, was less than enthusiastic. Finally, in a very grumpy mood, he announced that he was going out to make the pony a shelter and that, furthermore, he was going to do it alone. He wanted no help from me. He told me to take a nap with the children, as he headed out in the drizzling rain. It was one of the rare times that he told me what to do and one of the rare ones, too, when he didn't want my help. I gratefully, if guiltily, lay down for a nap, snuggled up in the deliciousness of the cool, cloudy spring afternoon. I soon fell asleep.

Several hours later, Edward came in to wake me up. There had been a catastrophe. He had hammered together a partial frame, with two upright boards and one horizontal board connecting them at the top. He had lost his footing in the slippery red clay mud and was knocked forward by a piece of lumber. He was thrust in between the two upright boards, his shoulders catching either side so that his chest came forward and both his shoulders were wrenched backwards. The pain was excruciating, he said, and he lay in the drizzling rain, calling out for help. With the windows closed and in a sound sleep, I had not even heard him. He was so frustrated and mad that he pulled himself up and, despite the pain, stubbornly finished the shelter. Only after it was finished did he come inside.

The pain was considerable, but he was too hardheaded to go to a doctor. After three days, I talked him into going for x-rays, and it turned out that both of his shoulders (his shoulders, not his collar bones) were cracked. The breaks were impossible to set, so he just had to tough it out. Unable to raise his arms past his waist, he was quite pitiful and quite helpless. He'd wake me up in the night to pull the covers up around his neck; and he ate with his face nearly in his plate, able to lift his fork only an inch or two. Drying off after a shower required a group effort, and we all took a towel and dried whatever we could reach.

To add insult to injury, this time quite literally, the first big wind blew the pony shed to pieces. We hired Dewitt Sexton, the babysitter's husband, to build us an authentic shelter down in the field, at the wood's edge. The structure housed Ginger effectively. Later on, as our farm efforts were fading, it was converted into a clubhouse—and, finally, ignominiously, it served as a place for the lawn mower.

We didn't fare much better with Ginger herself. It is true that she was well trained. She stopped automatically at the gate, waiting for permission to exit. She obeyed all commands. But she was ill-tempered, and no amount of training had tamed her mean disposition. She was generally unpleasant, even biting willfully and maliciously. She wasn't too keen on being ridden, and she'd buck the children off when she had enough. She ran away more than once. We called Uncle Windell and asked his advice. He told us in plain words just to "take a board and beat her"! Beat her? The very idea. Edward could never have taken a board to anything, not even to me, who doubtless deserved it a lot more than Ginger. Before the year was up, we found Ginger a new home and bade her farewell. The idea of having a pony was much better than the reality. We were not sorry to see her go.

The children suffered no real physical damage from hurtling through the air, just annoyance and a wounding of their dignity, but Ginger, or having Ginger, caused me to have a near accident. One Sunday afternoon after church, we tethered her out in the front yard to nibble the grass, tying her to the back bumper of our little white VW beetle. After a couple of hours, Edward asked Ed to put her back in her pen, and Ed did. Later that afternoon I drove to Athens. There was some sort of problem, and the little car twice jolted backwards. It was a weird sensation to be driving along at 55 miles an hour and suddenly have the car give one giant hiccup—then another.

After I bought my fabric at Jody's, off the Nowhere Road, I loaded the car to head back home. To my astonishment I discovered that I had been pulling Ginger's tether rope all the way. Ed had untied Ginger, as his father had asked, but not at the bumper, at her harness! The rope was still attached to the car. I had driven down the highway dragging a forty-foot tail, with my forward motion suspended when the tires from another car had rolled on it.

Our pony days were over for sure. And, honestly, after Mother (with some relish) kept telling me how Uncle Windell constantly impugned Edward's masculinity, my "uncle enthusiasm," little that there was in the first place, waned considerably. His confident assertion was based solely on the fact that Edward was an English professor. It didn't seem to register that Edward had been a marine in World War II and was still fathering babies well into his fifties. What a joke. I had gained by that time a fairly strong sense of myself, and I felt too old to put up with such nonsense. I have an enormous sense of loyalty, and the choice between Edward and my mean-spirited uncle was easily resolved.

MAN'S BEST FRIEND

Animal lovers are a special breed of people. Edward felt a kinship with all four-legged creatures, especially dogs. He contended that he actually preferred them to people, and, although said in jest, there was some truth to this. My own mother often commented that if there were such a thing as reincarnation, she wanted to come back as Edward Krickel's dog. One could certainly do worse.

The first "outside of class" discussion I had with Edward was about Happy, his Labrador retriever. I had gone out to eat with some other Wesleyan girls, or "Wesleyanns" as we were called, at the Shoney's in Macon where we discovered, sitting alone, our new English teacher, the one with the strange name. He appeared dejected, and we invited him to our table. He readily joined us. He was "down," he told us, because he had just come back from burying his dog, Happy. He needed cheering up.

Both he and his mother Daisy talked a lot about the two bulldogs they had when Edward was little. They were named Sergeant and Major. One of them, I can't remember which, kept watch over the family when Edward's father was out of town. In the 1930s in the heart of the Great Depression, there were no jobs and people were literally starving. Edward's father was fortunate to find work in Memphis, though it was on the other side of the state from Nashville. He spent the weekdays in Memphis and came home only on the weekends. As I say, he was one of the lucky ones, as many desperate husbands and fathers had to take to the road, walking from place to place looking for work. Sometimes they were even barefooted.

These unhappy itinerants stopped at houses along the way and volunteered to do chores in exchange for food and overnight lodging. Daisy never turned anyone away. She set up a bed in the basement and took in whoever stopped by. She also left a Bible on the bedside table, offering encouragement, as well as shelter and a hot meal. In those desperate years, everyone pulled together.

Although Daisy trusted these strangers, the dog was not so sure. He, whichever one he was, either Sergeant or Major, slept on the landing between the first and second stories of the house. Throughout the night he served as a sentry to protect his charges, including the little boys, in the bedrooms above. Interesting enough, Daisy said that no one ever breached her trust, except for the one man who used pages torn from the Bible as toilet tissue.

About a year after Edward and I were married, while we were still living in Dr. Bond's house down by the lake in Danielsville, we went to a party somewhere in Athens. We met a professor in the vet school who told us that they were in the process of performing tests on dogs, and among them was a full-blooded Labrador retriever. The next tests would be toxic, and she hoped to find a home for the young dog. On the spot we made the decision to become foster parents. We picked up the foundling the next day, and Edward named him "Danny Boy." I'm sure this entire process was illegal, and it's only after nearly fifty years that I venture to mention it.

Danny Boy turned out to be quite a character! When he first came to live with us, he was scared of the grass even, for he had lived his entire life on concrete floors and in cages. He trembled miserably. Under Edward's gentle guidance, he soon gained confidence, and when the first daffodil popped into bloom that spring, he assaulted it with great gusto, like Don Quixote charging the windmills. He kept us laughing, and he seemed to know that we had literally saved his life. His wagging tail and giant slurps showed us his gratitude.

Labs are bred to retrieve ducks and are natural swimmers. Danny Boy was no exception. In fact, he was absolutely obsessive about water. After he came to live with us, we took him swimming every day, loading him up in our VW bug. He associated the car with going to the water, and he jumped into everyone's car when they came to visit. It took a good bit of coaxing to get him out.

Whenever he traveled with us, he got excited if we passed over a river or creek. I'm talking about *really* excited. On our trips to Savannah, he'd start pacing every time we crossed a creek or river, always ready to dash in. We used to stop at Magnolia Springs, about halfway, just to let him splash into the water. It was not until later, thank God, that we discovered that alligators also liked that pond. Ranny saw a few sunning on the bank one time when he was visiting from Germany with Ann and Alfred.

We had to be careful everywhere we went, as Danny Boy was so attracted to the water. We had not rolled up the windows on one of our jaunts through Victoria Bryant Park, and Danny Boy actually leapt through the window of our moving car and raced down the bank to the creek. His enthusiasm and his adrenalin kept him from being hurt, and he never showed any signs of injury—or regret.

Danny Boy's other claim to fame was his delight in chewing any and every thing he could. He specialized in shoes. I think that he, having lived all his life in a cage, had to make up for certain puppy-hood deprivations. When my mother came for her usual three-week summer visit, she and I stretched out on the bed chatting while she rested up from her drive. Danny Boy was in our room, at the foot of the bed, and he was making all sorts of loud, smacking noises. Mother and I commented several times on how loud he chewed, when, suddenly we both bolted up. We realized that he had to be chewing something, and it was, unfortunately, one of her brand-new yellow shoes. They were both ruined, of course. We were exasperated, as much at ourselves as at him, because we had known that he loved to eat shoes, yet we had lain there and listened to him gnaw the leather with immense, quite audible pleasure.

When Ed was born, he came into the house, not only with a mom and dad, but with a faithful furry friend. Up to that point Danny Boy had been our only little creature, and he was terribly spoiled. Despite the warnings from my mother, Danny Boy never showed any jealousy of the baby, and they snuggled up together for many a nap on a pallet on the floor. Ed survived these communal naps, and we didn't worry for his safety, despite the horror and further admonitions of my mother.

Danny Boy worshipped Edward. Whenever Edward did anything, Danny Boy wanted to do it, too. If we picked wild muscadines and Edward plopped one into his mouth, Danny Boy pulled one off the vine with his teeth and gobbled it up. He wanted to be wherever Edward was and he joined me in being a worshipping groupie. That was all right until the day we moved. Danny Boy was at our new (old) house on Booger Hill, but when he saw Edward get into a truck and head down the driveway to get another load, he followed him onto the highway. He was killed by a car.

Within days of Danny Boy's death, we went looking for another Lab. I felt disloyal. I told Edward that I didn't think I could endure losing another dog, but he pointed out what pleasure he had given to us and what good care we had taken of him. He was right, of course. We answered an ad and drove to Covington, where we met a precious little black Lab puppy whom his breeders called "Dynamite," as he took off like a stick of dynamite whenever food was put in the communal bowl. He became our faithful companion for many years

Our house was on the corner of the Booger Hill Road and US Highway 29. There was a stand of trees and a deep embankment down to the highway, as well as woods and a long driveway down to Booger Hill Road. So adults and children were pretty safe and protected. But a steep embankment and woods are no deterrent to dogs and cats, so Danny Boy was not the only casualty. Dynamite, too, was struck by a car. Although he survived, he was left with a brain injury, which caused him intermittent but vicious seizures. His body would shake with paroxysms in such a violent way that it was painful to watch. After a minute or so, he'd stand up, look around, and walk calmly away, as if, ho hum, nothing had happened.

Particularly awkward was the time that someone brought over a female to breed with Dynamite. He did the doggy dating game and sniffed her appropriately. She met his satisfaction, but, instead of performing his manly duty, he proceeded to go into awful convulsions. We all looked away, and when we turned back, he had recovered fully, oblivious to anything else, and was taking care of business.

Dynamite grew old, with no other bad effects from his accident. One day he didn't come home, and we never saw him again. Edward drove around in his car, with no luck. He searched the sky, but there were no circling buzzards. We never knew what had happened to him. Privately, I think that he wandered off to someone's property, had a seizure, and was shot because the people thought he was rabid.

Living on the highway caused the demise of many a pet, but it also provided us with others. One was "Dingo," so named because she looked like an Australian dingo. She wandered up one day, and we fed her as we fed anyone who came our way. She and Dynamite developed a special bond, one like I've never seen before or since. They shared food and even bones, taking turns to chew and gnaw. They teamed up to hunt, with one crouching down in front of the bushes and the other one flushing out the prey. They really adored each other.

Ed and Dingo

Though not at all menacing, Dingo never warmed up like a domestic pet except to Ed, who was then about three. She remained skittish around the rest of us, and was an "outside dog." One night Dynamite, sleeping on the floor at the foot of our bed, started howling, a plaintive, lonely, bone-chilling howl, the first and last time that he made that sound. Edward and I were startled out of sleep, and he told me that when a dog howls that way it means that someone has died. He got up early the next morning, found Dingo missing, and started a search. She lay on the side of the road, injured but alive. He picked her up carefully, she not resisting at all, trusting us for the first time in her life. The vet assured us that, although her pelvis was crushed, she was miraculously all right otherwise. Nothing could be done for her injury, but she would survive. Relieved, we took her home, making her as comfortable as possible, outside, in front of the doghouse, with plenty of water and some food. She seemed calm and content. Dynamite lay down with her.

She died during the night. Apparently she had suffered undetected internal injuries. We buried her in what was becoming, sadly, our increasingly populated pet cemetery.

Over the years, other dogs wandered up the driveway. We usually advertised in the paper and found homes for them. One of the visiting dogs stood out from the rest. We were horrified one day to look out and see a hound dog inside the chicken yard, curled up next to the fence. Edward dashed out and coaxed the dog outside. He was obviously a hunting dog who had gotten lost from his pack and had a name and telephone number on his collar. We called the owner and went outside to wait. Amazingly, the dog had dug his way back into the chicken pen. He wasn't bothering the chickens at all, but was lying inside the fence minding his own business. When the owner arrived, he pointed out that his hunting dog was kept in a pen at home, with other hounds, and that he felt much more secure closed in than closed out, a canine version of the Stockholm syndrome.

Gypsy, Dynamite's daughter, was another of our Labs. She was nice and gentle and grew to be quite large, more so than was healthy. Mostly what I remember about Gypsy was her magnificent litter of twelve puppies. I had given birth to Elizabeth a couple of weeks earlier, and Edward teased me that I had only one pup, whereas Gypsy had twelve! He was very solicitous of her and daily mixed her up a potion of raw eggs, vitamins and cod liver oil, which was supposed to be very healthy for mother dogs. When I complained that he was paying more attention to her than he was to me, he replied that he'd serve me raw eggs and cod liver oil for breakfast the next morning. I just needed to give him the word.

We had another series of dogs, "Race," little black Lab, of a fine pedigree, "Domino," a mutt who had big black spots, "Cedar Oak," named by Ed, a non-descript stray who walked up the driveway one day, and "Hunter," a precious little boy Schnauzer. Race, Hunter and Domino were killed on Highway 29, and we found a home for Cedar Oak.

The first of our yard cats strolled up one day. We, of course, took her in and bought a supply of cat food. Not long after she came, one of our neighbors, little Tracy West across the Booger Hill Road, complained about her. I explained that "Snowball" was a stray, not really ours, but Tracy replied, "She's yours all right. Gladelle (the babysitter) let her off at your driveway, saying that you would give her a good home." That could well have been true of more than one stray. Edward and I were terribly naïve about such things.

When the girls got too old for a babysitter, yet were too young to be left alone, especially in our old, rather isolated home, I thought we ought to buy a small house dog. Edward claimed that he didn't like little dogs (I think most men feel that way), but, as usual, relented.

I declare that, when there were Labs in and out of the house, I swept up a whole bag of dog hair, enough to create an entire new puppy, every day or two, so my main priority was a dog who wouldn't shed. We decided on a Miniature Schnauzer. She lived with us only a couple of weeks, as she succumbed to the treacherous highway before long, running down the driveway and following my car to town.

A friend, Elizabeth Eidson, gave us her "stud puppy," a little Schnauzer, a few months later, whom we registered as "Liebken Katrina" and called "Kati." Of course, Edward fell in love with her and she with him. Kati spent endless hours snuggled up either in his lap or beside him on the sofa. He walked around with her peeping out of the oversized front pocket of the apron I had made him. They were mutually smitten.

Honestly, when Edward died, I assumed that Kati would grieve to death, too, but she didn't. She took up with me and didn't even seem reluctant to do so. We became good buddies. She followed me around and was a devoted companion. We cleaned the pool together, we pulled weeds together, and she walked outside with me many sleepless nights. She seemed delighted when I came home after work. Whenever I mowed the grass, Kati went with me. She was so cute when she jumped up in the air, almost vertically, as she cavorted up and down the hedges while I drove my big red Snapper and mowed the three acres of open space.

One hot summer afternoon my friend Sharon Conley and her two young children came for a swim. Kati followed us outside. Between the pool and the house was a hedge of abelias, the Latin word for "bees." It was always buzzing with both bees and butterflies. Sharon called out to her children: "Look, there are three Monarch butter-flies;" followed by, "Well, actually only two. Kati just ate one." Then, "Well, actually only one, as Kati just ate another." I was miffed! Kati, my sweet Schnauzer, wouldn't do such a thing. I didn't say anything, of course, only because they were my guests.

About that time, Kati jumped again up into the air. When she turned around, I saw hanging from her gray beard on the left side of her mouth one entire butterfly wing! That's what Kati had been doing all those times she was jumping vertically into the air. She was not entertaining me--she was snacking on butterflies. I guess that butterflies are not too smart, as they made themselves available again and again; no one passed the butterfly warning to his siblings. After all, even if "butterflies are free," they are apparently tasty and dumb.

Despite her predilection for butterflies, Kati was gentle and loyal. She was very protective, too, and would bark vociferously if anyone came to the door, for which I was thankful. Best of all, she did not stray to the highway. Ironically, Kati contracted the exact kind of cancer that Edward had died from, an adenocarcinoma. She had a mastectomy and the prognosis was dire, the cancer incurable. Miraculously, she survived, moved with me to Athens and lived about a year or a year and a half longer. She became ill, suffering from old age and senility, and Ed and Liz met me at the Comer Vet Clinic, where we put Kati "down," another interesting euphemism. Ed buried her at Booger Hill, beside the graves of our other pets.

The Setting of the Sun

WORDS

Words are sacred. The Bible tells us: "In the beginning was the word, and the word was with God and the word was God…." According to the gospel of John, the "word" preceded the creation of the heavens and the earth, the creation of the birds and the beasts. It even preceded the creation of mankind.

Words resonated early in my life. One of my earliest childhood memories was from the time that we lived uptown in Savannah on Hall Street. I must have been four or five years old. On warm nights we frequently walked through the neighborhood, in part trying to find a respite from the stifling heat. There was no such thing as air conditioning in those days, and everybody kept the windows open to catch the breeze. On Friday nights, our neighbors, the Garfunkels, met for their Sabbath meal. The two brothers lived next door to each other and they, their families, and their parents gathered around the dinner table at sundown. Their strong, masculine voices filled the neighborhood, and beautiful prayers hung in the sultry, Southern air. Although I could not understand Hebrew, I knew these beautiful chants were intensely reverent and extraordinarily important. My neighbors were handing down the stories, father to son, to grandson, through thousands of years, beginning with groups of desert dwellers who gathered together at nightfall, when the sun disappeared over the horizon. These solemn songs recounted the history, both the disappointments and the triumphs, of the Jewish people. I could not have articulated this then, but I could feel it. Something deep in my little soul was stirred.

I was envious when Jewish boys went to Hebrew Schule in the afternoons after elementary school. They complained bitterly, but I would love to have gone in their place. It was all so mysterious, and for all I knew it could have been a blood-letting cult, but I was intrigued. I wanted to know. I wanted to be part of this mystery, but the secrets of the bar mitzvah were not open to a Gentile girl.

One day I learned, far later than I should have, that not everyone in the world spoke English. I was dumbfounded. I don't know what I thought Hebrew was, but, after all, although the boys studied Hebrew, they still spoke English! I assumed that everybody did. I was excited to learn that this wasn't true, and I wanted to peer into the mysteries of other languages.

In high school, I took the so-called "dead" language of Latin, which I maintain is not really dead at all, but which has merely taken on different disguises in our modern world. I loved Latin. I took it for four years, despite the fact that I was the only fourth-year student in the school. I met Vergil then and Aeneas, too, though I disliked Aeneas intensely and still do, that self-righteous little prick.

As a freshman in college, I entered the world of Homer with breathless wonder, discovering the exquisite mysteries of Greek mythology. When I visited Delphi in 1996, I felt the secrets and heard the whisperings of the wise Sybil through the rustling winds in the mountaintop pines. The *Iliad* and the *Odyssey*, with their rich language and even richer images, spoke to the great questions of the universe. And, more importantly, they spoke to *me*. Their magnificent lore, handed down through hundreds of years, gave "life" to the rising and setting of the sun, the phases of the moon, the storms at sea, and all the other strange, otherwise inexplicable natural phenomena. The stories of these myths and the gods and goddesses who "peopled" them were personifications of the human emotions of love, fear, grief, happiness, jealousy. They speak as vividly to me now, as they have to countless others over several thousand years.

I was awed by the stories of the Old and New Testaments that my Sunday school teachers talked about on Sunday mornings. David and Jonathan, with their great and tortured love, and Saul, the father of Jonathan, who really preferred David. Solomon, the wise, who saved the infant's life, and Ruth, who was ever faithful to Naomi. The trials of Job, which I don't understand even now. The return of the prodigal son with full celebration, though the faithful son was ignored. I couldn't comprehend that as a child, but I can as a mother. I memorized blessings and prayers. I listened to nursery rhymes and sang simple songs as I jumped rope with my friends. Unaware of their importance, I was learning my own heritage and establishing my own values.

I've studied and read for decades now. A gathering of words is magical and profound. Edward always claimed that a poem has a life of its own. It is an independent entity and has significance beyond the scope of the poet's imagination. Upon reflection, I realize that the poems which echo in my heart and head are those which invoke profound maternal insights. I remember the Inuit mother who cries out with haunting grief over the impending doom of her convicted son. He was guilty, and the sentence was just, but she was still his mother, he still her son, and her agony was gripping and deep. Anna Akmatova, her own son in a work camp, stopped my heart with the scene of Mary in the crowd around Jesus's torture and crucifixion. Akmatova described the faces of the onlookers, all except for one, the most important one. In breathtaking understatement, overwhelmed herself by Mary's enormous emotion, the poet wrote the ineffable: "No one looked at Mary/ No one would have dared."

Edward was a wordsmith. He was a genius with words, oral, written, imagined, or real. He could quote endless lines of poetry or novels, and he could take an essay and, with a few strokes of his pen, perform magic. It was effortless for him to insert a mere word here or a phrase there, Flaubert's *mot juste*, which turned out to be just the right word in just the right place. I loved to hear him read, night after night, books to the children, as they balanced on the wide arms of his chair in the upstairs hall. I loved to listen to his strong, soothing voice when he talked away my midnight demons time and time again. His words, calm, comforting and assured, wrapped around me like a warm, soft down comforter.

All the graduate students in the Romance Language Department had to study the history of the French and Spanish languages. It sounds like a deadly dull experience, but, instead, it was fascinating. We were able to take a single Latin word, and through a predictable set of changes, discover the current word, however much changed and disguised, in any Romance language, specifically French and Spanish. I loved the sound changes, the simplification of structures, the changes of the meaning of a word which adapted to the usage and needs of various cultures. I loved the way one can discover history through language, the certain times that we adopt "loan words" from another language, and which words we adopt. I was enthralled.

After studying the histories of the French and Spanish languages, I yearned to take the history of the English language. I had long since finished my PhD, but I was happy when I was able to fit the class into my busy summer schedule. It was the worst course I've ever taken. The entire heritage of the English tongue was reduced to a few scientific sound analyses, with an emphasis on American dialects. There was no literature involved, no etymology, no morphology, no lexicography. How wretched! It was as if one reduced a human being to a study of x-rays, bone scans and body fluids, never considering the mind, the soul, the heart, the wonderful complexity of God's so-called crowning creation.

It was through that experience that I understood what my Old French professor had meant when he claimed that he was a philologist, not a linguist. A linguist is one who studies language scientifically, noting especially the sterile sound changes, the Great Vowel Shift, and other such tedious minutiae. A philologist, on the other hand, is a lover of language, the sounds of it, the meanings of it, the subtlety, the sheer thrill of the living, changing word. My Romance language teachers, though dealing with sound changes, too, had dealt with the life of the word, the real living evolution of language, the magic of it all. I decided that I was a philologist, too.

Edward and I treasured words together. Part of our delight were the times that words and knowledge became tangible. Forgetting for the moment our own *hubris* and the consequences, most often we shared experiences which were charming and sometimes profound. One otherwise ordinary afternoon, when we were walking in the woods, we came upon a natural spring bubbling silently out of the earth, trickling into a tiny little stream. We were both, without words this time, just feelings, struck by the stillness and the quiet profundity of nature's gift. Conscious of our closeness, we were in awe.

We had met Niobe, the queen of Thebes who had fourteen of the most beautiful and talented children ever born, seven sons and seven daughters. She urged her minions to worship her instead of the goddess Leto, the mother of Artemis and Apollo, on the grounds that

Leto had but one son and one daughter, whereas she, Niobe, had seven each. Niobe's *hubris*, her arrogant challenge, brought down the anger of Leto, who exacted her revenge. She ordered her two children, Artemis and Apollo, to strike all of Niobe's children dead, and they stifled the fourteen beautiful mortals' lives with swift and certain arrows. Beyond grief-stricken, Niobe cradled the still body of her youngest daughter in her arms. Then she herself died and was transformed into a stone from which formed a stream of endless tears, flowing forth through eternity, as if the earth had overflowed with weeping. In the stillness of the woods that day, we had discovered Niobe, the stone and the tears, and the tragedy hushed my breath.

Both lovers of literature, Edward and I met over books, he my Shakespeare teacher at Wesleyan. We thought words, we laughed words, we played words. We delighted in them almost as much as we delighted in each other. We fought words, too, with great relish and, I must admit, amazing frequency.

One spring the native honeysuckle and wisteria had invaded our long spirea hedge, literally choking it to death. Edward and I set to work. We put on our gloves and yard clothes, long pants and loose long-sleeved shirts, and attacked the jungle-like vines, clipping the long trailers and pulling up the stubborn roots. It took us weeks, several hours a day, and it was hard work.

About the same time I started to read for the first time Edward's favorite novel, Ford Madox Ford's *The Good Soldier*. I picked it up more out of duty than anything else, in my mind a supportive companion, or, I guess, a "good soldier." The novel made me furious. The attitude of the narrator, John Dowell, with his aggressive misogyny and cold detachment, was maddening. I hated the "good soldier" who was not at all good. I hated the implications of the "saddest story," which was maddening, but not at all sad. Nothing was as it seemed. Nobody was who he or she pretended to be. I fussed and fumed. I ripped the roots from the ground. I pulled honeysuckle as it had never been pulled before. The more I read, the madder I got. The madder I got, the harder I worked. Edward indulged me for a while, but then he protested. He didn't pull weeds with quite as much vigor.

I know and I knew even then that he saw more in a book than the narrative story line; he considered the craft, the novel's style, language, subtlety, and nuances. I still dealt with passion only. He tried to explain the greatness of the book to me, but I couldn't get past the narrator, who was, in Edward's words, but in my terms, "an unmitigated ass." The very thought of playing destructive parlor games with real people's lives was repugnant, and the thought of the novel even now sets my jaw in a tight lock. But I did enjoy the argument, and it clearly helped getting the intrusive vines ripped out of the ground. We salvaged our hedge.

Even after Edward got sick, we talked, sometimes all night, talked and listened to music. We said everything that we needed and wanted to say to each other. There was great satisfaction in that. Even so, I wanted to run away, not by myself by this time, but the two of us, so that we could take refuge in each other, far from the madding crowd, even if we had to take his sickness with us. He talked until he literally drew his last breath, and his last words were funny, then loving, then spent.

After Edward died, it took me nearly six months to place a marker at his grave. Somehow I couldn't do it. Even though I knew it had to be done, I felt an overwhelming resistance. I had already taken care of all the necessary business, the will, the death certificates, the Social Security for the girls. I had had the swollen doors planed down and locks installed. I was teaching again. I was carrying on as needed and expected.

But the thought of a marker, with Edward's name on it, caused a deep heaviness in my heart. When his good friend Ernest wanted to visit his grave, I had to admit that I had not placed a stone yet. I was ashamed. I knew what had to be done, and I finally trudged, alone, to Elberton, the Granite Capital of the World. I stopped at the first granite store on the right. I'm a private person, good at keeping my emotions safely in tow. But when I walked into the store, my tears streamed uninvited and unchecked. I was embarrassed, but explained that I needed to place an order and that they must, please, ignore my distress. Although it was awkward for us all, we completed our business.

Several weeks later the granite store called. The marker was ready. It was a late March morning, drizzling, foggy, and generally unpleasant, when I met the stone layers at the Danielsville Memorial Gardens, that cold, desolate strip of land, naked except for the impersonal rectangular slabs in their eternally ordered rows. I took Edward's little Schnauzer, Kati, and we waited. Kati and I walked up and down the narrow lane, back and forth in front of the plot where Edward's parents had been buried and his ashes had been placed. Finally, the huge flatbed truck arrived. It was larger than it should have been, larger than it needed to be, I remember thinking. With ropes and pulleys they lowered the stone and placed it where I showed them.

Of all the awful moments during that last year, this was the most painful. It was because of the words. Those words, which told Edward's birth and his death, were coldly etched on his bronze veteran's marker. Our wedding date was chiseled in stone. They held a power, a terrible reality and finality which lay heavy on my chest. It was excruciating. Nearly destroyed, I limped home with Kati, got my things together, and went off to work, duty-bound like my puritan mother and grandmother before me.

Two days later, I had heart by-pass surgery. Everyone was surprised, even the doctors, because I was young and otherwise in good health. I was not surprised. How could my heart not be broken?

How could I possibly survive when the real purpose of my life lay in the indifferent ground, when that strong voice was hushed, when those wise and comforting words would be just an echo?

The surgeons mended the parts that they could, the parts that they could see. The other parts I've had to wrestle with by myself. That's been nearly twenty years ago. I picked up the pieces of my life and of what was left of my damaged heart. And I've trudged on, as duty demands. But, if I indulge in true candor, I admit that not much has seemed terribly important after that, with surprisingly few exceptions. It's like the numbness of the shock of death never really leaves.

Though I didn't like *The Good Soldier*, from time to time I am jolted in recalling the powerful first lines: "This is the saddest story...." I can't say them without a catch in my voice or even think them without a start in my mind. My irritation is somewhat mitigated, as they are truly the most haunting words I've ever read. Maybe Ford Madox Ford was a genius after all. Edward was always spot on about such things.

The Alpha...The Omega...And the Letters in Between

I can close my eyes right now and picture the first time that I saw Edward. I was a student at Wesleyan, a women's college in Macon, Georgia. The campus had been much a-buzz that fall, twittering as only a gaggle of silly young women can, about these soon-to-be new faculty, Dr. Raindrop and Dr. Kringle. We made inane references to their unusual names, even jingles about Kris Kringle and about the raindrops falling on our grades. Giggling young girls live even outside Jane Austen novels. It turns out that their names were Reindorf, the head of the Spanish Department, and Krickel, the head of the English Department. The first didn't intrigue me at all, but, ah, the second....

I had signed up for a Shakespeare class, and I was eagerly perched on my front-row seat, waiting to get a firsthand glimpse of this new English professor. In he came, sidling into the small classroom, hugging an armful of books. He carefully stacked them, one on top of the other, on the scratched-up antique desk in the front of the small, conference-sized room. He then took one book from the pile and, holding it like a security blanket, settled back, and kind of jostled himself a niche in the worn-out desk. He began to talk. No notes. No note cards. No overhead projector. No PowerPoint. No syllabus. Nothing, except his voice. And his vast, vast knowledge. In delivering this first "lecture" (though "conversation" might be a better description), he referred to book after book, making whatever point he wanted, suggesting that we check out certain references or assertions on page 25 of this book or page 783 of another. He knew everything in all these books, even to the pages and footnotes. In fact, I got the impression that he was having an adoring conversation with his books as much as with his students. It was the most incredible thing I'd ever seen. I was at the same time both drawn to his soft, unassuming Southern voice and undone by his incomparable brilliance. I was smitten. Always an avid student and a lover of learning, I had had many crushes on my teachers before, but this was different. And I instantly knew that it *was* different, a knowledge of the heart as well as the mind. He, aha, was to find out before the year was over.

We didn't date in Macon, but instead went out in groups sometimes to eat, but most often to "happy hour" at one of the local bars. I never saw him alone outside of his office or classroom. We talked on the phone but one single time. The summer after I graduated, he visited me one weekend in Savannah with Harold Wilson as chaperone. We met one other time at Windell's house in Atlanta.

In the spring of my senior year, I panicked. I had no idea what I would do after graduation. I don't think that the thought had ever occurred to me. My religion professor, Clifford Edwards, suggested that I go to graduate school. It was too late to apply competitively, but he urged me to contact the state university, which we both assumed was in Atlanta. I immediately applied to the Classics Department and to the Romance Languages Department at the University of Georgia, which turned out to be in Athens, and received a teaching assistantship in French. In September I headed to Athens, scared to death. I was assigned to teach two freshman French classes, I who had just graduated myself and who had no experience whatsoever. I was allowed to enroll in one graduate course, the History of the French Language I.

Edward had planned to return to Wesleyan in the fall, though he didn't like the college at all. He complained about the non-intellectual atmosphere, the provincialism, the petty lack of imagination of the administration, and the poor caliber of the students. In retrospect, I don't think that the situation was as bad as he perceived it; it was merely an unhappy time of his life. Besides that, all faculty everywhere seem to have the same or similar complaints of their college posts. Part of it is the result of being trained as critical thinkers. Frankly, I had been as unhappy at Wesleyan as he, but even then I realized that it was part of the game: Thoughtful students were supposed to be unhappy.

During the late summer, just before the quarter was to begin, Dr. Ed Parks, a University of Georgia English faculty member, dropped dead, literally dropped dead, in Park Hall. Edward's longtime friend Marion Montgomery called him immediately, and Edward drove the hundred miles from Macon to Athens and interviewed with Dr. West, the chair of the department. Dr. West was relieved to find at the last moment someone qualified for the position, and Edward was thrilled to be leaving Wesleyan. So, quite unexpectedly, it turned out that Edward was coming to Athens, too.

In the mid-sixties, there were only three or four apartment complexes in Athens. With my friend Sandra Mock, I drove up to finalize my assistantship papers and to find a place to live. Being from such a large family, I don't think that I had ever spent more than one or two nights by myself, and I was worried about how I would cope. Though insecure about living alone, I didn't want a roommate hanging about all the time. I'd never in my life had any real privacy, and this was my chance.

I decided on the "high rise" at the University Garden Apartments on Baxter Street, so named because it was all of four stories tall, the tallest building in town! I met the resident manager, Pat Scott, who had been a friend of Ranny's at Emory. There was a vacancy right above Pat and Shelly's apartment, and I hastily put down a deposit. That gave me some sense of security, as I figured that I could bang on the floor in case of intrusion by some unspecified nefarious character. (I never knew exactly what I was so afraid of, but "he" was as real to me as Santa to a six-year-old.) Pat was also a graduate student in Romance Languages. Edward and Harold drove to Athens that same weekend, and he rented a little bungalow on Holman Avenue. That fall, fresh from his divorce, our courtship began in earnest.

When I met Edward, he had been in his early forties. To me that was a major factor in our happy relationship. We didn't have to "grow up" together, as he was "seasoned," experienced, and confident. He didn't have to discover who he was; he already knew. He had been married for sixteen years and had a young son. The only serious regret I have about our marriage, and about Edward, specifically, is that his son, August, was never a part of our lives. There were nominal reasons, of course. It was never convenient with August's mother for him to visit or to go on vacations with us. Edward visited him in Columbia in the early years, but those visits became rarer and rarer and finally ceased. Edward was an honorable man, of course, and he fulfilled his legal obligation of child support. He also paid August's private school tuition in Macon and part of his tuition at Vanderbilt. He paid alimony until the day he died. In fact it was not until years after we were married that

Edward brought as much money "home" as he sent to South Carolina. However faithful Edward was to provide financially for August, he was never really a presence in his life, except the few months when August was a graduate student in the Classics Department here in Athens. I am saddened that, due to the rupture of his parents' relationship, August didn't know the same man that we did.

After Edward and I both moved to Athens, our time together took on a familiar, comfortable pattern. I taught a first-period French class, he a second-period English class. We met during the third-period class hour for breakfast at the Mayflower Restaurant on Broad Street, directly across from Moore College. The plump middle-aged waitress became our confidante. She was the first person that we told when we decided to get married. She was the first person we told, two years later, that we were expecting a baby. Thirty years later, when Edward and I went to turn in his retirement forms, we decided to pay a nostalgic visit to the Mayflower, which we hadn't frequented for years. Our waitress had long since left, but we felt a certain satisfaction that we had finished his career full circle, at the little "mom and pop" restaurant where we had done all our courting.

Although I loved the idea of life on my own, in a nice apartment with a swimming pool, I confess that I hated night time to come. The darkness had always fallen heavy on me, and I had brought to Athens all my fears and insecurities. I was miserably frightened every night. I set up all sorts of booby traps before I went to bed, a chair wedged under the doorknob of the door leading to the outside hall, even a string of bells fastened across my bedroom door to jingle if there were ever any movement. My mind was never put to ease, and, whenever I was able to fall asleep, I did so with my back pressed up against the wall and my eyes fixed on the door, waiting for God-only-knows what! There was little rational about me then. All my machinations were fruitless, and it turned out that the joke was on me.

Edward and I had decided to get married. Rather than his asking me or my asking him, we just both felt the rightness and the inevitability, and accepted it, like putting on a warm, well-worn overcoat. We had planned to marry in June, but one morning it dawned on us how foolish it was to wait. We were both certainly of age, and it was wasteful to continue to pay another six months' rent on separate houses. We would marry over the Christmas holidays, and he would give up his lease and move in with me. I was into numerology in those days, and I figured up the precise date according to the numbers. I was born in 1942 and would turn twenty-four in early December and he was born in 1924 and would turn forty-two on the twenty-eighth. The year was 1966, the sum, of course, of 24 and 42, so it was crucial that we marry before the year was up. We chose New Year's Eve, three days after his 42nd birthday. The whole world celebrates our anniversary.

After finishing up exams, both the ones I gave and the one I took, I turned my thoughts to the holidays. I tidied up my apartment and went to the laundry room in the basement to wash my final load of clothes. In my exhaustion and excitement, I locked myself out of my apartment. The resident manager, my friend Pat, was out, so I called Edward on the phone. He came right over. He decided that the best thing to do was scale the outside wall up to my second-floor patio, in hopes that I had left the sliding door unlocked. He tried the glass sliding door, but it had been carefully and firmly locked by the always-scared-out-of-my mind me. On impulse he pulled the door on the other side, the one that was screwed into the wall. It readily gave way.

My reaction was mixed, to say the least. It was a relief to get in and to finish packing, but, then, I realized that I had locked and barricaded all my doors when one of them was never even attached in the first place. It had slid open as if it were buttered on all sides.

From Savannah we drove to Florida, so that I could meet Edward's parents. He had not seen them in years, but I could never have married a man whose family I didn't know. They were not able to come to the wedding, but Edward's brother, Jack, and his family were. The wedding took place and our life together began.

I remember when Edward was diagnosed with terminal cancer. Horror stopped me in my tracks. I had worried constantly about his health when we first married. After all, my father had died when he was in his forties. But I had gotten so involved with living that I forgot about death. I had actually been brooding on the fact that I had not cried in years, wondering if I had become heart-hardened and insensitive. In truth, the reason was simply that I had nothing to cry about. How smug I was and how quickly I was humbled.

Though strong around the family, which is the duty of a wife and mother, and competent in the classroom, storms roared through my solitude. Driving the fifteen miles to and from Emmanuel, I tried to let all the anguish out, and I screamed at the top of my lungs. But pain and grief don't work that way. They never leave. Whenever anyone was around, I appeared to have control of myself, but the truth is that in my silence, I still screamed, just not with my voice. My mind was on fire, and my heart was shattered.

The only time that I lost my composure was when I went to the attic to get out all the Christmas decorations. Suddenly I was slapped into the reality that this would be our last Christmas together and, in abject despair mixed with fury, I hurled the boxes of ornaments down the steps. Edward, helpless at the bottom, said quietly, "Sallie, sometimes I don't understand you at all," but I think that he really did understand. Most of the ornaments were salvaged, as they were well packed in the first place, but never again has putting up a Christmas tree brought joy to my heart.

I don't have to close my eyes to remember the last time we saw him. His once vigorous body was wasted and nearly useless, a final ghost emerging from Auschwitz or Dachau, his eyes sunken like a doomed, haunted character from Dante. Though certainly diminished, he still had his voice, and it was clear, if muted. He refused narcotics, except for a very few at the last day or two, as he explained that he preferred to be with us, vibrant as possible, as long as he could.

It was a Saturday night, and all of us were with him: Ed, who was in his first year of marriage, Liz, a sophomore at Brenau, Mary, a freshman in high school, and I. With us were his precious Schnauzer, Kati, a hospice nurse, and Susan Collins, Dr. Willy's assistant. It was nearly midnight. We were in the downstairs parlor, where we had made a makeshift bedroom. The latest stack of books was on a bedside table, though he was able to concentrate on only one paragraph at the time. I had called the hospice nurse to come help me change his sheets without moving him, as he was in serious pain by now. She came reluctantly, as it was late Saturday night and she was leaving for vacation the next morning. It was obvious that she didn't want to be bothered. She showed me how to change the bedding with him in it and said something or other about pulling the draw sheet up so that he would be higher up in the bed, not crumpled in the middle. He muttered wryly: "Well, you'd better hurry." He permitted her to apply the first morphine patch, which he had refused until that night. Then he whispered: "I love you all, especially Sallie." A final gift: that kind, protective reassuring voice, strong even in its weakness, gave us courage in our darkest hour. Then he closed his eyes.

What I've just written, I've needed to write, to tuck away. But what's ever so wonderful are all the years between the first hearing of that voice and the last. We had such a splendid life together, not always easy, but always valuable. We were blessed with three interesting, intelligent, and challenging children. We had lived the promises of the Alpha, the emptiness of the Omega, and the fullness of all the life in between.

When Edward closed his eyes, his life was, in truth, not over. We each carried away part of him, part of the *real* him. We encourage each other enormously. He is still the topic of most of our conversations, the children's and mine, and I doubt if we ever reach a decision of importance without "consulting" him--thinking of what he would have advised or, especially in my case, what would have pleased him.

We all have carried on with our lives, strengthened by his courage, kindness, magnanimity, acceptance, even his preferences. Finding something that he wrote or valued is like finding a treasure. Inexplicably I have a sudden love of opera, which had always been one of his passions. I prefer hot tea now. I have discovered in myself a sense of patience that I've never had before. Like Edward, I can wait endlessly and patiently reading a book without minding at all.

And, woe unto me, I can never seem to finish a chore, though I'm not yet to the point of leaving a bag full of garbage in the middle of the kitchen floor.

Acknowledgements

My first thanks go to Bilbo Books and its editors, Bowen Craig and Bill Bray, who spurred me on to write a memoir and encouraged me through the years. The little writing group they established provided gentle support, with an added bonus of getting to know people through their own stories. I'm grateful to the staff of the Athens Tech Library, especially to Sheba Grafton and Elizabeth Bates, for their technical support and for soothing my many crises. Elizabeth was an excellent typist, intuiting what changes I "meant" to make. Paula Dixon scanned my pictures and "dropped them in," and Anna Shelton formatted the final copy, both tasks for which I have equal bafflement and appreciation.

It's nice to have smart friends. Donna McGinty, Ted and Gay Miller, Sandra Cummings, and Anne Williams read the manuscript at various stages and gave me insight and direction. Dot Montgomery and Bill Burke read the penultimate version with care and made further suggestions. Finally Sonya Strickland did a magnificent job of handling the nitty-gritty corrections of the final copy. It's equally nice to have intelligent relatives who were willing to plow through the manuscript and check for accuracy: my brother Windell Bradford, my cousin Melanie Hale, and my three children, Ed, Liz, and Mary.

Finally, I'm grateful to my grandchildren. As I watch them growing up, I see sparks of brilliance, kindness, and love which are reminiscent of their grandfather. I hope that they will always be mindful of their heritage and touched by the spirit of kindness, gentleness, and incomparable brilliance of Edward, our dear guardian and guide.

CPSIA information can be obtained
at www.ICGtesting.com
Printed in the USA
LVOW10s1325301017
554285LV00017B/653/P